PRAISE for SUSAN SILVER & ORGANIZED TO BE YOUR BEST!

(Also see the back cover comments)

- **Winner of the Benjamin Franklin Award, presented during BookExpo America (the American Booksellers Association national convention).**
- **Selected by more than 10 book clubs!**
- **More than one-quarter million copies in print!**

The title of the book says it all. *Organized to Be Your Best!* is the single best resource that I know of for anyone who wants to get more control of their time, computer, paperwork, work space or life in general. It's a state-of-the-art tool kit, resource guide, time management seminar and personal consultant all rolled into one.
—**Michael LeBoeuf, Ph.D**, Author of *Working Smart* and *How to Win Customers and Keep Them for Life*

Organized to Be Your Best! is a must read for today's busy career professional. This user-friendly guide is comprehensive in its content and engaging in its style. It *is* the bible of organization.
—**Lee Gardenswartz, Ph.D.** and **Anita Rowe, Ph.D**, Co-authors, *What It Takes*

Worth a year in college.
—**Fred DeLuca**, President and Founder, Subway Sandwiches and Salads

I was literally drowning in paperwork. Then I bought your book. It was the perfect solution. Order is finally being created from chaos. Thank you for a terrific book.
—**Kori Lee Garner**, Reference Librarian, University Library California State University, Fullerton, California

I bought your book on a Saturday, finished reading it Sunday morning and went to the office Sunday afternoon to organize my desk. I'm looking forward to organizing our whole company to be the best!
—**Mark Taylor**, President, Evcor Systems Designers, Plymouth, Michigan

Your book has everything and it's clear and concise. I think it's absolutely fabulous!
—**Lesley Goranson**, Administrative Services Manager, SOFTBANK Expos, Foster City, California

It's obvious there's much work and love put into *Organized to Be Your Best!* It's a motivating book and the resources are excellent!
—**Elaine Wilkes**, President, Show & Tell Multimedia, Los Angeles, California

A practical approach to improving organizational skills...a sound how-to, recommended.
—*Booklist*, the literary review journal of the American Library Assn.

more...

From advice on managing time, to assistance on creating efficient work space, *Organized to Be Your Best!* has it all. It showed me how to tame my chaotic schedule, clear the clutter from my home office and generally bring order to my life...the most helpful book on the subject that I've come across.
—**Elane Osborn**, Novelist, *Skylark*, Reno, Nevada

Organized to Be Your Best! is an excellent resource. It's the only book of its kind to cover organizing of computer files. I've recommended it to over a thousand clients and students.
—**Harriet Schechter**, author of *Conquering Chaos at Work*, Professional Organizer and Owner, The Miracle Worker Organizing Service, San Diego, California

I've found your book to be really helpful, especially the time management and computer organization material. This ought to be standard issue for administrative people.
—**Alan C. Macdonald**, Vice President, Citibank, New York City, New York

This book has truly made it possible for me to increase my productivity by one and a half fold. My filing system is manageable and understandable for the first time in my life.
—**Robert Simon, M.D.**, Chairman of the Board, International Medical Corps, and Professor and Chairman, Department of Emergency Medicine, Cook County Hospital, Chicago, Illinois

...brilliant—definitely the best I've ever read—and I've read a lot. I liked that the focus initially was on goal determination rather than just purely getting organized. You named names, lots of resources and how to find them easily. There's a lot of focus on computer applications; I'm impressed with how computer literate you are.
—**Margaret H. Briggs**, Ph.D., Speech-Language Therapist, Pasadena, California

Thank you for your book. Even the title is an inspiration to get started. In addition to providing a wealth of information, it is also well written and enjoyable to read.
—**Patricia L. Stewart**, AT&T Marketing Manager, New Jersey

Your book is great, fills a gap and is readily useful to organizer colleagues.
—**Paulette Ensign**, President, Organizing Solutions, San Diego, California

Organized to Be Your Best! will help anyone achieve his or her goals. I heartily recommend it.
—**Robert Kotler, M.D.**, FACS, Author, *The Consumer's Guide to Cosmetic Facial Surgery*, Los Angeles, California

Thanks for writing this book! With multiple meetings every day, I am always at a loss for time. Your book has some great ideas that I'm implementing. Now I will get more out of every day!
—**Mark Stevenson**, Special Agent, Northwestern Mutual Life, Bennington, Vermont

Organized to Be Your Best! is an invaluable training tool that I used with participants in Personal Productivity Management training programs at the Jet Propulsion Laboratory. Each participant received a copy of the book, which served as both training material during the program and a take-away resource they used after the program. What's great about this book is that it shows such a wide variety of useful ideas and has something for everyone. It has both depth and breadth and does not have to be read sequentially.
—**Nancy Ferguson**, Former Training Specialist, Jet Propulsion
Laboratory, Pasadena, California

The impact of the time I spent with you continues to multiply. It has really helped me stay on top of deadlines. I am saving time because I have the tools to move through my paperwork more quickly. Thanks for your ideas, coaching and advice!
—**Terry Preuit**, Training Director, Los Angeles, California

Finally...a book on organizational techniques that I can use to help coach my clients toward peak performance! Your straight forward, immediately applicable book fills a critical gap in my coaching library.
—**Lois P. Frankel**, Ph.D., Partner, The Frankel & Fox Group,
Consultants in Employee Development, Los Angeles, California

Susan Silver offers a wealth of practical advice and ideas from which even the most diligently organized of us can benefit.
—**Sanford C. Sigoloff**, President and CEO, Sigoloff & Associates, Inc., Los Angeles, California

Concise, easy to read and so appropriate for today's work environment.
—**Dave Webb**, Supplier Standards Manager, Purchasing, Finning Ltd., Vancouver, British Columbia, Canada

As an attorney in a solo practice, I'm trying to make the office more efficient. The book was helpful for my legal assistant and me to organize our work and our office. It gets right down to the brass tacks.
—**Shirley A. Bass**, Attorney at Law, Portland, Oregon

What a pleasure to tell you how much I enjoyed reading *Organized to Be Your Best!* I'm very excited about the useful information it contains; it has given me the inspiration to actually put your ideas into use, right now!
—**Eadye Martinson**, Executive Secretary, Everett, Washington

Two hours with Susan changed my life. I turned a wasted room into a wonderful working environment. I had thought I should be able to do it myself. Wrong! Her guidance was what I needed.
—**Sharon Bloom, Ph.D.**, Psychotherapist, Los Angeles, California

more...

We all felt the opportunities presented by you for organizing our daily life in the office were without equal. Thank you for increasing our office's efficiency, positively! Your sessions were a catalyst to which our entire staff responded so enthusiastically that we are still buzzing over your presentation, discussions and the projects you inspired. And I have a new "bible"—your book!
—**Robert Aronoff**, Former Controller, Weight Watchers of Southern California

Susan has a remarkable talent for identifying habits and work conditions which are unnecessary complications and prevent you from becoming more productive. She has a first-rate ability for selecting the tools or ideas that are best suited to your style and needs. Add to this the fact that she is a delight to work with and you have an invaluable consultant who can make a real difference in your productivity.
—**Waltona Manion**, Public Relations Professional, San Diego, California

Organized to Be Your Best! is concisely comprehensive, giving insight into the overall organizational plan while focusing in on its components—an excellent guide through the organizational maze!
—**Meryl Perloff**, ASID, Meryl Perloff Interiors, San Luis Obispo, California

I have just finished your book and found it terrific! I believe that the basics in an office library are: 1) a good dictionary, 2) a good grammar book and 3) a copy of *Organized to Be Your Best!*
—**Sharon Leahy**, Vice President, Tri-United Realty Development & Management Associates, Skokie, Illinois

It's amazing! Your book worked! I work for an electrical utility in a small town in Northern Ontario, Canada. We inherited a young manager a couple of years ago and haven't seen the top of his desk since then. Last week I gave him your book opened at Chapter 4 and mentioned he might find some useful ideas. I saw results the next day. All his notes were in one pile and by the end of the week, his desk was completely cleared. Thank you, thank you, thank you.
—**Peggy Wikiruk**, Billing & Accounting Clerk, Ontario, Canada

Your book is definitely unique in its approach. You did a great job on the book.
—**Nancy Tawney**, Director of Development, Florentine Opera of Milwaukee

Organized
To Be Your
Best!

Simplify and Improve
How You Work

S U S A N   S I L V E R

ADAMS-HALL PUBLISHING
www.adams-hall.com

Library of Congress Cataloging-in-Publication Data

Silver, Susan
    Organized to be your best! : simplify and improve how you work / Susan Silver
      p. cm.
    Includes index.
    ISBN 0-944708-61-7 (cloth) -- ISBN 0-944708-60-9 (softcover)
    1. Business Records--Management--Data Processing. 2. Information resources management. 3. Time management. I. Title.

HF5736 .S543 2000
650.1--dc21

00-033198

Cover design by Hespenheide Design (hespenheide@hespenheide.com)

Adams-Hall books are available at special, quantity discounts for bulk purchases for sales promotions, premiums, fund-raising or educational use. For details, contact Adams-Hall Publishing at 1/800-888-4452 or www.adams-hall.com.

First printing 2000
Printed in the United States of America
20 19 18 17 16 15 14 13 12 11 10 9 8 7 6 5 4 3 2 1

CONTENTS

INTRODUCTION:
How to Benefit from This Book   1

1 HOW TO BE POSITIVELY ORGANIZED!   5

Quick Scan   5
Creating Balance in Your Life   6
How Organized Are You At Work? Self Survey   7
Targeting Achievable, Challenging Goals   8

2 TIME MANAGEMENT: What You Really Need to Know   13

Quick Scan   13
How to Plan and Prioritize   14
How to Choose the Best Time Management Tools:
    Calendars, To-Do Lists, Master Lists, Ticklers, Planners,
    Organizers, PIMs, PDAs, Pocket PCs and Web solutions   17
Resource Guide   34

3 HOW TO HANDLE TOO MUCH TO DO
    IN TOO LITTLE TIME   37

Quick Scan   37
How to Control Interruptions At Work   37
Five Secrets to Tame Telephone Time   39
How to Delegate Your Way to Success   40
How to Juggle Multiple Priorities   42
How to Avoid Rushing   43
Ten Terrific Time and Energy Savers for Terribly Busy People   44
How to Finish Your Work and Still Have Time For a Personal Life   45
Resource Guide   46

4 MASTERING YOUR DESK AND THE PAPER JUNGLE   47

Quick Scan   47
The Myth of the Messy Desk   47
How to Turn Your Desk Into a Self-Cleaning Oven   50
   Daily Paperwork System, Catching Up With Reading   50
Other Ways to Put Paper in Its Place!: Preventing/Conquering
   Long-Term Paper Buildup, Scanners and Software, Recycling   57
Resource Guide: Paper Management Supplies and Accessories,
   Desk Accessories, Other Organizers   61

5 FOR COLLECTORS ONLY:
   HOW, WHEN AND WHAT TO SAVE   68

Quick Scan   68
Types of Collectors   68
Making Decisions About Collectibles   69
To Save or Not to Save...That is the Question!   69
How to Prevent Long-term Buildup   73
Resource Guide: Artwork, Blueprints, Photographic Materials,
   Files, Records, Literature Organizers, Computer/Software Donations   74

6 WORK SPACE BASICS: Enhancing Your
   Physical Working Environment   79

Quick Scan   79
How to Organize and Maximize Your Work Space:
   Location, Layout, Proxemics, Your Work Style   80
Furnishings That Fit: Furniture, Equipment, Ergonomics,
   Accessories and Supplies   86
Your Total Environment: Aesthetics, Color, Personalization, Air,
   Temperature, Personalization, Comfort, Safety, Lighting, Privacy   99
Resource Guide   103

7 UP-TO-DATE PAPER FILES AND BEYOND   105

Quick Scan   105
The Three Filing Phobias   105
How Do Your Files Stack Up? Survey   106
Five Easy Steps to an Organized Filing System   107
Three Filing Tips For Every Manager   117
Resource Guide: Filing Supplies, Color Coding, Automated Solutions   119

8 POWERFUL COMPUTING: PC File Organization, Housekeeping And Backup — 127

Quick Scan — 127

PC File Organization Strategies: Partitioning, Separating Program and Data Files, Your Desktop — 128

The Rewards of Computer Housekeeping: Clean Hard Disk, Defragmenting, Compression, Viruses, Floppy Organization, CD-ROM/CD-RW/DVD Organization, Disaster Prevention — 133

Back It Up!: Backup Tips, Types and Storage Devices, Selection Criteria, Web Backup and Storage — 142

Resource Guide: Disk and File Management Programs, Hard Disk/Data Maintenance & Recovery — 150

9 MORE WAYS TO MANAGE YOUR WORK, PROJECTS AND INFORMATION — 153

Quick Scan — 153

Work and Project Management Shortcuts: Forms, Checklists, Charts, Capturing Creative Ideas, Project and Work Management Software — 154

Top Tools and Systems to Manage Information Resources and Records: Contact Managers, Database Programs, Data Access and Search Tools, and Record Keeping Systems — 163

Resource Guide — 168

10 WORKING WITH OTHERS — 173

Quick Scan — 173

Why Everyone You Work With is Your Customer — 173

Challenging, Changing Times Present Opportunities — 177

Surefire Ways to Increase Quality and Teamwork: Whether or Not You're the Boss: Communicate, Involve Employees, Managers as Team Leaders, Team Meetings, Employee Involvement Programs, Camaraderie, Train to See a Gain, Cross Training — 179

How to Organize Others: Multiple Bosses, Projects or Priorities, Working with Temps, Leading by Organizing — 195

Resource Guide: Reading and Reference, Special Products for Special Needs — 200

11 USING COMPUTERS AND TECHNOLOGY
        TO IMPROVE COMMUNICATIONS AND QUALITY   202
Quick Scan   202
Control Your E-mail: E-mail Management and Organization Tips,
    E-mail Writing tips, Instant Messaging   203
Value Voice Mail and Telephone Time   211
How to Max Your Fax   215
Unified Messaging   218
Collaborative Computing: Intranets, Extranets, Web-based Teamware   219
Resource Guide on the Web   221

12 THE TRAVELING OFFICE: How to Get Things Done
        On the Road and At Home and Travel Smarter   222
Quick Scan   222
Working on the Road: Traveling Technology, Wireless Connections,
    Internet Options, Voice Mail, Faxing, Traveling Time Management,
    Keeping Up With Calls While Away, Handling Paperwork on the Road   223
Seven Travel Tips You Need to Know   236
Resource Guide: More High-Tech Travel Tools, Accessories,
    Services and Web Sites, Portable Office Products, Travel
    Resource Information, Products and Services   247

13 SURFING THE NET: Search Tips, Tools, Shortcuts and Safety   252
Quick Scan   252
Internet Safety, Privacy and Protection   253
Browsing/Surfing Tips: Mouse, Keyboard and Other
    Navigation Shortcuts   255
Internet Search Tools   256
Resource Guide   258

14 POSITIVELY ORGANIZED! IN ACTION   259
Quick Scan   259
Your Positively Organized! Plan of Action   262

AUTHOR BIO   264
A Personal Note from the Author   264

INDEX   265

INTRODUCTION

HOW TO BENEFIT
FROM THIS BOOK

This book is the answer for you if any of the following questions are true. Are you

• overwhelmed with today's instant communication overload—especially e-mail, voice mail and faxes?

• swamped with paperwork or inundated with information?

• struggling with too many priorities and always in a time crunch?

• on overload with your workload?

• suffering from excess stress every day?

• out of balance with little or no personal time?

• interested in using your computer or the Internet more efficiently?

• working in a chaotic or cluttered environment?

• lacking a sense of teamwork with others?

• juggling multiple offices or traveling extensively?

• expanding your business?

• just looking for more ideas to help you grow professionally and personally and experience a real sense of accomplishment?

Why You Need This Book Now
More Than Ever Before

If you answered "yes" to even one question, this is the right book at the right time.

Even if you've read other similar books (including a prior edition of *Organized to Be Your Best!*), this is the time to make a real commitment to yourself.

This is a time of great change and challenge in the work place when good organizational skills are a necessity. They'll support you in your fast-paced, high-demand work place—whether it's located in an office building, a home, a car or other mobile/alternative office.

1

People today are working harder than ever. The average workday throws 200 plus messages your way ranging from e-mail, voice mail, pages and faxes on top of meetings, travel time and your "normal" tasks and projects. That doesn't allow much time for just plain thinking or even sleeping in some cases. No wonder Americans put in the most annual hours of work per person of any developed country! Compared to a decade ago, Americans are working an additional month's worth of hours.

To get through the day, you almost can't do one thing at a time. Multi-tasking can help you get more accomplished but it may be just overloading an already overloaded brain that needs time to process information not just receive it. To make sense of all this information, time has to be allowed for the brain to filter and organize all this input.

But usually no such time is permitted since both the amount and the pace of information are speeding up. Getting information or documents overnight is often seen as too slow.

Most of us operate in a "just-in-time" or "last-minute" workplace where time urgency, getting things done *now*, not tonight and not tomorrow, is the rule—as well as a leading cause of stress.

Adding to the stress is the inability to separate work and home life when so many work hours are demanded and instant communications allow work to follow you around the clock like an ever-constant shadow. Weekend work has joined nightly work as an accepted part of work life. The norm is working longer hours with fewer resources—and on your personal time. Business and personal schedules are often combined since the line of separation has become so blurred or nonexistent.

What's more, virtually every home has become part office. You may probably (or will soon) be one of the majority of Americans who do some or all of their work at home. Even with all the available technology at your fingertips, you'll still be struggling most likely with a lack of time, space—and sleep.

One *Wall Street Journal* article even reported there's a new luxury symbol and sign of success: getting eight hours of sleep a night. With our 24-hour, seven-day-a-week economy, work never stops. Since work follows us home, getting some sleep in this "24x7" world is sometimes the only way to avoid work!

We're talking about survival in a world of instant communications, exploding technology and multiple, changing priorities and deadlines—where doing more with much less (especially staff) is the norm and where you need to continually build your skills and marketability and keep your options open.

And talk about change! Did you know that more than 50 percent of the 1980 Fortune 500 companies no longer exist? Who knows—you may even end up working for yourself by default or choice—an option I've chosen and relished. Incidentally, wherever you work, take charge of your own career and destiny, remembering ultimately, you always work for yourself.

Moreover, good solid organizational tools, habits and systems can greatly help to expand your marketability, your options and your satisfaction.

The Positively Organized!
Program For Action

This book is different from others because it is *interactive*. This book is as close as possible to having a personal consultation with me right now. Together we will use the Positively Organized! Program for Action. Tried and tested over the years, this is a proven program designed for professionals who already possess strong determination and clear goals. I always use it in my consulting/coaching work as well as my training programs. The Positively Organized! Program recognizes the level of success you have already achieved and keeps on building and refining. It also gives you immediate access to *solutions*—specific tips, techniques and tools you can use.

In the Positively Organized! Program, we're a team—you're the player and I'm the coach. As a coach I require your full attention and commitment and I, in turn, will help you see what could be working better for you. I will point out the best strategies around so you won't have to waste your precious time and energy reinventing the organization wheel.

Take what you *read* and translate it into *action*. You'll be able to create a simple plan of action for tackling your desk, paperwork, projects, filing cabinets or storage areas.

Or maybe you and a colleague will read this book and together you'll create a joint action plan to improve a communication system, implement a fail-safe method for follow-up or create an office paperwork procedure that simplifies how you work.

What's in It for You

This book will help you reduce your stress, find extra hours in the day for the most important activities in your life and achieve more of your goals. Hopefully, in the process, you'll discover your own personal sense of achievement—what it really means to be *your best*.

If you share this information with others, you have a chance to improve quality, service and teamwork where you work.

You'll also discover handy desk accessories and helpful office products, including many for your personal computer and mobile office.

And you'll learn that more important than having the right equipment and tools is having the right *habits* to use the tools. You'll create your own personal organization system—because there's *no one right way to get organized*. We're all different and this book recognizes and appreciates those differences.

Even if you have the previous editions of this book, you'll discover all kinds of new products and ideas in this edition because there's no one right way to write a book either. In fact, you may notice I've even modified the title for this edition. Just as I encourage all of my clients to continue striving to be the best they can be, so, too, I work at making each succeeding edition the best it can be. And it appears to be working; you're reading an award-winning book with more than one-quarter million copies in print that's been selected by more than ten book clubs and continues to receive praise from readers just like you. No wonder it's called the Bible of Organization!

It's my goal that you'll not only get many good ideas from this book but that you'll also *apply* those ideas in your work and your life.

How to Save Time
When Reading This Book

This book is easy to use and will save you time because it has been specially designed for you, the busy professional. Special features make this book instantly accessible and usable. There is a complete table of contents and a useful index for easy reference. Also, there are brief "Quick Scan" summaries at the beginning of each chapter, distinct subheads in the chapters to help you read more quickly and plentiful resource guides at the end of Chapters 2 through 13.

And what's more, **you don't have to read the whole book!** Outside of Chapters 1, 2 and 14 (which are "required reading"), read only those chapters that apply to you.

The "Quick Survey" in Chapter 1 will let you see immediately where to fine tune and where to do a complete overhaul. After the survey, go to the detailed table of contents and mark those chapters that relate most directly to the items you marked that need improvement. The "Quick Scan" summary at the beginning of a chapter will help confirm whether you should read the chapter. Whichever chapters you select, *be sure to read Chapter 14* to actually put the ideas from this book into action.

So grab a pen, pencil or highlighter or some Post-it Flags for selecting key chapters and indicating key points. On your mark, get set, get organized—to be the best you can be!

1

HOW TO BE POSITIVELY ORGANIZED!

Quick Scan: This chapter is "required reading" because it helps pinpoint where you are now and where you'd like to be with regard to balance in your life as well as your organizational skills. Through the Quick Survey, you'll assess your organizational strengths and weaknesses at work. Next, you'll identify your goals and values. Finally, you'll reassess your survey results in light of your goals.

Take a deep breath and relax. *Positively Organized!* does *not* mean being *compulsively* or *perfectly organized*. It's being **only as organized as you need to be**.

Your own style and degree of organization at work will depend on a number of factors—your level of activity, whether you're part of a team and/or have any support staff, the image you want to project, if you deal face to face with the public and how you prefer to work. It's up to you just how much organization you need.

Being Positively Organized is *not* just having your papers in order; more important is having your life priorities in order. It's a question of balance between work and personal; between micro and macro; and between the details and the big picture.

There's no one right way to "get organized." As you'll soon see in this book, there are many different organization tools and habits you can use. In fact, I define an organization system as the combination of appropriate *tools and habits* to get a job done or to reach a goal.

There are also different organization styles that reflect both the choice of tools and habits, as well as how they are used. Styles often develop because of "brain dominance." Brain research indicates that most of us develop a dominant right or left hemisphere of the brain upon which we depend. If you are more "left-brained,"

5

you will tend to like more order, structure and routine; "right-brained" individuals prefer variety and flexibility. I believe it's possible to modify your natural "style" to a certain degree but it's important to become aware when you're going against the grain.

For example, a left-brained individual may prefer a clean desk and office where everything is put away. As a consultant I would help that person set up out-of-sight systems. But if a client comes to me stating an aversion to a "neat-as-a-pin" office, I would help design systems that are interesting, flexible and within eyesight and easy reach. As you're reading the book, be aware of your current style and perhaps your ideal style, as well as which products and ideas immediately appeal to you and which do not.

Be wary of *extremes*, however, for which this book will not be helpful. If your natural style (or that of someone with whom you work or live) is extremely rigid, compulsive to a fault and demanding of others, you could be suffering from Obsessive Compulsive Disorder (OCD). While there are many different manifestations of this disorder, one type includes arranging and rearranging rituals that are performed routinely and compulsively. If you think either you, a loved one or a coworker suffers from OCD, contact the OC Foundation at 203/315-2190 or **www.ocfoundation.org** for information and support.

This book will not be too helpful either for an extreme style that craves too much stimulation and variety. If it's difficult or impossible to stay focused for very short periods of time without getting distracted, Attention Deficit Disorder (ADD) may be a problem and professional counseling by someone specializing in ADD should be sought. One resource is the American Coaching Network at 610/825-4505 or **www.americoach.com**.

Creating Balance in Your Life

"Work has become our religion" according to Benjamin Hunnicutt, a University of Iowa labor historian. For too many of us, when we are not working (or shopping), we don't know what to do with our time. Over the last decade, Americans have increased their working hours. Too much time with work means less time for family, especially a spouse. Children also may feel the effect of parents working longer hours, including work done at home where the dividing line between work and home is hard to set.

On the other hand, some people are recognizing the value of working less and are tapping into "voluntary simplicity," one of the leading lifestyle trends. In fact, Trends Research Institute reported that many people have voluntarily "downshifted" and are working fewer hours for less pay in order to spend more time with families or pursue other interests.

Creating balance in your life involves two main steps:

1. Zero in on your professional and personal goals—decide how to spend your time by determining what's really important and has meaning to you (and possibly the world, too).

2. Use these goals to help you stay on course in allocating your time between professional and personal demands.

Next take a look now at how organized you are at work. Then, you'll have a second chance to evaluate your answers once you've identified your goals later in this chapter.

How Organized Are You at Work?

As a consultant I usually begin working with clients by giving them a quick survey, which helps them determine their own organizational strengths and weaknesses. Here's one for you that ties in with the subject areas covered in this book.

Benefits Are the Key

Just why is visualizing and listing benefits so crucial? A benefit is the reason why you do something. It's the motivation behind an action or activity and it should be connected to at least one of your major goals. You'll need a *compelling* benefit to justify spending the time and effort required to organize anything. *If there's no real payoff to getting more organized, you won't.*

Organization gets put on the back burner because it doesn't appear to be a top priority. Your benefit has to be strong enough to make organization a top priority and to counteract all the reasons and excuses that justify this "back burner syndrome."

Make organization a top priority. Take it off the back burner and make time for it *every day*. Get into the organization habit. It will give you a professional edge, not to mention more control and less stress.

Once you've identified at least one top benefit, keep it uppermost in your mind. Second, keep reminding yourself about the benefit while you're reading this book and when you're applying what you read. You (and perhaps your work group) are very much like athletes in training who need to remind themselves constantly about what they want to achieve and why. You need to do the same.

Read and react quickly to each of the following items on Figure 1-1 on the next page and check off the appropriate letter that describes how effectively you and/or your workgroup handle each item below—**O** for Outstanding, **S** for Satisfactory or **N** for Needs Improvement. If an item is not applicable to you, then write N/A.

Figure 1-1. A QUICK SELF SURVEY

ORGANIZATION AREA	Your Rating		
	O	S	N
1. Your system for planning, prioritizing and accomplishing work and achieving your goals. [Chapters 1, 2, 3, 9, 11, 14]...			
2. Your paperwork. [Chapters 4, 5, 6, 7, 9].....................................			
3. Dealing with interruptions. [Chapter 3]......................................			
4. Your ability to easily access needed information. [Chapters 2, 4, 7, 8, 9, 11, 12, 13]......................................			
5. Your telephone time. [Chapters 6, 10, 11, 12]............................			
6. Managing papers and possessions. [Chapters 4, 5, 7].................			
7. Your follow-ups. [Chapters 2, 3, 4, 9]......................................			
8. Your reading load. [Chapter 4]..			
9. Your filing system. [Chapters 4, 7]...			
10. Your desk and work space. [Chapters 4-6]................................			
11. Your personal computer organization. [Chapters 8, 9, 11-13]..			
12. Making habit changes in how you do things. [Chapter 14].......			
13. Your attention to quality and/or service. [Chapters 2, 9-11].....			
14. Juggling multiple projects and priorities. [Chapters 2, 3, 9, 11			
15. Instant communications (fax, voice & e-mail). [Chapter 11]....			
16. Work flow. [Chapters 4, 9-12]...			
17. Records management. [Chapter 7, 9, 11].................................			
18. Your portable, on-the-go, traveling office. [Chapters 2, 12]......			
19. Communications and teamwork [Chapters 10, 11, 12]...............			

How to Select the Areas
Most Important to You

Look at the "Ns" you've checked. Decide which three Ns are most important to you right now. Star these three items. Keep them in mind as you decide which chapters to read.

Take a moment now to reflect on what it would mean to you, your business, your career and your life to improve your top three starred items. Think about the *benefits* that you would experience. Take 60 seconds to jot down as many benefits that come to mind on a sheet of paper or in a notebook or right in this book if it belongs to you. Star the most important benefit to you.

Targeting Challenging,
Achievable Goals

Your benefits will come into focus more clearly once you've identified your current goals. Organization is a tool to help you achieve your goals.

As Yogi Berra once said, "If you don't know where you're going, you'll end up some place else." This is the first secret to being organized—Positively Organized! All the organizational tools and techniques in the world and this book are useless if you don't know where you're headed, that is, what you want to accomplish at work and in your life. Keep in mind that it doesn't matter how fast you're running if you're going in the wrong direction.

Start with an up-to-date list of goals. Not having this list is like taking a trip without a map. Goals give you focus, purpose and direction. Goals can help you attain something you don't yet have or better maintain something you already do. Don't underestimate the power of combining these two types of goals; "maintenance" goals can keep you nurtured and anchored in the present, instilling a sense of gratitude while "attain" goals let you yearn and strive for an even better future.

Effective goals are simple, clear-cut and direct. They should also reflect both professional and personal values—what's most important and meaningful to you and if possible, your life mission. Chiropractor Dr. Mha Atma Singh Khalsa stated it well in his newsletter: "Discover and clarify your mission in life—your overriding purpose."

Radio talk-show host Dennis Prager suggests his listeners ask themselves the following question after each day of work: "Are you proud of what you did today?"

Write down your goals on paper periodically during the year (this means more than once!). Make appointments with yourself to plan your goals on paper. Twice a year may be sufficient—in January and then again in July. Others prefer quarterly goals.

How to Write Down Your Goals

Use the Goals Work Sheet in Figure 1-2 to identify the "what," "why" and "how" of each goal.

Begin by listing "what" you want to attain or maintain and the extent or degree of accomplishment. In describing your goal, ask yourself what you want to **do, be** or **have**. Be as specific as you can. Write your goal in the present tense for a maintenance goal and in the future if it's not a regular part of your life right now. (Or you may prefer to write all goals in the present tense, making them double as positive affirmations of what you want.) Here are three "do, be, have" examples of personal and professional goals:

Do: I exercise three times a week; I play volleyball on Sunday, tennis on Tuesday and racquetball on Thursday.
Be: I am a peaceful person who greets problems as challenges and opportunities. (Here's an affirmation style goal.)

Have: I will have a job in my chosen field that is financially and personally satisfying by this time next year.

Answer "why" by listing any benefits and results you expect from accomplishing your goal. The "why" should also state the value this goal has for you in your life as a whole. If you choose goals that conflict with your life values, you'll be setting yourself up for sabotage and failure. Let's suppose, for example, one of your goals is to get a promotion within the next few years and to do so will require that you put in many more hours at work. But one of your values is to lead a balanced life that includes plenty of time spent with your family. You could have a conflict on your hands—a real values clash.

Your goals need to be in harmony with your most important life values. Taking the "do" goal listed above, here are some benefits or results to be derived: feeling fit; increased energy and vitality; getting those endorphins flowing; decreased stress; feeling more relaxed (exercise is one of the four natural tranquilizers—laughter, music and sex being the other three); having more fun; a better social life; and balancing a hectic lifestyle.

Answer "how" by listing specific ways you plan to achieve your goals—any strategies, action steps or tasks, in addition to the amount of time required (per day, week, month or year). Assigning deadlines—or "lifelines" as one person I know prefers to call them—will make your "hows" much more specific and helpful. Some specific "hows" for the "do" goal could include: calling to make reservations; confirming tennis and racquetball times with a partner; writing down activities and times in a calendar; and putting out sports clothes the night before by the door.

The Power of the Pen

Putting your goals in writing helps affirm your commitment. Your chances of achieving your goals are much greater when you write them down. It makes your goals more real. It also helps plant them into your subconscious. One professional woman I know writes down her goals each year in January, seals them in an envelope, opens the envelope at the end of the year and discovers she has accomplished almost all of them.

Now take five to ten minutes to complete the Goals Work Sheet in Figure 1-2 to quickly jot down three or more of your goals, including the "what," the "why" and the "how" for each one in Figure 1-2 (or better yet, make a photocopy of the page before completing the form).

Figure 1-2. GOALS WORK SHEET

Date:_____

WHAT is your goal?	WHY do you want this goal?	HOW will you proceed?

Aim High

Who says you have to accomplish all your goals? There's a saying that goes like this, "If you accomplish everything you planned, then you haven't planned well enough." You *should* plan a little more than you may actually do; practice aiming high because you'll probably accomplish more than if you lower your expectations and make them "realistic."

Techniques to Ensure Success

So aim high and use these eight ways to increase your chances of reaching your goals:

1. Put your goals in writing.
2. Read them daily before you do your planning and before you go to sleep.
3. Take some action on your goals every day or at least every week.
4. Share them with one other person (and listen to theirs). But only share them with other people who also set goals of their own and reach them. Those are the

kind of people who will be most supportive.

5. Every week write down and accomplish smaller goals that relate to your long-term goals. List these weekly goals where you will see them every day.

6. Review and revise your goals at least twice a year, always making sure they reflect your deepest values.

7. Let them *inspire*, not haunt you.

8. Include both professional and *personal* goals to increase the balance of your life. Make sure, too, that your goals harmonize with those of your career, position or company; if they don't, you could experience some conflict in your life.

Now review your survey on page 8. Find your starred items and notice the chapter references. See which chapter numbers come up most often. Now go to the table of contents and select the most important chapters for you to read. Keep in mind, too, that you should make Chapter 2 and Chapter 14 part of your "required reading" no matter which "elective" chapters you choose to read.

Now look at your goals on page 11 and note which chapters will best help you reach those goals. And remember, the idea isn't to be organized for the sake of organization. It's being 'positively organized' in order to be your best—that means the best *you* can be at whatever you do in your life.

2

TIME MANAGEMENT: WHAT YOU REALLY NEED TO KNOW

Quick Scan: The second of three "required reading" chapters, this one gives you the secrets to getting the most important things done in your life. Learn the art of planning and prioritizing and why time management is the foundation for good organization. See a wide variety of quality computerized and paper-based time management tools and why it's important to select the right one(s) for you.

Every problem with organization is in some way a problem with time. If your time isn't well organized, chances are your papers, projects and priorities won't be either.

Time management is the foundation of good organization. Its purpose is to help you do the most important things in your life.

Many people think the purpose of time management is to get as much done as possible. Not so. Let me repeat: **it's getting the most important things done**.

Do you *often* have days when it feels as if you have accomplished nothing? If so, you aren't taking advantage of time management. You're not doing the most important tasks and activities.

Have you considered what "most important" means? Is it something that has an urgent deadline? Is it something your boss wants? Is it something *you* want that relates to one of your goals?

It can mean all of these. But watch out if you're only making *other people's demands* the most important things you do. To be your best, make time every day to accomplish something that *you* consider important.

Activities you deem important come out of the values and goals you identified in Chapter 1. (If you haven't read that "required" chapter please do so now.) Without clear-cut goals, your time management decisions will be made in a vacuum or else they will be all externally determined by outside circumstances and people. You won't be in charge. So take charge and start choosing activities that contribute to your long-term goals.

Time management is the great simplifier, putting things in focus and perspective. Time management is an awareness of time coupled with the ability to choose and control purposeful activities related to your goals. It's the basis for decision making.

Time management is making choices about activities that have meaning to you. These choices should balance short-term and long-term, urgent and less urgent, internal and external activities. Time management helps you control what you can, when you can.

Time management is also using the right tools and habits to improve *how* you do something. Effective time management tools and habits can improve the quality and quantity of your work, help you make better decisions and increase your performance.

How to Plan and Prioritize

Planning and prioritizing are two essential habits that are the bread and butter of time management. Use them to balance long-term and short-term goals and activities.

Why take the time to plan and prioritize? Research indicates that for every hour of planning, you save three or four hours. Effective planning and prioritizing ("P and P" for short) will help you get the most important things done each day, week, month and year.

You've already started with long-term P and P in Chapter 1. Long-term goal setting is a real time-saver because it's a handy yardstick against which you can measure all your day-to-day P and P decisions.

Learning Your ABCs and Numbers

To master P and P, begin by learning to identify your "ABC" priorities. Author Edwin Bliss, in his wonderful book *Getting Things Done*, differentiates between these three priorities. He says A priorities are "important and urgent," as in crisis management. B priorities are "important but not urgent," as in long-term goals. You should try to spend most of your time on As and Bs. C priorities are "urgent but not important." Try to spend as little time on Cs as possible.

You're probably pretty good at handling As, which fall in the "fire-fighting" category, but how many Bs do you work on each day? **Make time every day to work on your important-but-not-urgent B priorities and goals.** A good source for these priorities are the goals you listed on your Goals Work Sheet in the first chapter.

Another way to describe A, B and C priorities is to substitute these three words: "must," "should" and "could." In other words, an A priority is something you *must* do, a B priority is something you *should* do and a C priority is something you *could* do.

And here's a trick using numbers that I learned from colleague Marjorie Hansen Shaevitz when she and I each spoke professionally at the same conference. Using a scale from 1 to 10, ask yourself these two questions if you're indecisive about whether to do an activity:

1. How much do I really want to do this activity (against the backdrop of everything else that is going on)?
2. How important is this activity?

Add D, D And D to Your P And P

To get the most important things done each day, add three other ingredients to your planning and prioritizing: **discipline**, **dedication**, and **desire**.

There is no substitute for a daily dose of **discipline**. Build planning into every work day and give it as much importance as if you were going away on a two-week vacation. (Did you ever notice how good you get at planning and prioritizing the day before you go away?)

Build a specific time slot into your daily schedule to work on top projects or priorities—and stick to it. For example, authors set aside certain hours of the day to write.

No matter what else happens, keeping that commitment to yourself will make you feel good about the day and your accomplishments. Nothing beats out single-mindedness of purpose when it comes to getting the most important things done.

What we're talking about is real **dedication** to your most important priorities. Start out the morning by asking yourself, "What are the most important items for me to handle today that would allow me to call this a successful day?"

And take time to acknowledge your accomplishments each day. Pat yourself on the back. This is a good way to spark your **desire**, which in turn will fuel your dedication and discipline. Keep relating your activities to your goals, which should also feed your desire.

Six Ways to Maximize Your P And P
When You Make Your To-do List

Now that you've learned the ABCs of planning and prioritizing, you're ready to use them plus these six ways to improve your **to-do list**—a daily or weekly list of activities that reflects your goals and priorities and helps you see the most important things you need to accomplish.

1. **Plan tomorrow, today, and put your plan in writing.** Take five or ten minutes today to type (or write) tomorrow's to-do list so you can start tomorrow fresh. (If you're an early riser, set aside some quiet time at home or at work to plan before the day really gets going.) Planning and prioritizing on computer (or paper) lets you see what you need to accomplish and when.

2. **Revise your plan—stay flexible and use common sense!** Check today's list several times throughout the day and if necessary, rearrange, postpone and yes, even procrastinate on purpose. "Planned procrastination"—consciously choosing to put off—is what prioritizing is all about. Remember your to-do list is a guide and no one gets everything done. Use common sense as you plan out your priorities. If something comes up during the day that bumps another item in importance, so be it. If you're using a paper-based system, write in pencil so you can easily erase and move items on your list. Weigh the value of doing an item at a particular point in time. For example, it may be better to call John Smith at 1:00 p.m. today, even though John is only a "B" priority, because you're sure to reach him at 1:00 p.m.; otherwise you'll be playing telephone tag with him for the next two weeks—which would be a major time waster.

3. **Make at least one, screened-time appointment with yourself each day.** Give yourself at least one hour of "screened, prime time" every day to work on top priority work. "Screened time" is quiet, uninterrupted time allowing you to concentrate and "prime time" is the time of the day when you're most effective. You can screen your time by doing any of the following: coming in or starting an hour early, continuing to work an hour later, having your calls screened by an assistant or colleague (and offering to do the same for them), working in another location (at home or a quiet, inaccessible office), closing your door, activating your voice mail system or your answering machine and writing in a one-hour appointment with yourself on your calendar.

4. **Consolidate activities and avoid "laundry listing."** If you're tired of making long, laundry lists of unrelated to-do's, then shorten your lists and group like items together. Have one section of your to-do list for scheduled appointments. Try grouping activities by category (such as "calls" and "correspondence"). Use priority groupings where you first list your top A priorities of the day—limit the number to three or four—and then list your B priorities.

5. **Make time every day to work on B priorities.** These are the priorities that

most closely tie in with your goals. But most people tend to put Bs on the back burner, selecting only the more pressing, fire-fighting A priorities.

6. **Write down several key goals, activities or projects for the week.** Select no more than four and write them some place where you'll see them every day as you do your daily planning.

How to Choose the Best Time Management Tools

There is no one best time management tool. There are, however, the best tools for you at this point in your life and career to help you plan, prioritize and get the most important things done.

One thing is certain. The more complex and demanding your life and career become, the more you need time management tools that can help you keep track of the complex demands on your time.

There are three broad categories of time management tools today: 1) paper-based, 2) electronic or computerized and 3) electronic-paper hybrids.

Recognize which basic category or approach appeals to you and will adapt to your workstyle and lifestyle. Whichever way you go, select the least number of tools.

The simpler, the better. But don't force yourself to use a tool that you've outgrown or that no longer meets your needs.

You'll see a wide variety of tools in this book, many of which can be used alone or with other tools. Some tools, such as a PDA (personal digital assistant), hand-held devices or contact manager/personal information manager software, are complete systems with many built-in features that often eliminate the need for other tools.

What's so great about today's time management tools and systems is that they work the way you choose to work. You have more choice and flexibility today when selecting and customizing the features you need. (Remember, though, not to feel guilty if you don't want to use each and every feature that comes with a system—use only what you need.)

In this section we'll start with the more traditional paper-based systems and then go to computer and other electronic systems. The seven main types of time management tools are: 1) calendars, 2) to-do lists, 3) master lists, 4) tickler systems, 5) planners/organizers, 6) computer software programs including personal information managers (PIMs), contact and productivity programs and Web-based solutions, and 7) personal digital assistants (PDAs) and other electronic devices. Be thinking about the following criteria as you evaluate these time management tools for yourself:

Size—what's the right one for you?

Portability—how portable does it have to be?

Accessibility—how easy is it to find information?

Compatibility—how easy is it to use it with your computer and existing software?

Features and adaptability—how important are they to you, as well as others with whom you work?

Looks, image and appeal—what is appropriate for your position and lifestyle?

Consider, too, your own personal style. Are you a person who likes to see the big picture, prefers a more detailed look at life or likes a combination of both? Do you want to use a computer or hand-held device as your only organizer? Are graphics and design just as important to you as function? Do you prefer simple or complex planning? These are some questions to ponder as you select time management tools. In most cases, go with your gut reaction; if you don't like a tool at first, chances are you won't down the line either. But if you're the kind of person who takes time to warm up to new ways of doing things, then give it a shot.

Calendars

The most basic planning and scheduling tool is the calendar, which can track future dates, events, meetings and appointments over a long range of time—at least a year out.

Everyone needs a calendar but not everyone is using the right calendar or using it correctly. Calendars come in all shapes, sizes and configurations and often by many a name: date books, diaries, appointment books, desk calendars, desk pad calendars and wall calendars. Calendars are also part of other planning tools such as PDAs, notebook organizers, PIMs and contact manager software programs, all of which will be discussed shortly.

Don't underestimate the importance of your calendar selection. Since this is an item you use daily, you should give your selection some thought. Don't be afraid to change to a different one, even in mid-year. Ask yourself these five questions:

1. Do you have more than one calendar?

2. Is your calendar either too small or too big?

3. Is it easy to miss seeing important dates (because they're hard to spot, there isn't enough room or your calendar is too cluttered)?

4. Are you afraid of losing your calendar?

5. Is it troublesome to carry it with you when you're away from the office?

If you have one or more "yes" responses, consider reevaluating your choice of calendar according to these criteria:

• You should not have more than one calendar unless you have a staff person and/ or a foolproof routine to maintain the additional one. (Keep personal and professional items on the same calendar.)

• Select a calendar whose size and style are adequate for your work and appointment load. Don't force yourself to use a calendar you've outgrown even if it is the middle of the year; switch to another one.

• Maintain a reliable backup system. What would happen if you lost your calendar? Do you have photocopies of the most important pages? If it's computerized, do you have backups?

• Your calendar should be accessible to you, both in and out of the office.

• Your calendar should have the right "look" for your profession and it should appeal to you in terms of appearance and ease of use.

If you're trying to cram too much information into your calendar or appointment book, consider a larger format or a different time management tool, such as a planner or an organizer. A calendar is for mapping out long-range plans; it's not generally the ideal tool for detailed, daily planning. If you're continually using many slips of paper to make notes to yourself because your calendar simply isn't big enough, you're ready for a change.

To-do Lists

Most people should use some kind of to-do list for daily or weekly planning at work and/or in their personal life.

If your work is very routine or very physical, it's possible you wouldn't need this tool. If you're a teller, a baker or a mechanic you probably wouldn't need this on the job. But if you're a manager or supervisor with administrative responsibilities besides hands-on work, you need a to-do list. And if you have a busy personal life, a to-do list is essential.

A good to-do list should have two basic sections—a place for **scheduled activities** and a place for your **nonscheduled activities**. Scheduled activities include appointments as well as blocks of time that you set aside to do specific types of work, e.g., projects, paperwork and planning. Nonscheduled activities are items on your to-do list that aren't scheduled to be done at any particular time of day; nevertheless, you should group certain common tasks together, for example, all your phone calls, e-mails or top A priorities. It's great if there's additional room, too, to record information related to goals and results. To-do list forms come in dated and undated styles and are available from stationery stores, suppliers and catalogs. You can buy forms separately or as part of a time management system or organizer.

It's important to see both your scheduled and nonscheduled activities at the same time and have them next to one another. Whenever possible or feasible, turn your nonscheduled tasks into scheduled ones because they're more likely to get done when you've attached a time frame or deadline. When you set time aside to accomplish a task, you're more likely to do it than if it's just an unscheduled item on a to-do list. If you've set aside time to do tasks and you have trouble gauging time, use an electronic countdown timer from an electronics store such as Radio Shack to help you stick to your schedule.

If you get tired of transferring today's uncompleted to-do's to the next day's list, consider using a two-page-per-week format You'll have a little less space to write, but you won't have to keep rewriting to-do's. You can also see your entire week, including any items that are incomplete. (A PDA, personal information manager (PIM) or contact manager program can also eliminate rewriting because they automatically transfer incomplete to-do's, as you'll soon see.)

Day-Timers, Inc. has a two-page-per-week format that includes three divided sections per day. You can use the first one for to do's, the second for appointments and the third for such items as services performed, time spent, expenses incurred or telephone calls made. There are four lines at the top where you can write your weekly goals.

Master Lists and Other Big Picture Planning Tools

If you have a large number of projects, activities and tasks (as compared to meetings and appointments, which go on a calendar), it may be helpful to group these items in special places other than calendars or daily to-do lists.

A **master list** is useful for listing activities that will occur over a period of time, from one week to several months. A master list serves three functions. First, it consolidates ideas you've been storing in your head and on your desk into one source. Second, it gives you an overview and some perspective of the "big picture." Third, you can use it to select items to place on your daily list. To make your master list more effective, categorize and prioritize it. Some people simply flag the most important items with a red star. You may want to combine a red star with a start date or a due date.

Others prefer to have separate lists. Some of my clients create two lists, one for personal and another for professional. Some create a separate list for each project or type of work. Usually the fewer lists the better, but the trick is to remember to use them. The more lists you have, the easier it is to forget to use one of them.

Whenever possible, put your master list on one page. Group activities by type and priority. You could use a simple master list in a chart format with three main categories in three columns such as: "calls," "correspondence" and other "to do's."

If you handwrite your list, use pencil (to write really small and get more items on a page, use a mechanical lead pencil with 0.5mm lead). Writing in pencil lets you erase and rewrite items when your priorities change. Keeping your master list on computer (with or without a printout) affords you that same up-to-date flexibility.

Remember to include some kind of deadline or time frame because almost nothing gets done without one. If you carry an organizer, hole punch your list and file it under "M" for "Master List"; that way you'll always have it with you.

Many PDAs, computer programs, planners and organizers provide their own master list sections or special planning forms. Some paper-based systems come with a monthly master list form.

If most of your items extend beyond a month, however, you may find yourself having to spend time transferring items to the next month's list. You may prefer an open-ended time frame "Items to Do" form. I recommend listing one numbered item per line and then putting any notes about a particular item number on the back, thereby keeping the notes convenient but separate. This form becomes a concise master list that isn't cluttered with any extraneous written notes or reminders and it can be used for a longer period of time..

If you work on projects with many detailed steps, use a **project sheet** or **project planner** in addition to or instead of a master list. Make a simple list for each project or buy project planning forms that are commercially prepared (see Day Runner and Day-Timers in the chapter Resource Guide). See also Chapter 9 for some other examples of project forms.

Memogenda is a thin, spiral bound book that is a combination master list and project planner. You can keep an up-to-date listing of all the things you have to do in one compact, lightweight source. It's available from Norwood Products in Nashville, 615/833-4101.

If you work with others on joint projects, you may prefer large **wall charts** or **visual control boards** that display activities or specific project tasks for many people to see at one time. Different varieties include "write-on-wipe-off" boards and magnetic boards with movable strips and cards. If portability is not a factor, these boards can be just the thing. See also Chapter 9 for more information on charts.

Tickler Systems

Almost all of us need to have our memories reminded or "tickled." A **tickler system** is a reminder system that tickles your memory. (By the way, the term "tickler" originally referred to a special feather that was used to tickle churchgoers who nodded off during a sermon.)

A calendar and a to-do list are the simplest tickler systems just about everyone uses. But you need more than these tools if you have many, many reminders or follow-ups that are too numerous or tedious to write down in the ways we've discussed up to now.

Tickler Card Systems

A **tickler card system** is useful if you regularly follow up with certain people over a period of time or have particular tasks to do on a project on certain days. A tickler card system typically consists of plain or colored index cards, monthly and 1-31 index guides and an index file box. A tickler card system is particularly useful for sales follow-up. You could use it for a prospect who isn't ready to buy your product or service today but could be ready over the next several months. You'd first prepare a prospect card with the person's name, address, phone number and e-mail address. Then you'd place the card behind a numbered tab (if you're calling within the next 31 days) or behind the tab for the month in which you plan to make the call. Each time you call or write you'd make a notation on the card and indicate your next follow-up action. The card keeps moving through the system until you decide to remove it and/or transfer the information into a computer or paper file.

Let's look more closely at how it works. You'll want to select the right size index cards—they come in different sizes—3 by 5, 4 by 6 and 5 by 8 inches. Decide what kind of data and how much you plan to write on each card.

Here's what you can write on each card. Begin with the name of the organization or the name of the individual, whichever name you're most likely to think of first. Then write the address and phone number and the key contacts and titles. Make a point of listing names of assistants, secretaries, receptionists or other staff members to whom you speak, too.

Write in an "action date" on the far left of the card for an action taken, e.g, actually talking to a key individual as well as entering the date when leaving a message in their absence. The day you send out correspondence or e-mail is an action date, too.

Keep a very brief summary of ongoing activity. For every attempted contact, write a date on the line at the far left. You may then want to use your own codes and abbreviations. You can use "TT," which means "Telephone To" and signifies you initiated the call. (Try to note the time you called, too. Especially if you reached the person on your call, you'll want to try to call back at the same time on subsequent calls. And, if you keep trying to reach someone at a particular time and you never get through, you'll know to avoid that time for future calls.) If you have to leave a message after you called, TT is followed by "LM," which indicates you "Left a Message." LM will then be followed by the name of individual in parentheses with whom you spoke. "Fol" plus a specific date and often a time indicates the next phone call Followup or appointment. You can also use "LMM" when you have Left Message on a Machine or voice mail, EM when you have e-mailed someone and "FT," when you have Faxed To someone—you get the idea.

If someone you've called isn't available, particularly someone you don't know well, ask the receptionist or assistant to take down your name and company and indicate you'll call back, preferably at a specific time. Ask the receptionist or assistant what time would be best to call back. Then jot down "IWCB," (I Will Call Back) on your card. This lets you put your name before a new contact or prospect without making any demands on the person. It's also good marketing to give your name repeated exposure and hence some familiarity. No call is ever wasted. It's a good way to make cold calls warmer.

To have more detailed information, you could set up a **prospect notebook** that contains correspondence and notes that are stapled together, hole punched and filed behind alphabetical tab dividers. (Or use an A-Z style desk file or sorter to avoid hole punching.) There they remain until the prospect becomes a client, whereupon the material goes into a client file folder. The prospect notebook is the longhand version of your marketing activity; the index card tickler system is the shorthand. And if prospects call you before the next follow-up date, you can quickly find the latest prospect information alphabetically in the prospect notebook.

Tickler Slip System

If you have a very busy office in which you're responsible for many details and delegations, the **tickler slip system** can be ideal. It works in much the same way as the tickler card system except you use preprinted NCR (no carbon required) forms, which are often in different colors.

Because you can make several copies of the original form, this system is particularly useful for activities such as delegations that involve other people. For example, if a coworker has agreed to complete a report for you, you would jot down the coworker's name and number, the report name and the due date on the slip. You could keep the original and give the copy to the coworker. You'd file your slip behind the due date (or a few days before) in your tickler slip system file box and your coworker would do the same.

Ideally, the party most responsible for the activity (in this case your coworker) would complete the report and give you a copy with the tickler slip attached. If the coworker does not follow through, your system is a backup that makes sure nothing "slips" through the cracks. But when both parties are using the system, greater accountability and responsibility is usually the result.

You may consider purchasing a tickler slip system such as the All-state Tickler Record System for attorneys (800/222-0510 [NJ] or **www.aslegal.com**) or Safeguard's General Reminder/Assignment System (800/523-2422 [PA] or **www.safeguard.com**), which all come with at least three-part NCR forms.

Desk Files or Sorters and Accordion Files

One of the best paper-based tickler systems that I recommend to almost every client is the **desk file** or **sorter**. The desk file opens like a book and has an expandable binding on the spine. Look for the style that has both 1-31 and January to December tabs. I use the desk file every day for follow-ups and action items that are connected to some paperwork, such as a letter or related notes. (I also use it for birthday cards to be mailed.) I keep the desk file conveniently located. (See Figure 2-1.)

The **accordion file** is similar to the desk file except it is enclosed on three sides and usually has a flap that folds over. I find it less convenient than the desk file/sorter. And if it's less convenient, you'll be less likely to use it. If, however, your paper-based tickler needs to be portable, the accordion file could be a wise choice.

File Folder Tickler Systems

Some people prefer a **file folder tickler system** that has file folders labeled both January to December and 1-31. A file folder tickler system can sit inside a desk drawer or in an upright rack or caddy on a nearby credenza, return or table.

There are many uses for such a system. One consultant I know uses a ruled sheet of paper in the front of each monthly folder to list follow-up calls for the month. He keeps corresponding notes for the calls inside an alphabetical notebook.

A file folder tickler system is also a great way to get reminder papers off your desk and into a chronological system. These are papers that require action on or by specific dates. They may include papers such as conference announcements, letters, memos, notes and even birthday or anniversary cards. If you like visual, tangible reminders instead of a note jotted down in your calendar or planner, this

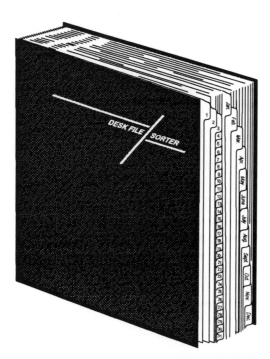

Figure 2-1. Combination 1-31 and January-December Desk File/Sorter by Smead

system could be ideal for you.

Suppose you have some notes you'll need to use at a meeting on the ninth. Get those notes off your desk (or out of a generic, overflowing "pending file") and put them behind the "9" tab.

A file folder tickler system is very similar to the desk file/sorter and accordion file in that it has file folders labeled January to December and/or 1-31 and it, too, is designed to handle paper-triggered actions. You can have more flexibility for tab names; for example, you could use weekly tabs. This system can sit inside a desk drawer or in an upright rack or caddy on a nearby credenza, return or table. Again, it's not quite as convenient as the desk file/sorter and some people are afraid that if it's out of sight in a file drawer that they'll forget all about it. Once it's a habit, however, and part of your daily routine, that shouldn't be a problem.

For convenience, you can buy preprinted file guides or Pendaflex hanging folder label inserts in 1-31, A-Z and January-December styles. Also available are Pendaflex Follow Up Tabs that run lengthwise across a hanging folder and have space for the file name plus two sliding signals that can be moved to indicate the month and the day of the month. Smead makes a Follow-Up Folder that allows you to easily change a deadline or follow-up date. Sliding signals across the top of the folder may be easily moved in the channel across easy-to-read printed headings for month and day.

Customizing Your Own Tickler System

Consider designing your own tickler system. One accounting firm created a simple reminder tickler form for use in its office file folder tickler system. Staff members complete the form, keep a copy and put the original in a centralized file folder tickler system arranged by the days of the month and the months of the year. One person in charge of the system makes sure that follow-through occurs.

When Terry Preuit was manager of a management development department, she worked with her staff to create their own customized tickler slip system. Their slip was a combination memo/assignment slip in four parts (see Figure 2-2). The sender kept two copies, one to file by project (so all correspondence and due dates for the project were in one place) and one to file by date (as a standard tickler reminder). The receiver got one copy. The department's program coordi-

```
┌─────────────────────────────────────────────────────────────┐
│              MANAGEMENT DEVELOPMENT MEMO                      │
│                                                              │
│   DATE:       _____        DUE DATE:_____      │
│                                                              │
│   TO:         _____                                │
│                                                              │
│   FROM:       _____                                │
│                                                              │
│   PROJECT:    _____                                │
│                                                              │
│   INSTRUCTIONS/MESSAGE:                                       │
│                                                              │
│   □ See me to discuss details      □ Handle/then brief me afterwards │
│   □ Prepare response then we'll discuss  □ Handle/update at next meeting │
│                                                              │
│   _____  │
│   _____  │
│   _____  │
│   _____  │
│   _____  │
│   _____  │
│   _____  │
│   _____  │
│                                                              │
│   □ Done/Date:_____        □ See Back/Attached     │
│   ORIGINAL - RECEIVER   CANARY-SENDER/DATE FILE   PINK-SENDER/PROJECT FILE   GOLD-LAURA │
└─────────────────────────────────────────────────────────────┘
```

Figure 2-2. Custom tickler slip designed by Terry Preuit and staff

nator received one copy that kept her up to date on the status of all major assignments, helped her field questions when the rest of the staff were unavailable and in general, cut down on "telephone tag."

If you handle recurring tasks, projects or reports each month, consider using the tickler card system developed by administrative assistant Judy Nowak. Judy uses two sets of 1-31 cards for two months in a row. When she completes a task on a card as it comes up chronologically, she immediately files the card behind the appropriate number for the next month when the task will come up again. In this way she "files as she goes" and doesn't have to file a whole group of cards at the beginning of the next month. She's all set to go.

Nowak also makes sure she never misses a deadline because she has a reminder card that she files a few days before the actual card comes up in her system. She moves both the reminder card and the task card to the next month's 1-31 set when the task is complete.

Computerized and Electronic Ticklers

Automatic calendar and reminder tickler functions are now a standard feature of many software programs (including PIMs or personal information managers and contact managers) as well as PDAs (personal digital assistants) and other hand-held computing devices.

Some of these programs and devices have alarms that ring to remind you of appointments and deadlines. Some will remind your computer when to do things; for example, you can set the alarm clock so the computer dials a phone number at a certain time. Some programs have a "pre-reminder" capability that lets you place a pre-reminder two to five days before your final deadline. The pre-reminder stays on your calendar. Computer analyst and writer Lawrence Magid jokingly calls programs with alarms and reminders "nudgeware."

These programs and devices are discussed later in this chapter as well as in chapters 9 and 12.

Paper-based Planners and Organizers

If you need portability and versatility in a paper-based tool, planners and organizers may be just the ticket.

What to Look for in a Planner

When you need more than a calendar or appointment book but less than a full-blown organizer, a planner may be the perfect solution. And in fact, every organizer should include a good planner as its main feature.

A good planner combines both long- and short-range planning. For long-range planning, you should be able to see the major events of the year and/or each month of the year. For short-range planning, you should have planning pages that present either the entire week (which is my preference) or separate pages for each day.

Your planner should have enough writing space. If you're adding notes all over the place, you could either be short on space or the format isn't working for you.

Decide whether you want a dated or undated planner. With the latter you will have to spend more time writing in the dates, but you also won't waste any sections of your planner if you should purchase it after the year has begun. With loose-leaf planners that isn't a problem, unless dated sheets are prepackaged by year or quarter.

If your planner comes with a telephone directory, try to find one with sections for each letter of the alphabet rather than two letters combined so you can use the sections not only as phone/address pages but also as subject dividers for resource information. For example, on an "R" page, write names that start with that letter and behind that page keep pages of resource information that start with the letter "R," such as "Restaurant" pages listing your favorite restaurants.

The size of your planner may pose some problems. You may want it to be small and compact enough to carry with you yet large enough to carry standard size papers. A tradeoff may be necessary. Choose the size that's all around the best for you. Lean toward the size you will use and select a planner that has the most important features for you.

Do You Really Need an Organizer?

Usually housed in plush ring binders, organizers help professionals manage both time and information. Organizers incorporate a variety of planning and scheduling tools, including calendars; daily to-do sheets; weekly, monthly and yearly projections; master lists; and schedules for special projects and activities.

Other features usually include a phone directory, sections for "fingertip information" referred to frequently, record keeping tools, special forms, compartments for credit cards and cash, pen and pencil holders and combination calculator/rulers. The Day-Timer combination ruler/calculator is an accessory for your organizer that's hole-punched, includes inches and centimeters and is solar-powered. Organizers are portable "Swiss army desks" equipped with many of the essentials professionals need close at hand. You can keep important resource or scheduling information handy—particularly vital if you're out of your office frequently.

A variety of styles and sizes adapt to many different professional needs. Some are small enough to fit in a coat or shirt pocket; others fit in a briefcase or purse; still others are self-contained mini-briefcases or combination organizer/purses that can be carried on the shoulder with a strap. Many come in leather and make for professional accessories that are attractive as well as functional.

Some professional women find the combination organizer/purse with shoulder strap particularly useful. It's portable enough for an organizer and large enough to carry items you would otherwise have to carry separately in a purse. Look for products that hold a loose-leaf style organizer and have at least one roomy outside zippered pocket or purse that is detachable.

Day-Timers, Inc. has several different shoulder binder/purse styles and sizes with innovative features such as handy card slots, utility pockets, a zippered compartment for valuables, pen loops, lipstick holder and a removable cell phone holder. In one, the purse actually unsnaps from the binder so each item may be used separately.

Franklin Covey also has a number of different organizer/purse combinations with useful features such as an outside pocket, a special cell phone compartment, a detachable purse and pen loops.

In the interest of health, I would suggest with any shoulder purse or organizer that you refrain from a) stuffing it to the gills and b) carrying it on your shoulder most of the time. I use the shoulder strap for convenience (or safety) when it's not feasible to hold the organizer in my arms like a notebook. It's not good for your spine to have anything weighing your shoulder down. It's probably a good idea to switch shoulders, but the best idea is to refrain from constantly carrying an organizer or a purse in this fashion. Another option, of course, is to select a smaller, scaled-down organizer with attractive shoulder style purses or wallets.

What I also like about organizers are the handy accessories and forms you can select to customize your system. One accessory I've enjoyed is an automatic pencil/pen combo writing tool. You can get such a tool with up to three different ink colors as well as the pencil. I've used a "tri-point" tool that lets me write calendar and to-do items in pencil, take notes in black ink and use the red to highlight or mark special notations. Both Day-Timers, Inc. and Franklin Covey have such useful writing instruments.

For pages you use constantly, Day-Timers has durable plastic "Tabbed Sheet Holders" (8 clear tabbed, punched pockets, 24 index sheets and 80 colored tab tablets). Day-Timers and Day Runner carry plastic, punched diskette holders.

Day-Timers offers a wide variety of loose-leaf forms. They offer colored ruled sheets, great for color-coding note taking by project or category type (e.g., correspondence and telephone calls). And Day-Timers has colored sheets that are "short-trimmed" so they won't hide the date at the top and are also "double-punched." The latter is great for taking notes on the other side of paper—have you noticed those rings always get in the way? Double-punched papers let you easily open the rings and turn the paper over so that you can write just as easily on the back as the front! Day-Timers even has a special "Double-Punched Narrow Hot list" with a salmon, green or blue border that's great to use as a traveling master list that eliminates transferring of items, moves easily throughout your organizer and because it's narrow, keeps most of your organizer pages in view.

3M has developed some handy personal organizer accessories. Here are a few of my favorites: Scotch Magic Pre-cut Tape Strips No. 673TP1 (you no longer have to take a roll of tape with you), multi-colored Post-it Flags in a thin pack dispenser (No. 683-5CF or No. 673LP1), a thin pack combo of Labeling and Cover-up Post-it Flags with Post-it Notes (No. 673TG1) and a thin pack with Post-it Fax Notes (No. 673LP6).

For years the organizer was my personal time management favorite but it's not for everyone (nor is any tool for that matter). If you're at your desk most of the day and don't move around from office to office or meeting to meeting, you may not need the portability and compactness of an organizer. Some people don't need to have that much information at their fingertips and find organizers bulky and cumbersome.

Others ask, "What would you do if you lost it?" Here are three measures to prevent the dire consequences of such a disaster. First, always photocopy any critical material and store it in a safe location. Second, use a computerized time management program or PIM (see the Resource Guide). With this option, you would print out your hard copies (which you can use in your organizer) and make regular computer data backups. Third, write the following statement on a business card that you laminate and attach to the inside front cover of your organizer: "REWARD: $150 for returning this lost organizer."

PIMs and Other Computer Solutions

The term "**personal information manager**" or **PIM** was first coined by Lotus Development Corp., who used it in conjunction with their former "Agenda" program. Lotus founder, Mitch Kapor, developed Agenda because he was looking for a better way to organize himself and his personal information.

There are many advantages to choosing a computerized time management tool such as a PIM. First, such a program combines most of the other tools we've discussed in this chapter (calendar, to-do list, master list, tickler system and planner/organizer) in one system. Some also provide sales and marketing tools and handle project management as well as other work-related information. Second, most PIMs can work/synchronize with a PDA (personal digital assistant) and can often connect you to the Web. Third, they let you quickly input and retrieve information—even complex or detailed information.

Fourth, because many of these programs allow you to print out information onto paper forms that will fit right into your paper-based personal organizer, you have the best of both computer and paper worlds. Fifth, with most such programs, you have the flexibility to store and arrange random bits of information such as notes, ideas, plans and activities in free-form style, linked loosely by categories that you create. Sixth, it's also easy to make backup copies for added protection.

The only downside is if your software is only accessible from a desktop computer, you're away from your computer much or most of the time (and you're not using a notebook computer, PDA or some other computing device) and you make lots of handwritten notes on your hard copy printout. It will be tedious to have to input all these notes into the program when you return to your office. And more than likely, you won't bother to do it and so you're defeating the purpose of using a computer program.

On the up side, PIMs keep track of your contact information, your to-do list, your calendar and often the schedule for your workgroup. Data can be transferred between and synchronized with your PC and a hand-held device (such as a PDA). If you have a mobile office, you may prefer to keep your PIM on a notebook PC that travels with you.

Contact manager programs handle your address book, allow you to keep track of the people you do business with and have detailed information about all contacts and information relating to them. They are designed to help with marketing and sales efforts. Most "contact managers," as such programs are called, have tickler, calendar and other time management features.

In fact, programs in each category keep expanding their features so don't just rely on the label given a program—look at its features to see if it has the features you need to manage your calendar, to-do's, tickler functions, phone and address database, projects and ideas.

An especially nice feature of a software program is that you can quickly search for information in a variety of ways. Let's suppose you want to find every contact you've had with a particular customer. You can search that customer by name and instantly find the information you need.

Just about every brand-name paper-based organizer has accompanying PIM software to make the transition to a computer-based system fairly easy. Try to determine in advance just how seamless that transition is; often the computer screens do not look like your paper-based systems, although the printout will. See if there is a "print preview" mode, so you can see in advance what the printout will look like so you don't end up wasting paper and time. Find out if there are any independent reviews on new software.

Notebook PCs can offer the advantage of having a portable computer that can perform all the functions of a desktop computer at any time. Some notebook (aka "laptop") personal computers have enough speed and disk storage to function as your sole computer. In other cases, you can use a notebook PC as your on-the-go computer that is an accessory to a desktop or networked computer.

PDAs, Pocket PCs and Other Hand-held Computing Devices

As small and as light as notebook PCs are, there are many devices that are smaller and much more portable. These include **personal digital assistants** or **PDAs** such as Palm, Inc.'s Palm series, **Pocket PCs**, Internet devices/appliances, Web phones and pagers. Some pagers and Web phones have PDA-capability built into them. The needs of your work as well as your personal preferences will determine what's the best solution for you.

These pocket-sized devices allow you to access your calendar, contact information and some or all Web sites as well as to send and receive e-mail and make notes. Additional features such as paging capability may be included, too.

How do you decide which is the right device for you? There are eight main factors to consider when making your decision:

1. **Screen size**—As the screen size gets smaller, it limits your ability to read lengthier e-mail and documents.

2. **Portability**—How small is small enough? How big is too big or too heavy to carry around? As devices become smaller, it's easier to lose them. Protect your information by using password protection features that may be built into a device.

3. **Cost**—As the needed features and number of devices multiply, so does the cost. You need to see what works with your budget.

4. **Keyboard**—Is there a keyboard with the device? Is it large enough to be usable? The smallness of a PDA can make it difficult to enter data unless it comes with a built-in keyboard. If not, consider having an external keyboard to connect to your PDA. There are portable keyboards that fold up into a very small size.

5. **Internet access**—Smaller devices are usually more limited in their Web site accessibility. Web sites often need to customize their content for a particular device so that the site content is readable by the device. This limited Web accessibility may change over time.

6. **Transferring files by e-mail**—See if the device has the capability to transfer files as attachments to your e-mail.

7. **Number of devices**—If you have too many devices, it can be difficult to keep track of them all. The more you have, the easier it is to misplace one. Instead, look for just one device that consolidates and simplifies. Otherwise, you may end up with your digital information stored in many places, too many places. If the same up-to-date information (e.g, your appointment schedule) is not on your desktop

computer, notebook PC, PDA, smart phone and your pager, you could have some problems.

8. Synchronization of devices—If you have more than one device, you better have the same information on all of them. You don't want to miss an important meeting or telephone appointment because different appointment schedules were stored on different devices.

The way for all of these electronic devices to have the same data is through *synchronization*. Check out software programs and Web sites offering synchronization solutions. Determine how easy (or difficult) it is to synchronize your devices. It may involve updating one device at a time, several at the same time or each device receiving the latest information each time it's turned on.

Also make sure you can synchronize (and do so easily) with your desktop computer software including personal/contact information software programs so data can be transferred easily between devices such as your PDA and your desktop computer.

Getting Organized on the Web

The Web also offers some time management solutions. Not only can you download demo software of either sample or complete programs, but you can also take advantage of simple PIM services that Internet service providers (ISPs) such as AOL are offering. Some ISPs let you store information on their servers; that could save you disk space but you may possibly leave yourself open to privacy or hacking problems.

Having your calendar and contact list on the Web may be a great convenience since you can access them from any location. And, you may be able to synchronize this information with your computer, PDA or other hand-held devices (such as your smart phone). The Web site may allow you to schedule group meetings, check scheduling conflicts and send out e-mail invitations and reminders.

Organizers on the Web include:
- AOL
- EXCITE (**http://planner.excite.com**)
- SCHEDULEOnline (**http://ScheduleOnline.com**)
- YAHOO (**http://calendar . yahoo.com**)

However, before you jump in and decide you'll use one of the online organizers, consider a few issues. First, if you use a notebook computer or a PDA, you can have all of your information at your fingertips. Second, accessing the Web through a traditional modem is not that fast and with a high-speed connection, privacy issues are more problematic.

And if you're with a company that has its own Intranet and a sophisticated MIS (management information system) department, chances are good your company has built-in software and computer solutions available today—check them out!

Resource Guide

Time management is an ongoing challenge and adventure. There are no magic wands but hopefully this listing will open your eyes to the many exciting solutions that are available.

Time Management Tools and Systems

Practically every time I turn around, I see a new time management tool or system. The following are among the best I've seen. See also Chapter 9 for additional ideas.

Calendars, Planners and Organizers

Day Runner organizers and refills are available nationally in office products and mass marketer stores in an affordable, versatile range of styles, sizes, features and accessories. Day Runner software is designed especially for paper-based system users and can be used with their specially-designed pre-formatted and pre-punched computer paper refills. Day Runner, Inc., 800/635-5544 (CA) or **www.dayrunner.com**

Day-Timers, Inc. planners and work organizers come in probably the widest variety of different sizes, formats, supplies and accessories. Check out their award-winning software (see the PIMs section later in this chapter). Free catalog. Day-Timers, Inc., 800/225-5005 (PA) or **www.daytimer.com**

Filofax small planners incorporate date book, project, expense and phone/address information in compact, attractive, leather binders. Available in department and stationery stores. Filofax Inc., 800/345-6798 (CT) to get names of stores in your area that carry Filofax or **www.filofax-usa.com**

The **Franklin Planner** is a full-featured organizer system. The Franklin Covey catalog offers a nice selection of high quality binders, accessories, forms and training materials. You can reach Franklin Covey at 800/654-1776 (UT) or **www.franklincovey.com**

Geodex Systems are binder-style organizers that are available in different profession-specific styles, as well as more universal styles. A Life Management format helps users identify a "Vision of Success," a personal "Purpose" and a "Life Plan" to balance your work, self and home (which includes family, friends and community). A wide selection of detailed forms are available. Anthony Robbins, Co., 800/322-6565 (CA) or **www.geodex.com**

Planner Pad is a concise, two-page-per-week, weekly planner available in three different sizes that has sections for things-to-do, appointments, expenses and plenty of space for your own categories. Planner Pad is a combination appointment book, daily to-do list and weekly master list. Planner Pads, Inc., 402/592-0676 (NE) or **www.plannerpads.com**

Pocket-it Organizers offer the practicality of 8½ by 11-inch sheets with the convenience of a small pocket-sized planner; they fold to the size of a 3-by-5 inch card for carrying in a slim wallet and then unfold for filing in a three-ring binder. Software is available, too. Success Organizer Systems, Inc., 800/955-0800 (UT)

QUO VADIS planners are readily available in stationery stores and allow you to plan by the week. I particularly like their **Prenote** and **Trinote** planners. You can reach QUO VADIS EDITIONS at 800/933-8595 (NY) or **www.exaclairinc.com**.

SCAN/PLAN The Creative Organizer Instant Information Scan System uses unique transparent plastic pockets that hold index cards and remarkably let you read and write on both sides of the cards without removing them! For cards you do wish to move, they move very easily. These versatile systems are great for managing time, projects and all kinds of information and come in a variety of different sized planners and accessories. You can use SCAN/PLAN with personal organizers or binders. You can use SCAN/PLAN with computers (templates for Microsoft Word and Office are also available). SCAN/PLAN, Inc., 800/SCANPLAN (800/722-6752) [CA] or **www.scanplan.com**

The **Time/Design Management System** is an integrated organizer that has planning, project and reference sections and focuses on self-management as well as time management. The Activities Checklist is a clever master list form that allows you to see the big picture as well as the details, helps with daily planning and eliminates unnecessary rewriting. Time/Design, 800/637-9942 (MA) or **www.timedesignusa.com**

PDAs, Pocket PCs and Voice Organizer

Palm PDAs come in different models that may include these features: date book, address book, to-do list, memo pad, expense report generator, calculator, ability to send and receive e-mail and faxes, Web access and synchronization software. Palm, Inc., 800/881-7256 (CA) or **www.palm.com**

Visor is a PDA that uses the Palm OS operating system and comes with an expandable Springboard module that may turn this device into a cellular phone, pager and digital camera among other things. Handspring, Inc., 888/565-9393 (CA) or **www.handspring.com**

Pocket PCs combine the compact size and convenience of a PDA with PC functions that include full Web browsing capability, e-mail with attachments, Pocket Word, Pocket Excel, the Pocket Outlook PIM and a super color screen. An e-book reader, an MP3 player and a voice recorder are built in. Hewlett-Packard, Casio and Compaq make Pocket PCs.

Voice Organizers are palm-size "offices on the run" that store phone numbers, appointments, reminders, memos and file folders and have optional PC links and recording space. Voice Powered Technology Intl, Inc., 800/255-2310 (CA) or **www.vpti.com**.

Time Management, Contact and Personal Information Managers (PIMs)

See Chapter 8 and the index for other products and especially Chapters 9 and 11 for more group scheduling, contact management and project management products.

Act! is a popular, award-winning contact management program. Contact Interact Commerce Corp., 888/265-1885 (AZ) or **www.actsoftware.com**

AnyTime Deluxe is a PIM that's easy to use, inexpensive and has a large selection of printouts. The program has a familiar, notebook-like interface that's intuitive, making the program easy to learn. Individual Software, 800/822-3522 (CA) or **www.individualsoftware.com**

Day-Timer Organizer is award-winning software that combines the power of the PC with the ability to print pages that fit the different formats of your paper Day-Timer system, as well as other popular paper-based binder formats; accommodates the different Day-Timer formats using special computer paper; and does group scheduling on the network version. Day-Timers, Inc., 800/225-5005 (PA) or **www.daytimer.com**

Goldmine is a top-rated contact manager program loaded with features. Goldmine Software, 800/654-3526 (CA) or **www.goldmine.com**

Lotus Organizer is an excellent personal information manager. Lotus Development Corp., 800/346-1305 (MA) or **www.lotus.com/organizer**

Sidekick is a fast, easy-to-use PIM. Starfish Software, 831/461-5800 (CA) or **www.starfishsoftware.com**

3

HOW TO HANDLE
TOO MUCH TO DO
IN TOO LITTLE TIME

Quick Scan: If you have an increasingly busy schedule in your professional and/ or personal life, you'll discover time-tested tips on managing interruptions, tele- phone time, delegation, multiple priorities and the "rushing game." See how to better balance the "great juggling act," make room for your personal life and start using ten terrific time-savers.

Rarely, if ever, do I meet people who have the luxury of working at a leisurely pace. There are always countless deadlines and shifting priorities, which all add up to mounting pressure.

The issue is not how much you have to do but rather how much you have to do that is really important. You learned how to sort the important from the less important in Chapter 1 and Chapter 2. You also learned how to organize work into categories and priorities so that you could see what you had to do.

The next step is to take a good hard look at *how* you work. See if there are better ways for you to get things done.

How To Control Interruptions At Work

The most common complaint I hear is, "There are too many interruptions." The main question to ask yourself is, "How many of these interruptions can I control, minimize or influence in some way?"

In my training programs I will often use the chart on page 38 to have partici- pants list all their typical interruptions:

Type of Interruption	I can control them...			How I could control or influence them
	Almost Always	Sometimes	Never	

First, jot down as many interruptions as you can imagine and be sure to include those from others as well as those you initiate *yourself.* How many times a day do you interrupt *yourself* to handle something now when it should be handled later, switch to something more pleasurable as an escape from the difficult task at hand or simply decide to do something easier?

Second, check whether each interruption is one you can control or influence "Almost always," "Sometimes" or "Never."

Third, for every interruption that enters your day, ask "Is this interruption *necessary?*" Some interruptions *are* part of your job. If you're a customer service representative or a receptionist, for example, telephone interruptions are your business. Even so, you can learn to maximize your telephone time so that you have more control. Write an "N" for Necessary next to each interruption that indeed needs to be handled.

Fourth, using your imagination, jot down anything you could do to control or influence each interruption in some way. It may be an interruption is necessary but could be handled later. Perhaps you could prevent similar interruptions from occurring in the future.

One large company I consulted with had its mail delivered three to four times a day. Each time the mail was delivered represented another possible interruption. How would *you* control these interruptions?

I'm sure you came up quite a few ideas. (It's always easier solving someone else's problem by giving advice; in fact, whenever you get stuck on a problem, take it to someone else for some fresh ideas!) Here are a few of my ideas:

• Handle the mail once a day and don't look at it during other times.

• Take a minute to scan the mail each time it comes for anything critical but process it only during a regularly scheduled mail appointment with yourself.

• Have an assistant or secretary scan it for you based on pre-established criteria.

• Suggest the company reduce mail delivery to twice a day.

The idea is to start looking for ways to control and prevent interruptions. Analyze interruptions carefully. Don't just assume they are all necessary. Become proactive, not reactive, whenever possible. And always use common sense and good judgment, especially when dealing with interruptions and concerns of other people.

Five Secrets to Tame Telephone Time

Many consider the telephone both a drain on time and the single greatest source of disrupting interruptions. Others, however, use it too much as an entertainment tool to escape from the tedium of e-mails and other work. Actually, the telephone can be your greatest ally if you follow these five essential ingredients to make your telephone time work best for you.

First, take control through preparation and planning. The key to mastering the telephone is doing much of your telephone work in advance, making more outgoing calls and taking fewer incoming calls. Whenever possible, set up telephone appointments. Prioritize and consolidate all callbacks. Prepare for each outgoing call or telephone appointment by having all the necessary material in front of you and *writing down* in advance any key questions or areas to cover as well as a projected time limit for each call.

Planning the time you call can be critical in preventing telephone tag. The busiest time for business calls is usually Monday morning, between 9 and 11 a.m. Sometimes calling before 9 a.m. or after 5 p.m. is a good time to catch those hard-to-reach people.

Deciding *when* to use the telephone instead of e-mail, for example, is also an important part of planning your calls. Some things are best communicated by phone—particularly sensitive issues or those requiring back-and-forth discussion. The telephone is usually better for building rapport and problem solving.

Second, remember what you say goes a long way with a PTA. Do you have a "Positive Telephone Attitude"? A PTA is essential for building rapport and good working relationships.

In particular, there is nothing like the power of praise when you're trying to accomplish your goals through the telephone. Acknowledge good telephone behavior by those who assist you, be they colleagues, contacts, prospects, receptionists or your own staff members.

I make a big point of thanking assistants or secretaries who have gone out of their way to take down a long message or connect me with someone who's been difficult to reach. I often will tell their boss. Fund raiser Suzanne Marx sends thank-you notes to secretaries and hotel operators as well.

A PTA also includes helpfulness and follow-through. A well-intentioned PTA becomes hollow indeed if what was promised isn't delivered.

Third, use concise communication. Be specific when you communicate. Corporate communications consultant Dr. Allen Weiner teaches professionals what he calls "bottom line communicating." I advise clients to focus on the result(s) they want before and during each call. Nothing will speed up a call like getting to the point sooner.

Try these two proven techniques: first, set time limits up front (e.g., "I've got five minutes to talk") and second, outline your calls (e.g., "I'd like to discuss these two questions...").

Even your voice mail or telephone answering machine message should be as concise as possible. We get a lot of compliments on ours: "Thank you for calling Positively Organized! Please leave your name, number *and the best time to call you back.*"

Finally, consider whether the telephone is your most concise and time-saving tool for any given communication and whether it should be used in conjunction with e-mail, fax or another communication channel.

Fourth, take notes and take action. Take notes during the call if you think you may need to refer back to the call in the future. Don't rely on a good memory and don't be tempted by the thought, "I'll remember this call."

Whether you take notes on computer or paper, always date the entry and list: a) the party who initiated the call, b) any main points to be covered and c) the covered comments, which you number as you go.

Right after the phone call, highlight key points and take any necessary follow-up steps, such as transferring information to your calendar or listing the next action step in your tickler system, PDA, PIM or contact manager software.

Fifth, train your telephone team. If you're fortunate enough to have someone else in your office handling your telephone, you have an opportunity to boost your effectiveness, provided you *train* that person how to screen and prioritize calls, take messages and use all of the effective telephone habits listed here. For more telephone tips, see also "Value Voice Mail and Telephone Time" in Chapter 11.

How to Delegate Your Way to Success

Whether or not you're in a position to delegate, delegation is a tool to help you increase your work output and performance in the least amount of time—provided you know how to use it and you understand what delegation really means. For the delegator, it's giving people things you don't want to do, or often, things you do. In fact, according to Ben Tyler, past Burlington Industries Transportation Division president, "It's giving up things you enjoy to someone else and recognizing that not only can they do it, but sadly, they can do it better." For the delegate, delegation is an opportunity to grow and develop and to shine.

Effective delegation requires four steps: 1) organize, 2) train, 3) entrust and 4) follow up and evaluate.

First, organize yourself. You need to see the whole picture in order to make delegation decisions. Think through the process. You'll also need a good personal organization system in order to follow up later. Top designer and entrepreneur Calvin Klein says he organizes himself first so he can delegate effectively to others.

Second, train your delegate. The amount of training and direction will vary according to the delegate's abilities and the nature of the assignment. Take time to clearly teach the delegate how to do something. Helping people be the best they can be is the highest and most productive level of delegation. It's important that you delegate to people whose judgment is similar to yours both to avoid conflicts and to have work done in a way that you'd do it.

Third, entrust your delegate with the assignment. Resist the temptation of peeking over shoulders. By the way, the dictionary definition of the verb "delegate" is "to entrust to another."

Fourth, follow up, evaluate and *praise a job well done*. Of course, you can't do this step if you haven't mastered step number one. So we've come full circle, back to organization.

If you find it tough getting people to follow through and give you things on time, do what Kathy Meyer-Poppe did when she was a director at Revlon. She told her staff, "This is what I need and this is the date I need it by." Then she wrote it on her calendar and her staff knew she had done so. They also knew she would ask for it if it wasn't done. But usually she didn't have to ask. She said, "They knew it was truly important when I said, for example, 'I need this by next Friday'—that I'm not just blowing in the wind." She stayed flexible, too; if her request was unrealistic, her staff told her and together they selected a new deadline and agreed on it. At times she suggested they reprioritize their work.

Reverse Delegation

You may want to try **reverse delegation** when someone higher up delegates something to *you* for which you don't have time. When Meyer-Poppe's staff came back to her to negotiate work assignments or deadlines, they were practicing a type of reverse delegation. This tool works best when you're organized and can clearly see the important things you have to do, how long they will take and how they relate to the goals of your delegator, your department and yourself.

This type of reverse delegation occurs when a person gives the delegated task back to the delegator. It requires great tact, diplomacy and communication skills. It also requires a thorough understanding of goals and objectives for the company or office and for the delegator. There has to be a real benefit for the delegator whenever you reverse delegate.

When I was the communications manager for an aerospace company, my boss wanted me to get involved in coordinating one of his new pet projects—the creation of a historical aviation museum. Since I had no interest in his project and saw no connection either to my job or my career, I suggested that he involve someone else who was far more qualified than I. Coming up with the name of someone else was an easy task; the company historian worked right next door to my office and was a natural for this project. I didn't know it at the time, but I was practicing reverse delegation.

There's one other type of reverse delegation that you should always practice whenever you're given an assignment or project. Take each of the four steps of effective delegation—organize, train, entrust, and follow up/evaluate—and make sure *you* are doing them. Organize yourself, get any necessary training or information, secure the trust or authority to do a job and finally, follow through on evaluating the job with your boss. This type of reverse delegation is a marvelous communication and self-marketing tool; it can show your boss just how well you work, not to mention how dependable and organized you are!

How to Juggle Multiple Priorities

When you handle many different projects, priorities and deadlines, you're very much like a circus juggler who runs around keeping a dozen plates spinning on sticks.

Sure, you can try to keep up this act all day, but you will certainly burn out before too long. Unfortunately, this method is used by far too many people. To prevent burn out, here are four tips that can help. (The first three recap key ideas you learned in Chapter 2.)

First, **plan and prioritize on a daily basis** and if necessary, several times a day. Do your main planning for the day, *the day before*. Then stay flexible in order to reprioritize, if necessary, throughout the day. Also, weed out those tasks that you really don't need to do. It can put a drain on your time and your brain to even think about activities that really won't make a difference in your work results.

Second, **use the right planning tools** that give you enough of an overview. I'm not talking about a flood of reminder notes scattered all over your desk. Effective planning tools could include a wall chart that shows upcoming deadlines, a project or time management software program that lets you see priorities in a variety of ways or a master list.

Third, to prevent having to remember too many things in your head, **use an appropriate follow-up system**. A tickler system that you use every day, for example, can save a lot of wear and tear on your gray matter.

Fourth, **use effective communication tools and techniques to get clarity** from those people making demands on you. Determine the real, not imagined, urgency of each request. Encourage others to indicate both the nature of the request and the specific time frame for its completion. Chapter 10 describes a simple form delegators can use for this purpose that's attached to paperwork landing on your desk. A written request doesn't interrupt you and lets you plan and prioritize similar requests and time frames more easily. As for e-mails and other "instant messaging," don't assume that the instant medium always indicates an equally instant deadline; always determine the deadline up front and negotiate it when necessary.

If several people from the same department or office are regularly making conflicting demands on your time, bring it up at a staff meeting for a brainstorming session. Often, people may not be aware of the severity of the problem. Involve them in a cooperative way, not through finger-pointing, but through an exchange of ideas that can solve a problem. (For more on problem solving, communication and teamwork, once again see Chapter 10.)

How to Avoid Rushing

If rushing makes you crazy, make a commitment to stop doing it whenever possible. As a famous Simon and Garfunkle song says, "Slow down, you move too fast."

Some rushing may be unavoidable. Beware though if it's a regular habit of yours. Advance planning can prevent most cases of rushing.

Be realistic about time by becoming more *aware* of time. Be honest with yourself about how long an activity will *really* take. Estimate the minimum amount of time and a maximum and then aim for an amount in the middle.

Things usually take longer than we think (the unexpected almost always comes up). And yet, Parkinson's Law says that work expands to fill the time available, which is to say that if you allow too much time to do something, you'll do it in that period of time. Sometimes the opposite is also true: work contracts to fill the time available; it's amazing how much you can get done quickly when you have to.

Follow your own time clock but speed it up and slow it down when necessary. If you practice setting your own realistic deadlines and time frames and sticking to them, as well as eliminating unnecessary or time-wasting activities, you will soon accomplish so much more and with less rushing.

My own mother used to rush all the time (and be late for almost everything) until she decided that the associated stress was just too much. She now allows more time to get ready for appointments and commitments and also does more advance planning. The combination results in less stress and greater respect from clients, friends and her daughter, the organizer.

Ten Terrific Time and Energy Savers
for Terribly Busy People

Here are ten things you may like to try to help you save time and energy and create more balance (they work for me):

1. Carry a PDA (personal digital assistant), other electronic device or paper-based planner all the time and type or write down things-to-do right away.

2. Consolidate similar activities, such as telephone calls, correspondence or errands and do them together. You'll save time starting and stopping different kinds of activities.

3. Buy in bulk ahead of time for frequently-needed items such as office supplies, gifts or cards. It's often more efficient to buy for long-range needs than to frequently run out to buy individual items.

4. Call to confirm appointments. Always call doctors to see if they're running on time before you go there.

5. Use voice mail and e-mail to prevent unnecessary interruptions and to give you more control over when you'd like to communicate. Ask callers to leave you the best time(s) to call them back. If you have a short phone message to leave someone, call at a time when you know their voice mail or answering machine is likely to be on, so you don't get involved in a lengthy, unnecessary conversation; better yet, e-mail short messages.

6. Sometimes do two things at once, such as listening to a self-improvement tape while commuting or reading while waiting in line.

7. Be creative, open-minded and look for better ways of doing things. Share ideas with your friends and colleagues. How do they organize their day and life?

8. Don't rush. There's a saying that the faster you go, the slower you are going to get there. It's the old tortoise and the hare story.

9. Make time for yourself every day ideally but certainly every week at the very least. Plan things you look forward to doing that nourish you. Make time for family and friends. Some alone time every day is also essential to reflect on your life and recharge your batteries.

10. Remember the core values that shape who you are and strive to live them

every day. These values will help you save time by eliminating meaningless activities and will encourage you to use your energy in more meaningful ways for yourself and others. You may actually discover a hidden reservoir of energy as you do activities that align with your core values.

How to Finish Your Work
and Still Have Time for a Personal Life

If your work hangs over you like a dark cloud and follows you wherever you go, it's time to stand back and gain some perspective.

I'm not concerned about an occasional heavy schedule or major deadline. But if you think about work all the time, take too much work home every night (where your office isn't in your home) or suffer from insomnia over work-related problems, you need a break!

In fact, you need more than a break; you need **balance**. Granted, your need for balance will be different at various times in your life. But the first step is developing some awareness of when you're losing your balance and then to take some realistic steps.

Alternative Work Arrangements

Don't overlook new alternatives to your worklife as a solution to your situation. Consider the following: 1) telecommuting and working from home at least part of the time; 2) having flexible hours so you can better balance your professional and personal life, 3) reducing your work hours or 4) changing careers so your workload isn't so demanding.

For some people, it's helpful to add more structure to their schedule. Establish a quitting time each day and stick to it! That's more difficult than it seems for the workaholics among us.

One company has started a "time management" program in which employees are urged *not* to stay late and are even pulled aside and told that it's the results that count, not the hours.

If you must work late once in a while, here are a couple of safety tips. If you need to sign in at the lobby: only write your first initial and your last name. Carry a cell phone for emergencies.

If you must take work home (and who doesn't these days), make an appointment with yourself. Decide to spend thirty minutes and thirty minutes only, for example, reviewing that report for tomorrow's staff meeting. (If necessary, use a timer.)

Make sure, too, you're not just playing a martyr role by taking on too much work or that you're giving in too much to your perfectionism ("no one else can do this as well as I"). Time management expert Mark Sanborn counters the myth that everything worth doing is worth doing well. He says, "Some things are worth doing well, some things are worth doing very well and some things are just worth doing."

Make an effort to talk openly with your boss or coworkers about your heavy work load. Don't just assume that there's no solution.

When Too Much Is Just Too Much

It does help to have a cooperative boss or coworker. If you're working, however, with someone who's out to sabotage you or the company or you truly do have too much to do and too little time, it may be best to look for a different working situation altogether. This is a last resort but consider it if you've tried the time management tools and techniques in this chapter (or book), all to no avail.

At every seminar I give there's at least one person in one of these "impossible situations," with an autocratic boss or a highly bureaucratic structure where no amount of organization could help. Or maybe you're currently involved in a down-sizing effort, alternately called "right sizing" or just plain "capsizing," depending upon which boat you're in. If you're in any one of these "impossible" situations, it may be better to cut your losses and bail out. (On the other hand, some of these down-sized organizations can provide you with some new, exciting, empowered ways of working—see Chapter 10.)

Don't take job stress lightly. According to the Families & Work Institute in New York, job stress is three times more likely to spill over into the home than family problems are to crop up at work.

Resource Guide

Newstrack Executive Tape Service is a twice-a-month tape cassette series that summarizes major newspaper and magazine articles related to business. 800/334-5771 (NJ) or **www.news-track.com**

Nightingale-Conant business and motivational audiocassettes. An excellent selection of tape programs to get and keep you inspired to and from work. 800/323-5552 (NJ) or **www.nightingale-conant.com**

Soundview Executive Book Summaries sends subscribers two or three eight-page summaries of business books and three one-page book reviews every month. You can also buy back copies of summaries. 800/521-1227 (PA) or **www.summary.com**

4

MASTERING
YOUR DESK
AND THE
PAPER JUNGLE

Quick Scan: If you're inundated with the "pile system" on your desk, if your work area is steadily shrinking into nonexistence and if desktop clutter has got you down and under, this chapter is for you. Learn why your desk represents the single most important part of your office, how to make it work for you and what to do about paperwork.

D o you know where your desk is? This question is usually good for some chuckles at my seminars. The problem is most people can't even find their desk. It's under here somewhere...

You're not alone. You and 60 million other people in the U.S. have a desk of some kind. When I refer to a desk, I mean any piece of furniture that is used as your primary working surface. It may be a large executive model with many drawers in a traditional office, a computer work station or a spare table in a bedroom corner.

Chances are good you spend many hours every day at your desk. Why not have it be the best looking, best functioning desk around? And when you're doing your New Year's Resolutions keep in mind that the second Monday of each January is National Clean Off Your Desk Day.

The Myth of the Messy Desk
No matter what you've seen on coffee cups, **a clean desk is the not the sign of**

an empty mind! I know those coffee cup cliches will try to tell you otherwise. But don't be fooled. Most people think and act more clearly at a clean, well organized desk.

Don't fall prey to the false notion that a messy desk means you're busy because you look busy. The reasoning is that if you look busy, you're productive. Take the advice of B. W. Luscher, Jr., from the U.S. Postal Service, who warns: "Don't confuse activity with productivity."

Far from indicating productivity, a messy desk signals a lack of dependability, control and focus, not to mention incomplete work, missed deadlines and lost information.

One manager told me about an employee who had a ton of stuff on her desk. As the manager put it, "All those piles of paper told me she was in trouble."

While the woman was on vacation, the manager went in and saw a six-month-old check lying there with a bunch of invoices. He also discovered an important letter to 20 people that had never gone out. The letter was to announce a meeting the manager had planned. The manager found the 20 letters stuck in a drawer together with papers to be filed. All the letters had been typed and the envelopes addressed. All the employee had had to do was mail the letters! When the employee returned from vacation, she was devastated to learn of her mistake—she could have sworn she had mailed the letters months ago.

What was her problem? The manager says it was a combination of many things. She was very social, always wanting to know what was going on with other people and didn't take care of her own business. The manager observed, "You've got to worry first about what's on your own desk." He also said, "You've got to be a team player and let someone know if you're falling behind." In a nutshell, what she didn't have were the right organizational systems—the right tools and habits that signify a pro who is organized to be her best.

The fact is you are not more productive when you're working out of a cluttered desk. Besides feeling stress, you're continually distracted by all the different papers, piles and objects that keep pulling at you. It's easy to go into sensory overload as your eyes keep flitting from thing to thing and your mind keeps worrying whether you're working on the right task. No wonder you're exhausted at the end of each day!

Here's a general rule of thumb: don't have more than one open paper file on your desk at any given time. You'll prevent papers from slipping into the wrong file. When it comes to desks, a variation of Parkinson's Law seems applicable: your stuff expands to fill the available space.

Think of a clean desk as a little gift you give yourself.

The Paper Explosion

Like most people, you're probably suffering from a paper explosion that never seems to let up. Despite computers, or rather because of them, we have more paper than ever before. The problem is three-fold: first, we produce paper documents faster and more easily now; second, most of us still crave hard copies because we like the feel of a paper document and third, we're printing out e-mail and information from the Internet.

Here are some interesting statistics: a) The annual rate of paper consumption in the U.S. has nearly doubled, b) people regularly underestimate how much paper they use and c) Washington, D.C., the world's paper capital, consumes so much copier paper that if laid end to end it would reach to the moon and back nine times over.

The amount of paper is even affecting office layouts. Rows of taller file cabinets are sometimes being used as space dividers.

Not a Storage Locker

Do not use your desktop for storage. It's a work surface, not a storage locker. Keep it clear, ready for action. Your desktop is prime work space and should contain only those items you use every day, such as your phone, calendar or planner, clock and possibly your computer. Keep your desk as clean as possible.

But how clean is clean? That depends on a number of factors. First, consider who sees your desk. Colleagues? Clients? Customers? Patients? What kind of image do you want to create before these people? It's quite possible your desk should be spotless before the public but can be more of a workhorse before other staff members.

Incidentally, if you're concerned with image, consider this: research reveals that the cleanest desks belong to those individuals higher up in the organization. If you're on an upwardly mobile career path, have your desk look the part.

Second, consider what your level of aesthetics and function dictates. Start to become conscious of what your ideal level of order is and work toward it.

Some people really are more comfortable with clutter and claim they would dry up in an orderly, "sterile" environment. Neatness counts but neat isn't always organized or necessary. If you're one of those people who prefers "organized clutter," more power to you.

Most people, though, have simply never tried working in a clutter-free setting for more than a day or so. The expression "try it, you'll like it" certainly applies here.

How to Turn Your Desk Into a Self-Cleaning Oven

Clients chuckle knowingly whenever I tell them, "Your desk is not a self-cleaning oven." They realize that they need to do something. Even with a self-cleaning oven, there are steps you need to take for it to work effectively: wipe up major spills, remove cookware and set the controls. So, too, there are steps to take with your desk to make it more automatic.

Clear a Path

The first step is "clearing a path," as one of my clients described the process of thinning out the paper jungle and cleaning out the dead wood from her desktop and work area.

Think of yourself as an air traffic controller and your desktop as the runway. You're in charge. You determine which papers, piles, and projects can land on your desk—and stay there.

Use the Accessibility Principle

I once had a client who sent me a snapshot of his terribly cluttered desk and office before we began working together. The caption read, "My office...where everything in the whole world is at my fingertips!"

Don't use your desk as one giant tickler system. You needn't be afraid that if papers and projects are out of sight, they'll be out of mind provided you do two things: 1) set up an appropriate **time management system** as described in Chapter 2 and 2) set up a **daily paperwork system**, which I'll describe soon.

Beware of the feeling that everything has to be so accessible. How many of those things on your desktop do you actually use every day? Every week? Every month? Every year? Make a list of the things you use every day. Of those things, which need to be sitting on your desktop? See if there isn't a better place, one that's accessible, but not on top of you.

Accessibility is the key word. It's the frequency of use that should determine accessibility. How often are you using all of your items? Maybe you started out using an item every day in the past and at some point you stopped. But there the item remains. As a general rule, **the more often you use an item, the more accessible it should be.** Give your desk an Accessibility Survey. Sort the items on your desk into the following categories of usage: daily, several times a week, once a week, once a month, a few times a year and rarely or never.

Remember, the frequency of use determines the proximity and accessibility an item should have. Keep close at hand only those things you're using every day or several times a week.

Begin to Sort

The Accessibility Principle lets you see the big picture on your desk. Now you're ready to start sorting and grouping papers and other items on your desk, such as supplies and mementos, using another principle: **things that you use together or that require similar action, go together**.

As you sort through papers and other items, start grouping them into broad categories by asking yourself questions such as the following:

1. Do you see active paperwork or files you're using daily or several times a week? Put them on one area of your desk for now. Attach a self-adhesive, removable sticker to label this and the other temporary piles you will sort.

2. Do you see "reminder" papers with information that should be recorded elsewhere, such as your calendar, planner, phone book or computer? If you can do it quickly, transfer this information; if not, stack these papers together.

3. Are there any items of indecision that are sitting on your desk because you haven't decided when to handle them or what to do with them? These items make up what attorney Robert Span calls the "problem pile." Pull them together.

4. Do you see reference or resource items that somehow landed on your desk and remained? File them now if you can do it quickly or put them in an area or box for filing later.

5. Is there material to read—maybe magazines, books or reports? Separate personal from professional reading. When possible, tear out articles you wish to read and recycle the rest of the publication.

6. Are there personal items related to a hobby or an interest that belong elsewhere?

7. Are there any supplies and equipment on your desk? Separate them by function and by frequency of use.

The trick is to start categorizing and prioritizing everything on your desk, focusing most of your attention on the active, action paperwork and projects and clearing away the clutter. See how many things you can remove from your desktop and store in other places. Even for items you use every day, don't clutter your primary work surface by putting them all on your desktop. They could still be very accessible in a drawer, on a credenza or on a table to the side. Remove any items you don't use.

Set Up a Daily Paperwork System

Now that you've cleared away some items and have begun to sort your desktop paperwork, you may be wondering, "Now where I am going to put this stuff?" When you don't know where to put papers, they inevitably end up staying on your desk or in the in-box on your desk. You may also be making extensive use of the "pile system," which has a way of spreading to every available horizontal surface in your work area.

Let's face it: most of us were never "paper trained." Setting up appropriate categories and containers in a **daily paperwork system** can help. The daily paperwork system doesn't take the place of your filing system, which is discussed in detail in Chapter 7. The daily paperwork system is for active paperwork that you process on a daily basis. It is a set of tools and habits to help you manage your mail, paperwork, projects and desk.

Begin by categorizing types of papers that come your way most often. Typical categories might include: "Action" (this week), "Financial," "Correspondence," "Calls," "Staff," "Reading," "Filing" and "Pending." You might also include specific category names for active projects you're using on a daily basis. Using the initial groupings you've already created as a guide, make a list of basic category names you could use for your everyday paperwork.

If you're having trouble thinking of ones that fit your needs, try this simple exercise. Next time you process your mail and other paperwork, have some 3-by-5-inch index cards handy. Go through your paperwork, making decisions about what to keep and what to toss. (For many people this is the most difficult part. Be willing to get in the habit of freely tossing—more on this in Chapter 5). On an index card, jot down the major category for each type of paper you're keeping (e.g., "Reports," "Must do today"). A broad category name will often describe the general type of activity or level of urgency. Do this for a few days or for one day if you have a lot of mail and paperwork.

Go through the cards and **select the broadest, the most general categories you'll use every day.** See if some of them can be combined. A category is a good one if you'll use it just about every day. Remember the purpose of these categories is for general sorting, not filing of paperwork.

After you've decided on your basic categories, set up the tools of your daily paperwork system using existing file folders, boxes, caddies or organizers. Label these containers with your categories. Ideally, get as much off your desk as possible. Containers should be accessible but they shouldn't crowd your space.

Set up a trial paperwork system. Buy a package of assorted colored, "third-cut," manila folders at your local stationery store. (The cut refers to the width of the tab in relation to the folder; third-cut folders have large tabs that are cut one-third the width of the folders.) See what you already have on hand in terms of boxes, trays and caddies. Even a simple corrugated cardboard magazine file or holder (as described in Chapter 5) works great to hold active files.

Don't invest in a lot of equipment; remember this is just a trial system. Some people, after getting all inspired about organization, rush out and buy too many accessories without first thinking through the system. I've walked into offices of some new clients only to find five name and address books or rotary files, ten letter trays and dozens of file folders—all of which had had "good intentions" but have since been abandoned. The supplies are not the system. They are part of the system. They are only the tools.

Start with a simple system. Select the smallest number of tools and label them with your category names. Arrange them in an easy-to-use, accessible location. A couple of pointers may be helpful. First, use vertical systems whenever possible, as horizontal ones tend to promote the "pile system" of stacking papers. (See Figure 4-1 for examples of vertical, desktop active file organizers.) You may have noticed that the pile system has a way of spreading to every available horizontal surface in your work area. Piles add to confusion and a sense of work overload.

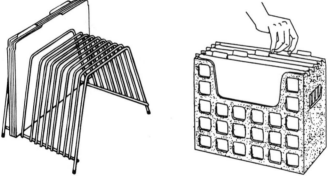

Figure 4-1. Colored manila folders for your daily paperwork system work great in a vertical wire rack (on the left). If you prefer a desktop file organizer that accommodates hanging file folders, consider the Oxford DecoFlex by Esselte Pendaflex, which comes with Pendaflex hanging folders.

Second, try the system out for two to three weeks, make refinements and then purchase any additional supplies you need.

Your daily paperwork system doesn't have to be visible; some of the best ones are "invisible." Use prime filing space in your desk or within an arm's-reach of your filing cabinet or credenza. If out of sight means out of mind, then perhaps a more visible system is indeed a good idea for you. But if you're the type of person who gets anxious just looking at paperwork, then design a more hidden, yet accessible, system and start using your time management tools to jot down things to do and remember.

Several tools may be particularly useful in your daily paperwork system. I use the **desk file/sorter tickler system** that is described in Chapter 2 to sort what would otherwise be miscellaneous follow-ups into an organized, chronological system. Also useful is the Pendaflex Sort-Pal, an expanding sorter file that organizes papers requiring specific routine actions, such as faxing, photocopying or signatures. It comes with six preprinted tabbed sections and includes blank labels to customize your own headings.

The Pendaflex Hanging Expandable File fits inside your file drawer and has nine expandable filing sections that grow as your daily paperwork system grows. A handy tool for your daily paperwork system, it comes with blank, self-adhesive labels so you can make custom headings for your paperwork categories.

With regard to in/out boxes, consider a number of possibilities. First, consider whether you need them at all. If you're the type of person who either doesn't get much mail or paperwork or who's very decisive and organized and immediately takes action on papers that cross your desk, you might not need them at all. Or perhaps you could get by with just an out-box.

But most people are inundated with paper that doesn't require immediate action. You might consider having more than one box, tray or folder designated for different types of work or priorities and training any coworkers who give you work to presort it into the appropriate container. It would be great if each person were to also use a work request priority form (as described in Chapter 10) indicating the level of urgency.

If such a system isn't feasible in your office, consider using the FIFO, First-In/First-Out, paper handling system available through Daisy Wheel Ribbon Co., Inc. (800/266-5585 [CA] or **www.daisyw.com**). This paper handler replaces the traditional in-box. Simply place the transparent acrylic unit on your desk so that the v-shaped opening leans toward you. Place papers upright so the print faces you and place additional papers, publications, files and so forth behind. This system allows you to automatically see and remove your paperwork in the order it was received. If you choose not to handle a particular piece of paper, simply place it behind the existing papers, marking it with the date or simply a check mark and it will work its way forward once again.

Ideally, you would not let the paper cycle through more than once. And of course, try to handle as many papers as possible the first time through the system. But we all have those "C" priority papers that would be nice to handle but simply aren't urgent enough for right now. The durable FIFO paper handler holds about 500 sheets of paper and can be used alone or with an optional out-box that fits underneath.

Survey Your Work Surface

Now that you've cleared a path and set up a daily paperwork system, look at your desktop. **Do you have enough work surface?** Many people put up with a desk that is too small to begin with and it becomes smaller and smaller as the paper jungle takes over. Now that you've cleared a path, try out your desktop for several days. See if you now have enough space to work.

Most people need at least two work surfaces in their office (not counting a return or table for computer or typewriter). The second surface should be accessible and placed within an easy swivel of your chair—behind you or at your side.

Don't use the extra work surface as a storage depot or junk table, however. This surface should only hold things that you use daily or several times a week. This surface is great for holding active, working file folders that sit vertically in upright caddies. You might use this surface for your stapler, tape and other supplies as well as reference materials, in/out boxes, mementos and index card files. Part or all of this second surface could be designated as a telephone station. A nearby table top, a credenza or even a two-drawer filing cabinet can work great as secondary work surfaces. If you prefer that spotless, executive, clean desk look, put items inside your furniture.

Make Appointments with Yourself

Setting up the tools of a daily paperwork system is only half the story; setting up regular routines and habits is the other half. Any organizational system, by the way, consists of two components—tools and habits. I often use this simple equation in my seminars: **a system = tools + habits**.

The trick to making your daily paperwork system work is simply, to work the system! Here are some habits and routines that can help you work the system—circle any that you could use:

• Schedule appointments with yourself to process paperwork. One training manager I coached schedules "personal administrative time" every week to work in her office. This time has become a "safety net" that allows her to stay in control of paperwork and priorities. She meets with her assistant every Monday to block out her self-appointments on their respective calendars. They both try to protect these appointments.

• Open and sort your mail every day you're in the office.

• If possible, have someone else open and sort your mail.

• Make a decision about each paper that crosses your desk the first time it crosses your desk. For the papers you're keeping, decide if they can be handled now or later. If a paper will take only a minute or two, do it now. If you're deferring papers for a later time, resist sticking them back in the pile or the in-box. Decide when you'll be handling each one and where each should go in terms of its function and meaning to you—i.e., where's the first place you're likely to look for the item and retrieve it for action?

• Keep it clean! At the very least, clean your desk and work area before you go home or stop work for the day. Or try the CAYGO habit—Clean As You GO— to prevent paper buildup during the day. And if filing is a real chore use FAYGO— File As You GO or do as Bill Butler from BCG International does—clean one file a day.

• Use time management tools such as your calendar, master list, organizer, PDA or PIM to record key information from papers that you can then toss.

• Consolidate information. Use notebooks, charts, forms, tickler systems and a good deskside filing system. (And read chapters 2, 7 and 9.)

Catching Up with Reading

Make separate reading appointments with yourself to keep up with professional reading. If your day is just too hectic, make a reading appointment with yourself on your personal time. One professional working parent I coached has made Wednesday night "Reading Night" where she, her husband and their eight-year-old son curl up and read instead of watching television.

When you read, try these tips: separate professional from personal interest reading; make clear decisions whether what you're reading is worth your time; read more quickly by reading selectively—check out headlines, subheads and first and last paragraphs; try using a timer or give yourself reading goals, e.g, two journals in twenty minutes; to increase your motivation, tell yourself positive messages about reading, e.g, how reading helps you control your paperwork, saves you time, helps you learn more about your field and makes you feel more professional.

Highlight anything you read that you plan to save so that you won't have to reread the whole thing the next time. I picked up a time-saving highlighting technique from my husband; instead of underlining or highlighting whole sentences horizontally, draw a vertical line (using any writing tool you prefer) alongside a sentence or paragraph. Star any points or paragraphs that are particularly pertinent. You'll be surprised at how fast you can highlight as you read. Also, jot down the name or subject at the top of a paper or article you're saving so that it can be quickly filed or distributed without having to reread it (also put the date on the paper so you can later easily spot outdated information without having to reread it).

Other Ways to Put Paper in Its Place!

Are you suffering from a paper mill logjam? If so, you may have a tremendous amount of paperwork to process in your job and/or you probably have some difficulty making decisions.

Start making decisions. If you're always drowning in paperwork, chances are you tend to avoid decisions. See if one or more of the following seven symptoms apply to you:

1. You're insatiably curious and love to learn to the point of distraction.
2. Perfectionism tends to rule in your life.
3. Everything always takes longer than you thought it would.
4. You're creative.
5. You distrust structure and/or authority.
6. You're afraid of making a mistake and taking risks.
7. **You don't have a current, written list of goals that you refer to every day.**

All of these can contribute to decision-making difficulties concerning paper. But remember, number seven is the most important. Making decisions about paper shouldn't be arbitrary. They need to relate specifically to your values and goals in life.

Without goals as a guideline, as a yardstick, it is very difficult to make decisions, including decisions about those papers on your desk.

Difficult decisions about paper often signal ambivalence or conflict about what you want to do now and in the future. "I might need this someday" is such a haunting thought, especially when goals are fuzzy at best. Remind yourself frequently about your goals—every time, in fact, you pick up a paper, a piece of mail, a file folder, whatever. Remind yourself whenever you put down a paper without making a decision. And remember, almost always the worst decision you can make is not to make a decision because this equation is almost always true: **No Paperwork Decision = Greater Paperwork Buildup**. (See also Chapter 1 on goals and Chapter 5 on collecting.)

Preventing and Conquering Long-term Paper Buildup

Certainly, decision making will be a contributing factor to preventing paper buildup.

Controlling your mail will also be a factor. The volume of mail sent by Americans grows every year and 44 percent of it is junk mail. Here are some tips to gain more control over your junk mail monster:

• Cut subscriptions to magazines and/or share your subscriptions with others so your name doesn't go on additional lists.

• Whenever you order anything by phone, fax, mail or e-mail, ask that your name not be sold, rented or traded.

• To help remove your name from many national mailing lists write to Direct Marketing Association Mail Preference Service, Box 9008, Farmingdale, NY 11735 (212/768-7277) or log on to **www.e-mps.org/en/.** You can also write to: Direct Marketing Association, Telephone Preference Service, PO Box 9014, Farmingdale, NY 11735.

• Remove your name from company report distribution lists if you're receiving reports you don't need to see.

• Reduce memberships in associations that no longer meet your needs.

• The Privacy Rights Clearinghouse has information on reducing junk mail and telemarketing calls and other issues in which technology is affecting privacy. Log on to **www.privacyrights.org**.

For existing long-term paper buildup, you have these four options available: 1) trash it, 2) quickly box and store it now and plan to sort it later as a long-term project after reading chapters 5 and 14, 3) read chapters 5 and 14 to do something about it now and 4) create a workable filing system that accommodates resource and reference information you want to keep and go directly to Chapter 7.

Choose an option based on how important these papers are to you. **Are they worth your time?**

Scanners and Software

There's another great solution to getting those papers off your desk—scanning them directly into your computer.

The scanner market has really grown and with good reason. The prices have come way down and the quality has gone up.

Make sure the software that comes bundled with the scanner can handle your text and graphic needs. You may also separately purchase document management software that helps you organize, file and retrieve scanned documents. (See Chapter 7 for examples.)

OmniPage Pro is award-winning OCR (optical character recognition) software that scans paper into editable, electronic Word documents, Excel spreadsheets or live Web sites without tedious retyping. It recognizes photocopies, faxes, small and large text, color and black-and-white images, multi-column documents, tables and spreadsheets. 800/535-SCAN (CA) or **www.caere.com**

The award-winning TextBridge Pro is OCR software whose accuracy rate, editability and formatting is excellent. It's easy to use, too. 800/432-9329 or **www.textbridge.com**

Up until now I haven't bothered listing any business card scanners in previous *Organized to Be Your Best!* editions. The accuracy is finally here with the Corex CardScan, which keeps getting rave reviews. If you collect many business cards, contact Corex at 800/942-6739 (MA) or **www.cardscan.com**.

The award-winning Visioneer PaperPort scanner with its compact design and small "footprint" is handy for scanning all different-sized documents, from business cards to newspaper articles (888/229-4173 or **www.visioneer.com**).

There are many other reliable scanners on the market today that can handle a larger volume of documents. Look for reviews in *PC Magazine* and *PC World* and check out models from Canon Computer Systems, 800/848-4123 (CA); Envisions Solutions Technology, 800/365-SCAN (CA); and Hewlett-Packard Co., 800/722-6538 (CA).

Computerize More of Your Paperwork

You can reduce paperwork by using computers more extensively and at the same time resisting the temptation to make all those hard copies. Instead, when the urge to print out hard copy seizes you, back up your work on a computer tape or disk more religiously instead.

A number of years ago I read an article in *PC World* magazine entitled "The Less-Paper Office" *not* the paperless office, which isn't realistic at this point in time. The article encouraged readers to embrace computerized work solutions. I have included computerized solutions throughout this book, in virtually every chapter, that can help you reduce or eliminate paper. You can put your calendar on computer (Chapter 2); use scanners as discussed in this chapter along with document management software (Chapter 7); use electronic forms and workflow (Chapters 9 and 11); put your business contacts on a computer database (Chapters 2 and 9); do document sharing and editing in which two or more people work off the same document on computer (Chapter 11); fax directly from your computer to another's computer (Chapter 11); and use e-mail (Chapter 11).

Recycling, Reducing and Reusing

If after all of the above, you end up with a lot of paper that best belongs in the trash can, please reuse or recycle as much of it as you can. And look for ways you can reduce the amount of paper you use.

We accumulate a lot of scratch paper in our office. I always try to reuse paper that has printing on only one side. I use the clean side for taking notes, for printing out drafts and for brainstorming ideas.

Remember to use both sides of a new sheet of paper when photocopying or printing whenever possible (but always first check with the manufacturer to see whether this could harm your copier or printer). An **auto-duplexing laser printer** makes this kind of printing easier.

Sometimes I get graphically interesting junk mail that I give to my nine-year-old to use in an art project.

I reuse mailers, boxes and manila envelopes and folders. I put large corrugated boxes that I'd be unlikely to use in our city's curbside recycling bin. It feels great to make these contributions to our planet!

For other recycling ideas, see the index or chapters 5, 7 and 10.

Shredders

You may have papers with private or sensitive information that should be shredded before they are recycled or thrown out. Shredders vary in their capabilities including the sheet capacity, the way papers are cut up, the speed and their workload (e.g., light, medium or heavy duty).

Five Easy Ways
to Organize Your Tax Paperwork at Home

Here's a good way to apply the principles, tools and techniques we've discussed thus far, especially if you sweat it out at tax time spending precious weekends trying to catch up on a year's worth of tax-related paperwork and record keeping. Follow these five simple steps:

1. **Create a pleasant, well-equipped work area**. Whether it's a nook, cranny, corner or an office with a door, your work area should be conducive to doing tax paperwork. It should contain all necessary supplies and equipment—such as computer, calculator, pencil, paper and files—within arm's reach. Make sure you have enough work space to spread out your paperwork. (For more on "work space basics," see Chapter 6.)

2. **Set up a simple daily paperwork system to store current bills, checks, receipts and records**. Notice the emphasis on current. Generally, you'll want to keep the current year's paperwork together, especially any tax deductible expense records. File current paperwork so that it's accessible. Select the right filing tools. If you're tight on space or you need portable containers, consider lightweight, plastic file boxes with handles. For faster filing, use different colored folders for different categories. (See also Chapter 7 on filing.)

3. **Separate and store past years' taxes and records**. Most records should be grouped by the tax year and stored separately from current records. Records that you'd refer to by category, such as those for car repair, home improvements and investments, should probably not be filed by the tax year. The main point is keep

current records, or those you use most often, most accessible and file inactive information in your filing cabinet or in file storage boxes.

4. **Do record keeping as you go**. Once you've organized your physical records and papers, you're ready for a written recordkeeping system. Keeping your checkbook register up to date is an important step. But if you have a lot of deductions, you'll want to organize and track this information by category as it occurs. Computer programs and even simple recordkeeping books can help. If you deduct car or travel expenses, for example, use handy auto expense booklets, which are small enough to fit inside your glove compartment, briefcase or pocket. Your PDA may allow you to easily track records, too.

5. **To make your system work, be sure to work the system**! Make weekly or monthly appointments with yourself and write them down on your calendar. Create a routine and then reward yourself each time you stick to your routine.

Resource Guide

Paper Management Supplies and Accessories

These selected office products here are handy items you may wish to add to your work area. Most are available in good office products catalogs or stores and in fact, it's helpful to look at a good catalog right now to see the products that are described here. Good office supply catalogs with hundreds of pages usually have two indexes—one listing manufacturers and the other listing general types of products. I've used the general headings you're most likely to see in these catalogs.

Binders and Accessories

Besides file folders (which are discussed in detail in Chapter 7), there are many other options to store and organize paperwork.

The **notebook** or **binder** in all its different sizes is still one of the best organizational and storage devices around for paper resources and records referred to frequently. Sure, it's easier to throw something in a file, but when you go to find it, the notebook wins hands down.

Use binders to store articles and clippings, updates, product literature, samples, ideas, active client summary sheets and the latest professional or trade information—the list is endless.

As a professional speaker and writer, I keep an **anecdote notebook** with alphabetical tabbed dividers. Under each letter of the alphabet, I have key subject words that begin with that letter. For example, under the letter "T" are the subjects, "Information Management," "Inspiration" and "Insurance." Blank sheets of white paper are labeled with the key words. Short clippings are cut and pasted or stapled onto the appropriate page. Longer articles I want to keep are labeled with key words and placed in plastic sheet protectors.

You say you hate hole punching? Then buy the three-hole pre-punched plastic sheet protectors with a margin that allow you to store 8½-by-11-inch papers without additional punching. They're called **top loading sheet protectors, page protectors** or **plastic sleeves** and are enclosed on three sides and "load" through the open end on top. They should be widely available or contact Centis (800/767-0777 or **www.20thcenturyplastics.com**).

C-LINE (888/666-5773 [CT] or **www.cdg.com**) makes them in several styles: clear, colored or clear with a colored edge. C-LINE also makes a combination sheet protector with tabs for indexing called "Tabbed Toppers." Or, if you prefer, you can use Avery Dennison's Extra Wide Index dividers specially designed for binders containing oversized sheet protectors. The point is if you're using sheet protectors and index divider tabs together, make sure the tabs are not hidden from view.

Pocket dividers also called **pocket folders** or **slash pockets** are handy for items that you don't want to hole punch and are smaller than the standard page size.

If you need to organize duplicate sets of binders with tabs but you don't want to bother with typing and inserting labels repeatedly into plastic binder tabs, consider one of the multi-colored index systems on the market that let you simplify the job considerably. The process is simple: you type a master contents page that aligns with the tabs and then you photocopy the page onto blank contents pages. Look for the Avery Dennison and Wilson Jones brand indexes.

Avery Dennison Ready Index is available in either the standard 8½-by-11-inch or 9¼-by-11-inch sizes for binders with oversized items such as sheet protectors. The 8½-by-11-inch is available in a wide variety of styles, including numerical, monthly and alphabetical and the 9¼-by-11-inch size is available in the numerical style. Ready Index works with laser and ink jet printers and copiers. Easy-to-use templates for Ready Index are built into many leading word processing programs.

Wilson Jones "MultiDex" features a slide out Quick Reference Table of Contents that allows you to see titles without having to flip back to the contents page in the front of the binder. It's available in five different numerical sets—5, 8, 10, 12 and 15 plus 1-31, Jan.-Dec. and A-Z.

If you are tired of three-ring binders that never close properly and snag important documents, look for binders with a locking mechanism, such as the Wilson Jones brand. You'll find the strongest mechanism in Bindertek's Law Files great two-ring binder (the ring is guaranteed for life) and lets you access, insert and remove documents easily. Also available are accessories for filing photos, bulky documents and important originals without hole punching. For more information contact Bindertek (800/456-3453 [CA] or **www.bindertek.com**).

For a whole variety of preprinted tabs for nearly every area of law, consider those by Legal Tabs Co. (800/322-3022 [CO]). The tabs are available on the bottom or on the side, plain or punched (3-hole side or 2-hole top). You can use them in binders or in file folders to organize your legal documents.

To easily make your own custom tabs for notebook dividers, look for Avery Dennison's Index Maker which comes with tabbed, reinforced dividers and clear labels, ready for laser printing or photocopying. You apply the self-adhesive labels directly onto the divider tabs. For ways to use Index Maker with software, log on to www.avery.com and search for Index Maker.

Business Card Accessories

If you attend meetings where you collect many business cards and you prefer to physically store them (rather than scan or input them into your computer as described earlier in this chapter), there are a few options. You could start a **business card notebook** with plastic business card sleeves that are tabbed. Label the tabs with either letters of the alphabet or names of organizations and associations. Before you go to a meeting, skim the cards and any notes you made on them.

Rolodex makes a variety of different business card files as well as some useful accessories. Some Rolodex cards are large enough to hold stapled or glued business cards (without having to recopy the information). There's also room for brief notes. To turn your file into more of a resource database, insert special Rolodex plastic divider tabs with your own category names to divide up your Rolodex. Use an alphabetical system within those categories, not the entire Rolodex. With several different subject categories, it's often easier to look up listings, rather than trying to remember exact names. You can organize your file with Rolodex colored cards and/or colored plastic card protectors. If your system is used all the time, get the Rolodex plastic sleeve card protectors, which are available in clear as well as colors.

While the most common brand name, Rolodex is not the only brand of card file. There are many brands as well as styles from which to choose. Compare card files available in office supply stores and catalogs.

Clips

To temporarily group and secure papers, nothing beats the paper clip. What you may not realize, however, is the variety of clips now available.

Rectangular clips hold papers securely and will not catch on other adjacent papers. **Binder clip** is the generic name for what is probably the most secure, slip-proof clip you can buy. Use binder clips for loose bulky papers that need to be held securely.

Plastic paper clips should always be used around computers because metal clips can become magnetized and can destroy computer data. They come in a variety of colors and so can be used for color coding different papers.

The **banker's clasp** has a strong grip and is useful for holding bulky papers. The raised short end allows you to easily and quickly slip the clip onto papers.

A **magnetic clip** attaches to the sides of metal file cabinets and is handy for attaching notes or information.

Color Coding

For color coding and drawing attention, here are additional products that will help:

Redi-Tags are removable, reusable color-coded tags that have a reusable adhesive on half the tag. They come in 16 different colors, three sizes and many have preprinted phrases. Many come in refillable dispensers. There is a "general office" series with such tags as "FILE," "FYI," and "RUSH!" There's also a medical series that includes "SIGN ORDERS" and "DICTATION NEEDED." If your local office supply store or catalog doesn't have this item, call 800/421-7585 (CA) or visit **www.btetag.com** for a store location near you.

Post-it Flags by 3M are versatile. Half of the flag is colored and may have a pre-printed message such as "Note" or "Sign Here"; the other half is a transparent surface upon which you can write with pencil or pen. Available in 10 colors, easy-to-use Post-it Brand Flags keep your paperwork organized. Use them for quick reference, easy retrieval and handy reminders. They are ideal for color coding, organizing and indexing. Both Post-it Flags as well as Pop Up Notes have handy, refillable dispensers that are available.

Avery Dennison's **See-Through Color Dots** are useful for highlighting directly on an item, such as maps, blueprints and graphs, where it's important the information not be obscured. Available in four colors, these ¼- or ¾-inch dots are removable. One manager uses them on her voice mail log where red dots are for "immediate call backs," blue for "action items" to do now, green for "correspondence" where she needs to send something and yellow indicates "for information only" with no response needed on her part. (If you need more colors and can use permanent, opaque dots, look for Avery Dennison color coding labels, which come in 12 colors.)

To help you keep tabs on your paperwork, try Avery Dennison **SwifTabs** or

TABBIES index tabs. Both of these products are self-adhesive, durable and come in a variety of colors and styles. SwifTabs are made of plastic and TABBIES are made from laminated paper. Both are also available with preprinted months, numbers or letters. You can write or type on them. Use them on such items as computer printouts, reports or on spiral bound books. For TABBIES self-adhesive index tabs contact Tabbies, a division of Xertrex International, 800/822-2437 [IL] or **www.tabbies.com**.

And if you're looking for a great selection of paper, envelopes, presentation folders, paper accessory products and even software solutions, contact PaperDirect for their catalog: 800/A-PAPERS (NJ) or **www.paperdirect.com**

Other Paper Accessories

Abbot Office Systems carries versatile paper organizers. **Abbot Organizers** provide fast, organized access to information that's frequently referred to; they're available in a Deskside Wall Organizer model that displays 20 sheets, Desktop Units (that display 20 to 120 sheets) and Rotary Display Systems (that display either 50 or 100 sheets).

StationMate Project File by Abbot keeps up to 25 projects in easy view. The cascading design holds 25 translucent pocket files in five colors. Each pocket file is sealed on two sides, holds up to 50 sheets of paper and includes a fifth-cut tab with an adhesive label.

Stacking Storage Drawers are versatile drawers that not only can be stacked but also each drawer can accommodate one or two partitions enabling you to section off each drawer into two or three compartments to eliminate wasted dead space. Different style drawers (all with insertable label areas) let you store a variety of materials—literature, forms, binders, supplies, stationery, magazines, reports, disks and multi-media. Quantity discounts are available on these Abbot products. **800/631-2233** (NJ)

3M Organization Cabinets are lightweight, compact cabinets ideal for holding paper, letterhead, transparency films, forms and more.

Desk Accessories

In the office supply world, the desk accessory category includes everything from basic desk or letter trays to designer desk sets with matching components. As a general guideline, I advise clients to use the minimum number of accessories and those with the smallest capacity. It's just too easy to start stockpiling stuff.

I also urge clients to lean toward vertical rather than horizontal containers and whenever possible, to put papers in files rather than piles. Of course, the type of paperwork will often determine which format you should use. A horizontal container often works best for frequently used forms, which often flop over in a vertical container.

But you'll generally want a vertical container for active files (look at the many examples in this section).

Your in/out box or basket system will most likely be horizontal because you're probably processing different sized papers. But remember these tips: keep the depth of containers to a minimum, maintain high access and visibility and clean out trays regularly.

Balance good function with good design. Upon getting organized, some clients reward themselves with attractive desk accessories. Check out well-designed products in office supply stores and catalogs. Also look at the Hold Everything stores and catalog (**800/421-2264** [NV]). The Reliable Home Office catalog is an excellent choice, too, at 800/326-6230 (IL) or **www.reliable.com**.

Desk Files

Take a look at some products to help you set up your daily paperwork system for your active working files and paperwork.

If your work load fluctuates constantly, you may prefer a modular system that expands and contracts with your work. The **Eldon Add-A-File Filing Vanes** are individual sorting units that interlock to hold files, folders, notebooks, stationery and other items.

Step files give great visibility to your working files. The **Rogers Wire Step Sort-a-File** features eight graduated steps for visible access to files and includes plastic tips to protect surfaces. **Fellowes Strictly Business Visible Folder File** is a low-cost step file made of corrugated fiberboard with five tiered compartments that can be used vertically or horizontally.

Compact enough for a desk, **The Folder File Holder** and **The Hanging File Holder** by Eldon combine exceptional flexibility with high visibility and ease of retrieval. A simple adjustment in the base permits the use of letter-size, legal-size and international-size manila folders for The Folder File Holder or hanging folders for The Hanging File Holder. When not in use, they can be folded flat for easy storage.

Other Organizers

Here are some other items to organize your desk and paperwork, some of which may not be familiar to you.

A **collator** (Figure 4-2) is designed to manually collate (organize) documents but I recommend it for holding large, bulky, active client or project files that you want to be accessible. It's great for CPA or legal files and comes in 12,

18 or 24 expanding sections. We use it in our office above our printer to store paper, letterhead, folders and mailing envelopes.

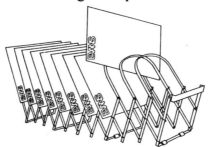

Figure 4-2. Evans recycled aluminum collator

If you're short on work surfaces, try using **wall mount files**. Sometimes these files are referred to as **pockets** and they can be used on walls as well as on the sides of desks. Some come with magnets and attach to metal surfaces such as filing cabinets. They don't take up much space and they can hit the spot when you need a holder for paperwork at the location where they will be used.

If you have lots of literature or inserts you're pulling together to put into kits or notebooks, consider **literature organizers and sorters**. Your selection will depend on a number of factors: the number of separate inserts you use, the quantity of each insert you need to have on hand, the space you have available, the frequency of use and your budget. (See Chapter 5 for illustrations of literature organizers and sorters.)

Don't forget your basic **letter trays**, which are useful for in/out boxes or to hold papers to be filed or read. Look for stacking letter trays that leave space between trays and that use supports to connect trays. Some people prefer wire letter trays because you can easily see what's in them; others prefer plastic or wood trays that keep paperwork less visible. If aesthetics are important, select a line that has coordinated desk accessories. Consider getting shallow trays to prevent paper buildup unless you need deep ones for thick folders or reports.

To keep other materials, manuals and references neatly organized around your computer or desk, consider the **Oxford DecoRack**. To keep your small supplies organized, use a drawer organizer. To keep your drawer organizer from sliding around, use **3M brand Mounting Squares** or **Mounting Tape** on the bottom. By the way, 3M also makes an adjustable width **drawer organizer (Model C-71)** that offers one-hand dispensing of tape and Post-it brand products, as well as spacious compartments for other desk supplies.

Stationery holders are great for letterhead, forms and envelopes and come in many different styles and formats. Some sit out in the open and others fit inside standard desk drawers.

5

FOR COLLECTORS ONLY: HOW, WHEN AND WHAT TO SAVE

Quick Scan: If you're an inveterate collector or you're in a profession that simply requires you to save many records, documents or resources, this chapter is for you. Here are some guidelines that will help you save only the essentials.

I'm convinced the world is divided into two groups of people—those who save and those who don't. And there has to be a Murphy's Law somewhere that says, "If you're a collector, you're probably living or working with someone who isn't."

I admit it. I'm a collector. Not only do I have many interests and avocations (I suffer from the "Da Vinci Syndrome"), but I have chosen occupations that attract collectors. I have been a school teacher, an editor and a manager. Today I am a professional speaker, trainer, writer and consultant and I continue to maintain well-organized resource material.

I am not against collecting. Certain professions demand it. But collecting requires strict guidelines and routines if you ever hope to stay in control.

Consider the degree your collecting habit is taking control over *you*. Recognize that it can be tamed and turned into a constructive resource that will give you a professional edge.

Types of Collectors

Sometimes it's helpful to see the different kinds of collecting traps we fall into. People with a "possession obsession" like to buy new things and add to their growing collection. And once something enters their environment, it remains for the duration.

"Chipmunk collectors" don't go out of their way to purchase new possessions. Instead, they squirrel away everything for the winter—*every* winter. "Waste not, want not" is their motto. Chipmunks were taught to hold onto everything for dear life. Beware of thoughts like these: "I might need this someday" or "Somebody else might need this" or "This could really come in handy."

Compulsive hoarding may be a type of obsessive-compulsive disorder (OCD). This type of collecting can result in tall piles of old newspapers, broken items or even trash. (See p. 6 for more information on OCD.)

People who love the printed word are "information junkies." These are people who love to learn, read, write, improve themselves and find out what the experts have to say. And even if you're not an information junkie per se, you still live in an "information age," where there are more than 1,000 specialized publications every year and 1,000 new book titles each day throughout the world. The sum of printed information is doubling every eight years; the millions of computers in the world have greatly contributed to the problem of information overload.

If you can relate to any of these collecting habits (and most of us can), you'll want to keep reading. Any of these habits can become nightmares in short order if you don't put a lid on them. The way you do that is by learning to *make decisions* about paper and possessions. But as we discussed in chapters 1 and 2, decisions aren't made in a vacuum.

Making Decisions About "Collectibles"

The secret to making decisions and controlling paper and possessions is simple: know your goals and values. Know what's important to you and what's really worth your time and energy. According to Roy Disney, Walt Disney's brother, "Decisions are easy when values are clear."

Once you're clear about your values and goals, you're ready to establish some stick-to-'em criteria. The problem people have when they're going through papers and possessions is that they aren't using the right criteria. As a result, every item requires a major decision from scratch.

To Save or Not to Save...
That is the Question!

If you're suffering from "Discard Dilemmas," the following two general guidelines can help you with troublesome papers:

1. When in doubt, *save* tax, legal or business items.

2. When in doubt, *toss* resource information, especially information you seldom,

if ever, use.

When you're in a discard mode (or should we say discard mood), use these simple guidelines along with the following criteria:

Nine Questions to Toss Out When Deciding What to Save

1. Do you need the item now?

2. Was it used last year? More than once?

3. Will you use it more than once next year? (How likely is it that you will *ever* need it?)

4. Would it be difficult or expensive to replace? Could you get it from someone else?

5. Is it current (and for how long?)

6. Should it be kept for legal or financial reasons?

7. Could someone else use it now? (Or could someone else wrestle with this decision instead of you?!)

8. Does it significantly enhance your work or life?

9. Is it worth the time and energy to save?

Go back and star any that you could use. Keep them right in front of you as you make your discard decisions. Add any others that specifically fit your situation.

Or follow the "cardinal office rule" of Richard Riordan, who advises, "Don't keep it in *your* file if someone else can keep it in *theirs*."

The Sorting Process

Now that you've established your criteria for saving (or tossing), you're ready to begin the actual process of sorting your collectibles. Your best bet is to make it a game with definite time limits. You can spread out your game over a period of time, doing a little this week and a little next week. Or maybe you prefer to dig right in and work for a few days straight, such as over a weekend. Or instead, try this one on for size: pretend you have to move your office in less than 24 hours to a space that is half the size. (Got your adrenalin flowing yet?)

Whichever is your style, choose blocks of time without interruptions, as this is real mental work that requires concentration. Block out at least a few hours. Have on hand the necessary supplies—a trash basket (or barrel), a pencil, a timer, empty cardboard boxes (Fellowes Bankers Boxes or other cardboard file boxes with lids are great) and space to work.

Tackle a small area at a time—one pile on your desk, a file drawer, a section of a file drawer, etc. Begin where the need is greatest. If your file cabinets are packed to the gills, start there. If you haven't seen your desk in years, there's no better place to begin. It's best to choose something small and be able to work through it. Set your timer to establish a reasonable time limit (an hour or less).

Begin by sorting through the designated area, deciding what to save, what to toss and what should be stored elsewhere. As you decide which items to save, sort them in categories based on types of items (e.g., books, files, supplies, personal items to take home), as well as *how often* you intend to use them (e.g., daily, several times a week, once a month). **Only things you use or refer to regularly during your working hours should be in your office**.

The process is not simply willpower, of sitting down and forcing yourself to go through your stuff (although a little willpower won't hurt). What you need is a **plan of action**, particularly if you have "long-term buildup." (Chapter 14 will help you design a simple plan of action—you may wish to read that chapter before attempting to tackle long-term buildup.)

Write as you sort. It's helpful to list your criteria and your sorting categories as you do the process. This list, along with a written plan of action, will help you tremendously. Carefully number and label boxes and drawers *as you go*. Keep a written record of any items going into storage.

I use my computer to keep a record of boxes that are stored off site. It's easy to update my word processing document, which is named "Files." I also keep a printout of "Files" in my manual filing system. My boxes are labeled alphabetically (I'll double up on letters should I ever get to "Z," heaven forbid!) I share an off-site storage room with my husband, who uses a numbered box system.

An attorney who is a solo practitioner keeps track of open and closed client files with index card boxes—ones for "Open" files and others for "Closed" files. Each card has the name of a client, the number and location of files for the client and when those files were opened or closed. The cards are filed alphabetically in the appropriate boxes (open or closed). Such a manual system would work even better on computer.

What if you inherited somebody else's clutter? I received a letter from Sharon Lawrence, a student of mine who ran into this problem several months after taking two of my seminars. She had just accepted a position as a financial management analyst in a California county administrative office. She writes:

> I have a new job and a new challenge to being organized. I left my organized office for a complete disaster area. I couldn't believe my new office; when I walked in, my mouth fell open. There were three inches thick of papers strewn over the entire surface of the desk, a bookcase

> filled with a year's worth of obsolete computer printouts and two file cabinets filled with five-year-old data, which belonged to other analysts. I informed my boss that I couldn't function until I had gotten organized. It was hard to know where to begin. By the end of the second day, I had thrown away four trash cans full of obsolete reports and duplicate copies of letters and reports. I had also managed to clear the desktop. I was still faced with four piles of paper which had been sorted into broad categories. Working a little each day for two weeks, I have now managed to organize the piles of information into file folders. I have also given away two file cabinets and distributed their contents to the appropriate analysts. People now walk by my office and say things like, "Wow, what a difference!" I tell them about your classes and how this is the new me.

This is great, you say, if you know what you're going to need on the new job. But what if the job isn't second nature to you? When Nancy Schlegel became a systems engineer for IBM she waited a year before she tossed out information. "After a year, I knew what I needed and what I didn't and I was in a better position to set up a filing system."

Where to Store It

Deciding where to store your records and resources depends on four factors: 1) up-to-date sorting and purging, 2) frequency of use, 3) size, shape and quantity of materials and 4) proximity to related items.

First, have you completed the sorting and purging process before you buy that extra filing cabinet or bookcase? Where to house something should only be considered after you decide *if* you should keep it.

Second, the more frequently you use an item, the more accessible it should be. Identify *prime* work areas in your office—those areas that are most accessible. If your desk top and a deskside file drawer are the most accessible areas, do they contain items that you use most often in your office?

Third, the size, shape and quantity of your resources will suggest the types of containers, accessories or pieces of furniture you select to hold those resources. If you have 12 inches of file folders you probably won't be choosing a five-drawer lateral file cabinet. If you're a graphic designer or a printer you may need special cabinets to hold large, oversized art boards.

Fourth, things that go together should generally stay together. Try to group similar types of books, files and supplies together. Sound like common sense? You'd be amazed to see how many items that are unrelated to each other end up together—sometimes for years.

How to Prevent Long-Term Buildup

Having a philosophy about paper helped Kathy Meyer-Poppe when she was Revlon's Corporate Fleet director. Her philosophy was, "File a paper or toss it out—it's either important enough to be filed right then and there or it's not that important. So throw it away."

Bill Butler, president of Butler Consulting Group in Indianapolis, cleans one file a day. Butler says, "One file you can manage. As a result, you have fewer files, which means fewer places to lose things."

There are no rules to maintenance. You may like to adopt Butler's "one file a day" or Poppe's "file or toss" routine. On the other hand, once a week or once every six months may work better for you. Or perhaps you want to wait until the need arises—bulging file cabinets or an impending move. Some people tell me the only way they can get organized is by moving—so they actually plan a move every few years!

It can be thrilling to "clear a path" as one client described making headway on her collection. It's also thrilling for me to get letters like the following from Coleen Melton, a California art teacher:

> I'm writing to report to you that my goal is accomplished: 20 years of art placed into retrievable order thanks to your "Positively Organized!" class and your notes of support. I even have my husband wanting to organize his filing cabinet, and that is a miracle in itself.

Even lifelong collectors can learn and use the art of organization.

Giving It Away

Sometimes it's easier to get rid of things if you have someone to whom you can donate items. Often, you can get income tax credits, too.

For small donations, contact local charitable organizations such as Goodwill Industries or the Salvation Army. To learn about computer-related recycling, log on to **www.best.com/~dillon/recycle/** or check **www.microweb.com/pepsite/ Recycle/recycle_index.html** for a state-by-state directory of organizations that take used computer equipment and contact the following:.

Association of Personal Computer User Groups (APCUG) lists local (and international) user groups, many of which have community service projects dedicated to collecting, restoring and donating computers to schools, churches, senior centers, etc. **www.apcug.org**

The **Computers for Schools Program** places donated equipment in schools located in more than 30 states around the country and offers many local pickups of donations. 800/939-6000 or **www.computersforschools.com**

The **East West Education Development Foundation** accepts any type of computer equipment, including components and circuit boards and software; what they can use is matched up with other working components and sent to nonprofits and what can't be fixed is recycled (617/261-6699 [MA] or **www.bitwise.net/eastwest/**)

Green Disk is an award-winning company featured in *TIME* magazine that provides high security recycling and disposal of media including old floppy disks (except 5¼-inch disks), CDs, videotapes and jewel cases. Green Disk outsources the nonprofit recycling work to a nonprofit organization that provides jobs for disabled adults. Green Disk sells their new, award-winning office supplies, which are made out the recycled material. 800/305-DISK (800/305-3475) [WA] or **www.greendisk.com**

The National Cristina Foundation links local organizations with companies and individuals wishing to donate; they can use all types of computer equipment and software. **www.cristina.org**

Share the Technology is a nonprofit corporation with a Web site that lists computer donation requests and offers from across the U.S. (and other countries). 856/234-6156 (NJ) or **www.libertynet.org/~share**

If you have excess new inventory or equipment to donate, including computer donations, contact one of the following organizations:

Gifts in Kind International can link you with local organizations in need of equipment; they prefer full working systems. 703/836-2121 (VA) or **www.giftsinkind.org**

National Association for the Exchange of Industrial Resources (NAEIR) only takes new items. 800/562-0955 (IL) or **www.naeir.org**

Resource Guide

(Addresses and phone numbers are included for mail order items and generally *not* for products that are widely available through office supply catalogs and stores. It's helpful to have a good office supply catalog handy while you're reading about the products in this guide.)

Art Work, Blueprints and Photographic Materials
Artist and Document Storage Files
Artists portfolios, art folios, art cases, presentation cases are all different names of portable containers for storing, transporting or displaying art work.

Check out good office supply or art stores and catalogs. For storage rather than display, consider the following items available in most office supply catalogs:

For Flat Storage

Plan Hold is a manufacturer of flat storage equipment that provides many different solutions. To get their catalog, call **800/854-6868** (CA) or visit **www.planhold.com**.

Safco has many flat storage solutions in its catalog. Here are some products to look for: the **Art Rack**, a modular, vertical filing system with eight large compartments; the **Safco Portable Art and Drawing Portfolio** is a low-cost, durable file with a handle that comes in three sizes and is useful for transporting art work, film, drawings and large documents (see Figure 5-1); **Safco 5- and 10-Drawer Steel Flat Files** are for serious, professional storage; **Safco Vertical Filing Systems** offer efficient systems for keeping large sheet materials well protected, yet organized and easily accessible; and **Safco Giant Stack Trays**, which stack up to five feet high, are economical alternatives to expensive metal files for art boards, blueprints, film, drawings, drafting paper and other oversized documents you want to store flat. These Safco products are available nationwide through office products dealers, industrial supply dealers and art and engineering dealers. For a catalog or more information, contact a local dealer or visit **www.safcoproducts.com**.

Figure 5-1. Safco Portable Art and Drawing Portfolio

Smead Artist Portfolio is another low-cost alternative.

For Rolled Storage

Fellowes Roll/Stor Stands and **Perma Vertical Roll Organizers** are good choices for deskside filing of rolled documents that you use frequently.

Plan Hold offers rolled storage solutions. See listing under "For Flat Storage" above.

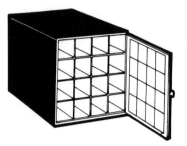

Figure 5-2. Safco Corrugated Fiberboard Roll File

Safco solutions include their **Corrugated Fiberboard Roll File**, an economical way to organize and store large materials that comes in three different tube lengths and in three different compartment configurations (see Figure 5-2); **Safco Tube-Stor KD Roll Files** also provide an ideal low-cost system for active or inactive storage and include two convenient label areas to list rolls and locations and built-in tube length adjusters; **Safco Mobile Roll Files** are good for active rolled materials that you need to move from office to office.

Photographic Storage—Slides and Prints

Abodia Lighted Slide Storage Cabinets organize and store slides for easy access, scanning, editing and assembling, and have a built-in, lit viewing screen. Cabinets hold from 1,000 to 65,000 slides. Contact Abodia at **800/950-7775** (WV) or **www.abodia.com**

The **"Century Photo Products"** catalog is an excellent source for photo, slide and negative pages and albums. Contact Century at **800/767-0777** (CA) or see **www.centuryphoto.com**.

Creative Memories is a great source for photo-safe albums, mounting products and album-making supplies and accessories. The albums have a unique flexible binding that allows the addition of many extra pages and provides for stress-free page-turning, keeping pages and photos mounted on them flat at all times. Creative Memories offers a good selection of albums as well as accessories, such as special plastic protectors and a compact paper cutter. Contact Creative Memories at **800/468-9335** (MN) or **www.creative-memories.com**.

Light Impressions is a photographic and fine art storage and presentation catalog featuring archival supplies and equipment. The following two Light Impressions items are of special interest to photographers: **Nega*Guard System**, which preserves and indexes hundreds of negatives, and **PrintFile**, a complete negative and slide filing and storage system that provides rapid access to negatives and slides. Printfile consists of transparent, polyethylene protectors in a wide range of styles and formats, many of which can be filed in binders. To get their catalogs contact them at **800/828-6216** (NY) or **www.lightimpressionsdirect.com**.

System 4000 slide cabinets offer a complete system for storing, viewing and retrieving slides and have a viewbox for viewing 120 slides at a time. Contact Miller Multiplex Display Fixture Company at **800/325-3350** (MO) or **www.millermultiplex.com**.

University Products Archival Quality Materials catalog offers a wide range of products including acid-free albums, papers and boxes to preserve photos, slides, books, prints, important papers and memorabilia. Contact University Products at 800/628-1912 (MA) or **www.universityproducts.com**.

Visual Horizons offers a good range and selection of slide storage solutions, as well as other presentation materials. Contact Visual Horizons at 800/424-1011 (NY) or **www.visualhorizons.com**.

Files and Records

When you have inactive records, look in your office supply catalog or store under the category "storage files." There you'll find boxes made of corrugated fiberboard that come in a variety of sizes and styles (see Figure 5-3). They usually come with lids. If you'll need access to files, consider getting drawer style storage boxes. Some of these are available with metal reinforcement, which provides greater durability for stacking.

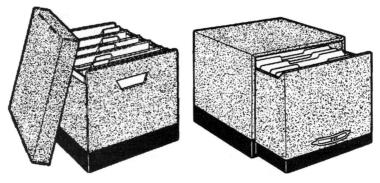

Figure 5-3. Fellowes Portable File and Drawer File

If you have many, many boxes of records you want to store off site, look in the Yellow Pages under a heading such as "Business Records Storage." See also Chapter 7 for more information on filing.

If you need permanent storage boxes that are moisture resistant, consider those made by Rogers such as Roger's Trunk Tote file box, which features a transparent snap-tight lid and durable construction. Use it for hanging files or for general storage at home, at work or on the go.

Literature Organizers

Magazine files or **holders** sit right on a shelf or table and are great for storing magazines, catalogs, manuals or reports. The Oxford DecoFile is made of high-impact plastic and comes in eight colors (which you could use for color coding different types of literature). Made of corrugated fiberboard, the Fellowes Magazine File costs less but will still do the job.

For an easy way to store thin magazines and catalogs in a three-ring binder without punching holes, use Baumgarten's **Magazine/Catalog Organizer** strip (**www.baumgartens.com**).

Literature sorters and **organizers** come in many different styles and sizes and are great for catalog sheets, brochures and forms that you use frequently or that need to be assembled into kits. See Figure 5-4. See also Chapter 4 for drawer systems by Abbot and 3M.

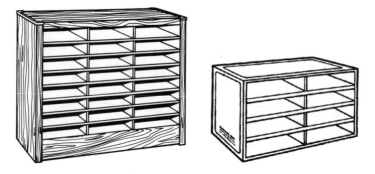

Figure 5-4. Fellowes Literature Sorter (left), Fellowes Strictly Business Mail/Literature Center

Donations of Your Old Computer Equipment
See pages 73 and 74, earlier in this chapter.

6

WORK SPACE BASICS: ENHANCING YOUR PHYSICAL WORKING ENVIRONMENT

███

Quick Scan: Whether you're planning a move or you just have a sneaking suspicion your office design is missing the mark, this chapter will reveal the physical features your office should have to be a more productive, comfortable environment. Many of these features are inexpensive and easy to implement. You'll be amazed to see how the little things can make a big difference in your office, especially if you're one of the tens of millions of people in the U.S. who now work or will work at home some or all of the time.

Do you feel like everything in your work space has been put in its place with Krazy Glue?

Once you get used to an office or work area, it usually feels pretty permanent. Everything seems as if it's always been there (and always will be). But when you become too used to your environment, you don't see the possibilities. Or if you do, you figure you can't do anything about them anyway.

I love the story that stockbroker Alan Harding shared at one of my seminars many years ago. Harding had wanted a window office. As he saw it though, he didn't need to change offices—he just needed to install a window in a wall that faced the outside. So Harding asked his boss to have a window installed but his boss refused. For most people that would have been the end of it.

Not for Harding. You see, he spent a good part of every day in that enclosed office. He had been with the company awhile and was planning on staying a good while longer. Since he really wanted that window, he decided to spend his own money to have one installed—to which his boss agreed.

But that's not the end of the story. After seeing how serious Harding was about the window, his boss then decided to chip in and split the cost. What's more, when Harding came in on a Saturday to physically do the installation, his boss ended up helping. Harding says, "The whole thing wound up as a cooperative effort." It's amazing what can happen when you keep open the "windows of your mind."

There are three types of physical factors related to your office over which you have some control: your physical space, your furnishings and your total environment.

How to Organize and Maximize Your Work Space

Look at where and how your work space is organized. Two space factors come into play: location and layout.

Location, Location, Location

Where is your main work area located? It sounds like a simple enough question. But you probably could provide many answers.

For example, any of the following could be truthful responses: in my den, near the freeway, 40 miles from home, next to the water cooler, on the fifth floor, far away from clients or close to the marketing department.

The last time you probably thought about your location was when you changed jobs or moved to a different office or to a home office. But so often we just forget about location factors. We may even experience some irritation and not realize that that irritation is directly related to our location.

So just take a moment to think about the location of your work area, to see if there are some aspects that really bother you. Take this little survey. Next to each item, write "O" for Outstanding, "S" for Satisfactory, "N" for Needs Improvement or "NA" for Not Applicable (or not important):

1. Commuting distance
2. Proximity to colleagues
3. Proximity to vendors or suppliers
4. Proximity to your market—clients, customers or patients
5. Traffic flow in or near your office
6. Privacy
7. Noise
8. Lighting
9. Proximity to equipment and supplies

10. Proximity to personal or professional services—e.g., restaurants, shops, attorney, accountant

Take a look at any "Ns" you've marked. Are there any ways you could change or modify undesirable locations? Don't just accept things the way they are, especially if your performance and productivity are really suffering. Be creative—like Alan Harding.

Latitude in Your Layout

Work spaces are shrinking and changing in their design. Spurred by a need to reduce rental costs and create a more egalitarian, team approach, large, open rooms with cubicles for everyone are replacing window offices for managers and windowless offices for the rest of the employees.

Keeping in mind the size limitations of your work space, take a look at your **layout**—the location and arrangement of the furniture and equipment within your own work space. There are two essentials of every good office layout: adequate **work space** and **storage space**. Sometimes it's hard to tell, however, if work and storage spaces are adequate, especially if a desktop hasn't been seen in years, filing is less than routine and a move hasn't occurred in more than a decade.

Differentiate between work and storage space. Unfortunately, in far too many offices, the distinction is nonexistent. Work and storage spaces are all lumped (and I do mean lumped) together. You'll be making great headway if you can separate these two basic spaces.

The biggest problem comes when your desktop becomes more a storage space than a work space. Too often the desk becomes a place where things are waiting to happen; instead, make it a place for action. Think of your desk as an airport runway. If you were a pilot, you wouldn't find spare parts in the middle of the runway. They would be in the hangar. So, remove the obstacles from your work surface and **clear your desk for action!** Get out of the habit of keeping everything at your fingertips.

How do you break the keep-the-clutter-close habit? First, **set up appropriate systems for paperwork and projects** (see Chapter 4 on desktop management, Chapter 7 on paper files and Chapter 9 on managing work, projects and information).

Second, **put only those items you use most frequently**—be they accessories, supplies, furniture or equipment—**closest to you**.

Third, make sure you have enough work space! I generally recommend at least **two surfaces plus adequate, accessible storage space** for most people. The surface right in front of you should be your primary work surface and ideally should contain only things you use every day. This is the area where you are doing your most common work activities. A secondary surface off to the side or behind you could be used as a work area for a particular activity, such as telephoning (unless that's a primary work activity). This secondary area could also provide storage for items you use frequently such as your daily paperwork system and stapler.

An **L-shape** layout uses two surfaces—a primary one such as a desk and another one off to the left or right side, which when attached is called a **return**. A return is a small, narrow extension of a desk that is designed to hold a computer. You can order a desk with either a right or left return.

It's easy to create an L-shape layout by putting a table alongside your desk. Or if you don't like using a desk at all, try two tables at right angles.

A **U-shape** layout gives you more work surface and usually more accessible storage.

A **triangular** layout takes advantage of a corner, makes good use of angles and plays up the importance of the desk as a focal point. A **parallel** layout places the main work surface, such as a desk, parallel to and in front of a storage unit (a credenza or lateral file cabinet, for example) or another work surface, such as a table. (See Figure 6-1 for these four layouts).

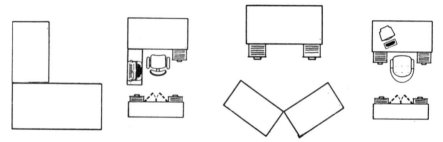

Figure 6-1. L-shape, U-shape, triangular and parallel layouts

Design Your Own Layout

I use a modified U-shape in my office—I call it a **J-shape**. I have combined modular computer furniture with two work tables and a printer stand. I also use two two-drawer filing cabinets and a small bookcase that provide additional work surfaces and storage space. Figure 6-2 shows my office furniture in two, mirror-image layouts.

Get objective about an existing or proposed office layout. Make a quick, little sketch of your layout. Or better yet, particularly if you're planning a move, buy some graph or engineering paper (quadrille pads work well), draw an outline of your office to scale and make paper cutouts of your furniture to scale. Cutouts work great if you have a small office space and your furniture is going to be a tight fit. Also, it's a lot easier moving cutouts around on paper than moving the

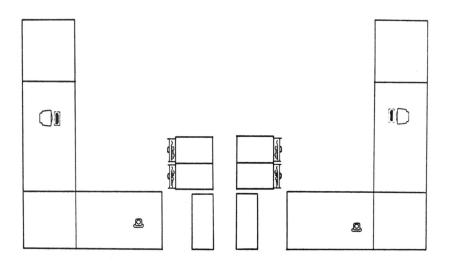

Figure 6-2. Because I have modular furniture, I've been able to use my J-shape layout and easily reverse it to better accommodate new office space.

real things. I've yet to see anyone throw out their back moving cutouts around.

Another option is to use Microsoft Visio, the award-winning, enterprise-wide business drawing and technical diagramming software program that has a space planning feature. (800/426-9400 or **www.microsoft.com\office\visio**).

Even if you're not moving, remember you're allowed to move things around. I consulted with a public relations executive who had one of the most beautifully designed and equipped offices I had ever seen. But she had been designed into a corner.

She had a huge pedestal desk, with a large, cumbersome chair. Behind her was a custom-built, corner credenza with all kinds of shelves and drawers, which she never used. Instead the surfaces of her desk and credenza were piled high with papers.

Why didn't she use the credenza? Simple—she didn't have enough space to easily move the chair and access the credenza. My solution: move the desk farther out from the credenza! Why hadn't she thought of moving the desk? Probably because the designer had indicated where the furniture was to go and there it remained. Also, the desk top was a heavy piece of glass. These factors suggested real permanence.

Alexis Kyprianou, a colleague of mine, related how she once had a boss who spent a lot of money on a design that wasn't functional. The boss insisted, "We'll make it work!" What he didn't realize was that it becomes *real* work when the design doesn't work.

Once people are in their offices or have been designed into a corner, the thought of changing a layout simply doesn't occur. Here's a chance to check out your layout. Quickly sketch out the main elements of your office space—furniture, equipment, walls, windows, light sources and plants. Don't worry about scale at this point.

Ask yourself these questions:

• Is your layout convenient?
• Are the things you use most often close at hand?
• Do you have enough storage and work space?
• Do you have enough space for your equipment, especially your computer equipment?
• Do you like the way your office is configured to meet with others—coworkers, clients or customers?
• Does your layout invite irritating distractions? (For example, do you always catch someone's eye as he or she walks by?)
• Do you have different areas in your office for different types of work or activity, e.g., telephoning, computer work, meeting with clients? How and where do you like to do various kinds of work?

All of these factors may enter into the kind of office layout you can live with. Some of these factors are very subtle but their subtlety shouldn't diminish their importance.

Proxemics

One subtle factor concerns **proxemics**—the study of spatial configurations and interpersonal relations. Do you know that the seating arrangements in your office influence the relationships you have with your colleagues as well as your clients? Your seating arrangements make subtle statements. If, in the first example in Figure 6-3, you are "A," sitting behind your desk, and you're meeting with "B," you are in a distinctly authoritarian, powerful position. This configuration may be totally appropriate when meeting with a client but if you're meeting with a colleague, perhaps the side by side configuration in the next example would be more effective.

If you have meetings in your office and you tend to run meetings in which you assert your authority, you would select a rectangular table, as shown in the third example, and sit at the head. If, however, you tend to meet informally and you're trying to foster that "good ol' team spirit," select a round table. Of course space considerations as well as purpose will affect your final layout decisions.

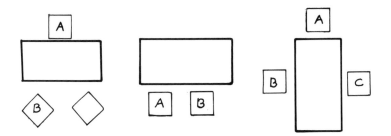

Figure 6-3. These three seating arrangements make three statements.

The Doorway

Decide, too, where to place your desk in relation to the doorway. If you're facing the doorway (or the opening of your cubicle) and you're in a high people traffic zone, you may find interruption is your constant companion. Turning your back to the doorway may appear too severe or even antisocial. You may prefer instead to angle your desk so as not to catch everyone's eye but to remain responsive.

When Kim Villeneuve was a divisional vice president for a major department store in Southern California, she changed her position toward the doorway, depending on the type of work she was doing. Since she needed to remain open to staff most of the day, she generally sat facing the door. But when she used the telephone and didn't want interruptions, she would swing her chair around to the credenza behind her. Her telephone sat on the credenza and there she did her phone work without inviting interruption. The credenza became an area designated for important telephone work, without interruptions of people as well as any distracting paperwork on her desk.

Your Home Office and Family Members

It's hard to work at home if you're continually interrupted by children or a spouse. Here are a few tips to help you complete your work. First, close your office door when you're working. Let that be a signal that it's worktime. Second, have regular office hours or use a sign on the outside of the door that says when you'll be available for nonwork matters. And consider having a clock there, too, to help children know when you'll be finished working.

Your Evolving Work Style

Finally, consider how you like to work when you design your layout and remain flexible. As your work style needs change, so should your design.

Dr. David Snyder, a physician in Fresno, California, had a desk in his private office with a credenza behind him. Then he eliminated the credenza. He used his desk to process patient files and other paperwork quickly and efficiently. He said, "I will never have a credenza again—that's where I put stuff I didn't have time to do."

Today he has added a two-drawer lateral filing cabinet behind him. The close proximity of the cabinet gives him access to reference files. He uses the top of the cabinet for his daily paperwork system, which includes a vertical rack that holds active project files.

Furnishings That Fit

Walk into your office as if you were walking into it for the first time. Pretend you've just arrived from Mars (some days don't we all feel that way!). Look at your office with fresh eyes and notice all your furnishings—your furniture, equipment, accessories and supplies.

Are they all well-organized, in good repair and well placed? Are they as functional as they should be? Do you have enough storage space?

Furniture and Equipment

With today's changing technology, workforce and work place location, *flexibility* is a key word to apply to your choice of furniture and equipment. **Modular** furniture (often called "systems furniture") with interchangeable components works great, particularly in today's smaller offices, because it's flexible, can save floor space and yet can increase the amount of work surface.

The flexibility and functionality of modular furniture is particularly important if you'll ever be moving your office. Since buying modular furniture for my office, I have moved twice. Each of my offices required a different configuration. Figure 6-2 shows how I was able to take my original configuration from my old office and simply reverse the components to fit my current office requirements.

Figure 6-4 shows an illustration of modular furniture. Notice how the combination of a single compact pencil drawer and notched side panels provide for completely unobstructed leg-room, protecting your knees as you swivel to different areas. If you have a mini-tower computer CPU on the floor, place it where it won't obstruct your leg room, such as under a connector, which is also shown in the figure.

If you need more drawers, consider getting a portable drawer unit or file cabinet on casters which is also shown in Figure 6-4. Sometimes such portable units are called **pedestals** and come in different styles. Some consist of two file drawers and function as a two-drawer file cabinet on casters. Other models, especially underdesk units, may come with one utility drawer and one file drawer.

Some modular work tables come with recessed, half-depth shelves underneath for storage that don't obstruct your movement.

As for equipment, if you're short on space or money and/or you have occasional needs, it may be time to look at a **multifunctional device (MFD)**—a multipurpose machine that combines a computer printer, a fax machine, a copier and sometimes a scanner. Having separate, standalone pieces of equipment is generally better for moderate or heavy copying, faxing or printing.

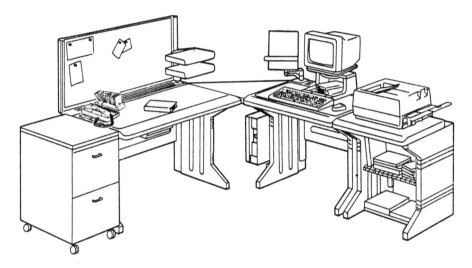

Figure 6-4. Modular computer work station components and accessories.

Ergonomics

Modular systems we've been discussing are a fine example of applying **ergonomics** to office furniture design. Ergonomics is the science of making the work environment compatible with people so they can work more comfortably and productively. Ergonomics looks at the dimensions of work tables, desks and chairs and matches them to the wide range of body sizes and shapes according to certain recommended standards that are illustrated in Figure 6-5.

When you pay close attention to these standards you can avoid such symptoms as fatigue, eyestrain, blurred vision, headaches, stiff muscles, wrist pain, sore back, irritability and loss of feeling in fingers and wrists. The longer you work at a desk or computer, the more you need to consider the importance of correct angles of eyes, arms, hands, legs and feet.

If you're looking for more information on ergonomics, visit **www.me.berkeley.edu/ergo** or **www.ocean.odu.edu/ug/ergonomics.html** or **www.hfes.org** or **www.tifaq.com**.

Because you can do almost everything today at the computer, you may find, like many people, you are sitting there for more hours every day than ever before. But this single type of repetitive activity is dangerous physically and mentally. You need to do different things throughout the day. Studies show that repetitive stress injuries (RSI) become more common starting at four or five hours of work in front of a computer every day.

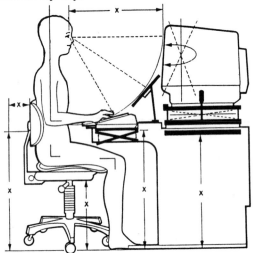

Figure 6-5. Ergonomics—The Human Factors

If your work simply demands you spend long hours at a computer, then the suggestions you're about to read are especially critical. This is the ideal time to become a clock watcher and take breaks at least every 30 minutes. Take a "micro break"—which could be a different work activity, a trip to the restroom or some simple stretches or exercises. In fact, there are even computer programs that you can preset that will pop up and remind you you've worked 30 minutes and it's time for a break or even help you go through a variety of such exercises. "ExerciseBreak" by Hopkins Technology is one (800/397-9211 [MN] or **www.hoptechno.com**). "ErgoSentry" by Magnitude Information Systems, Inc. (888/786-7774 or **www.magnitude.com**) alerts you once you've reached a time limit of actual work done on the computer and provides stretching exercises.

One study has even shown that sitting still for long periods in cars, planes or trains can cause blood clots, even for people in good health. Hopefully, this wouldn't apply to sitting in the same position too long in front of a computer but why take a chance?

Use a good **ergonomic chair** whose back and seat are adjustable. A good chair is more than a piece of furniture; it's a necessity for long hours of computer work. A bad one is literally a pain in the back. Adjust the height of your chair so that your thighs are parallel to the floor when your feet are resting flat on the floor. You should have lower back support from the backrest, which should adjust to fit your spine's contours and reach at least the lower part of your shoulder blades so you can relax against it. The seat of the chair should be curved and should have a "waterfall" front or downward-sloping edge. The chair should swivel, have a pneumatically adjustable seat height and back, have a stable, five-prong base with casters and be upholstered with one to four inches of thickness. Experts differ on whether armrests help you or create problems. If your chair has armrests, they should be adjustable and allow you to sit close enough to your desk. The armrests should support your arms in a natural position.

Apply ergonomics from head to toe. Position your computer to minimize glare from sources of light. Have a flicker free monitor to minimize stress on your eyes. Install an **antiglare filter** on your computer screen if it already doesn't have one to reduce glare, eyestrain and radiation. A **foot rest** not only supports the feet, but the angle is beneficial for the back and circulation.

Remember, too, that **good ergonomic work habits** will make a big difference in addition to selecting the right furniture and equipment. Be sure to stay at least 28 inches (about an arm's length) from your computer monitor, especially if it's a color monitor. (Electromagnetic fields are considerably weaker at that distance.) You should also maintain a distance of 4 feet from the sides or back of any other monitor in your workplace, even if a wall separates you from the other monitor, because electromagnetic fields are strongest at the back or side. (Keep laser printers and copiers also about four to five feet away from your body.) Some studies show that electromagnetic fields emitted from monitors (and other equipment) at unsafe distances may be linked to health problems.

Check to see if your monitor gives off too much static (which typically is not a problem with newer, low-radiation monitors). There are two telltale signs. First, there may be an accumulation of dirt on the plastic in and around a monitor that's very difficult to clean. Second, if after your monitor has been on for a few hours you turn it off and run the back of your hand over the screen, you should not hear popping, crackling sounds; if you do, then your monitor is giving off too much static. When there's too much static, an invisible cloud of microscopic particles floats in front of the screen and can cause eye irritation. According to computer expert John Dvorak, you should consider buying a new monitor if yours is giving off too much static.

It's also a good idea to pause every 20 minutes or so to look away from the screen and to change your close-up focus by looking at distant objects in order to prevent eyestrain.

Try to blink more often. Blinking moistens your eyes and reduces eyestrain.

We blink one-third as often while looking at text on a computer monitor. Consider purchasing prescription glasses designed for reducing the strain of viewing computer screens (PRIO glasses, **800/621-1098**).

A larger-sized monitor may also help you reduce eyestrain.

Don't underestimate the importance of ergonomics in relation to your **computer keyboard**. Increased use of computers can lead to RSI (repetitive stress injury). Remember that no one keyboard or keyboard accessory works for everyone. Listen to your body when you're using a keyboard as to whether it's right for you.

Do you like the touch and feel of the keys, the sound they make and the design of the keyboard? I like the clickety-clack touch and feel of the keys on my keyboard as well as the raised dashes on the "F" and "J" keys, which keep my fingers in correct alignment. Remember, you can easily buy a replacement keyboard for your computer if you're not happy with the standard issue.

In fact, your keyboard is one of the most important factors that determines just how happy you are with your computer as a whole. It's not expensive to replace your keyboard—it will typically cost you anywhere from $60 to $150.

How you use your keyboard, especially if you use it many hours every day, can have an adverse physiological effect on your hands. There are several ergonomic measures you can take to prevent hand disorders such as tenosynovitis and carpal tunnel syndrome. Take a five-minute break every hour to relax your hands. Wrists should be straight while typing and at the same height as your elbows. As you're typing, you may want to rest your wrists on a **wrist rest**, which either is built into your keyboard or you may need to use an additional wrist rest accessory. I'm using a comfortable, padded wrist rest attached to a platform called the Daisy Wrist Rest from the Daisy Wheel Ribbon Company (800/266-5585 [CA] or **www.daisyw.com**. I find it's very comfortable using my keyboard on this wrist rest/platform, which I place on my lap, with my feet supported on a foot rest. This also positions me more than 28 inches from the screen. (See also Computer Accessories for more on wrist rests.) For wrist rests and other products discover **your own comfort level**.

Another way to reduce the stress of typing is by using macros. A macro allows you to use as few as two keystrokes to replace many keystrokes or mouse clicks. Macros are often part of your existing computer programs or you can use the free program, TypeItIn, available at **www.fileworld.com**.

If your job requires you to open many envelopes each day, a battery-powered letter opener may save wear and tear on your body.

Positioning and **placement** of equipment is an ergonomic factor that also relates to left- or right-handedness. At my Positively Organized! seminars I'll often ask participants whether their telephone should go on the right or left side of the desk if they are right-handed. Answers are usually evenly divided between "left" and "right." The correct answer is "left." If you're right-handed you'll be writing with your right hand. So place the phone on the left so that the phone doesn't get in the way. You'll want to hold the phone with your left hand to your left ear, leaving your right hand free to write. (If you're using a telephone headset, placement may not be as critical.)

Consider, too, how you like to turn your body in relation to equipment. Do you prefer a computer or typewriter on a left or right hand return? Where do you want to place the copy stand and materials—on the left or right side of your computer or typewriter? (I have my copy stand on the left, which seems ergonomically to make sense since we read from left to right). Most people just don't stop and think about the things that they use every day.

Check to see that your work surfaces are the right height from the floor. Your keyboard should sit on a surface that's generally 26 inches from the floor but your writing work surface should be 29 inches high.

The **accessibility principle** should influence your decisions about equipment placement, too. Even a work surface has areas that are more convenient than others. Angle your computer, for example, off to the side for occasional use; place it right in front of you for frequent or constant use.

Trying it on for size is an important principle when shopping for workspace equipment as well as for clothes. Never buy a chair from a catalog; you should "test sit" any chair you buy. When it comes to keyboards, mice and trackballs, you should play with them first or if a mouse or keyboard is standard issue with your computer and you're less than pleased, then go out and test drive some others and don't be afraid to switch.

I personally think that posture and positioning are critical factors in preventing RSI, carpal tunnel syndrome, tendinitis and "mouse shoulder." The latter often results from reaching for a mouse and using it too much. But good design of keyboards, mice, trackballs or electronic touch pads may be just as important and may also build in some positioning features. Look for shapes and configurations that fit the size of your hands and fingers and for any features that reduce the amount of work your fingers, hands and arms need to do, e.g., some mice and trackballs are eliminating double clicking. As one article pointed out, no matter how ergonomically designed a product is, final selection boils down to personal preference because one size or style does not fit all.

You may prefer a mouse with a wheel in the middle that makes scrolling down pages easier. (I love this feature on my mouse.) If you're left-handed, make sure you find a mouse that works for you. You may want a kid-sized mouse for your children to use. To reduce strain on your body, you may want to switch between using a mouse and a trackball.

Create an Ergonomic Phone Area

Set up a separate, clear phone area where you can handle calls without the distraction of other work. When you don't have to shuffle through other tasks and projects, you can really focus on each call. Your area should have enough writing surface and be close to files and other telephone information you may need. Telephone equipment should ideally include: a clock (or if necessary, several clocks for different time zones); a timer (if you have trouble keeping track of time and length of calls); a voice mail system or a telephone answering machine; a speaker phone with on-hook dialing, automatic on-hook re-dialing and automatic memory dialing; and a **telephone headset** if you're on the phone at least two hours every day and/or you need your hands free for writing or typing while on the phone.

I've used a headset for years. The small price tag for a headset is certainly well worth it for convenience as well as for your health, too. A telephone headset can help prevent neck and back aches and trips to the chiropractor. For more information, see the "Telephone Accessories and Features" section later in the chapter, as well as "Accessories and Supplies" in the Resource Guide.

Use the speaker phone when you're on hold so you can do other work while waiting. You can also use it for a conference call in your office, provided that confidentiality isn't a problem and the speaker phone sound quality doesn't bother the person(s) on the other end.

Accessories and Supplies

In my consulting work I notice that clients either have too few or too many accessories for their paperwork, telephone and computer. Those who have too few generally lump their work all together on the desk, on tables, on shelves, in drawers and on the floor. Those with too many (if one pencil holder is good, six are better) collect accessories along with good intentions. They buy a new accessory every time they're inspired to "get organized." Soon the accessory becomes just another catchall rather than a clearly defined tool. The original purpose is too soon forgotten.

Remember, to keep it simple; sometimes the simplest, least expensive accessories can save you a lot of money. You might even avoid the "$12,000 paper clip." It's the little things that count as one man found out after losing two $12,000 copiers because of paper clips that somehow became lodged inside. This man now uses a $3 magnet attached to a piece of Velcro tape on his copier to hold paper clips. (By the way, we use Velcro tape to attach a writing instrument to each of our office phones or any place where a pen or pencil has a way of just walking off by itself.)

Any time you add a new accessory to your environment, define its purpose and *get in the habit of using it*. And from time to time, check to see if it's doing its job. If it has outlived its usefulness, get rid of it!

Let's look at some of the most useful work space accessories (see also chapters 4, 5 and 7).

Paperwork Accessories

One of the most versatile paperwork accessories is the **expanding collator**. It comes in plastic or aluminum with 12, 18 or 24 slots. If you're a CPA or an attorney, use it for large, bulky active client files that you're referring to daily or several times a week. (While it's always safer to put client files away each night in filing cabinets, using the collator is a good intermediate step for anyone who is still piling files on couches and floors.)

Use the collator near your copier or computer printer to store large quantities (up to 500 sheets) of different types of paper.

You can always use the collator for its original purpose, too—collating! It's great for assembling or sorting literature and handouts. (See Chapter 4 for an illustration of a collator.)

The **stationery holder** is a wonderful accessory to hold letterhead, envelopes, forms and note paper. Some stationery holders are designed to fit inside a desk drawer; others sit on top of furniture or on a shelf. Place a stationery holder where you'll be using it.

Magazine files or **holders** are indispensable boxes for storing magazines, catalogs, directories as well as current project files. They're usually made out of plastic, acrylic or corrugated fiberboard. (See Figure 6-6)

Figure 6-6. The Oxford DecoFile

When you type, use a **copyholder**. There are many different styles (see Figure 6-7) but the main idea is to get one that can be placed at the same focal distance as the screen. It's hard on the eyes to keep refocusing to accommodate different focal lengths. The Curtis Clip attaches to the monitor and swings out of the way when not in use. It may not be feasible to use such a clip all the time; you'll probably want to have at least one other standard copyholder.

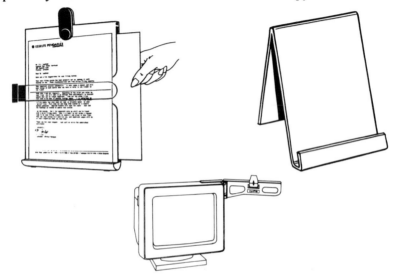

Figure 6-7. The Oxford CopyKeeper (includes a sliding guide and side storage compartment for "to-be-typed" materials); the Oxford CopyCaddy holds thicker material; the Curtis Clip can attach to either side of your computer and gives you good ergonomic positioning.

If you have wall partitions, consider installing a **wall unit paper management system**. As office space decreases into more flexible, partitioned "cubicles," using vertical wall space for accessories makes sense. Wall systems help you get paper off your desk and yet make it accessible and organized.

If you do a lot of hole punching, stapling, folding or trimming, consider getting accessories to help you automate these processes. **Electric hole punches** and **staplers** and **letter folding machines** can save you a lot of time and reduce the stress on your body.

Don't forget about color coding. Simple, small colored adhesive dots on locks and matching keys will help you save time, too.

Telephone Accessories and Features

Selecting a basic desktop telephone today has become a major decision given all the different features and accessories that are available. Look for these features:

- speaker phone with on-hook dialing
- automatic on-hook re-dialing
- automatic memory dial
- compatibility with your headset, telephone answering machine or other tele-communications equipment.
- voice mail system with multiple mailboxes

If you're on the phone a lot (at least two hours a day) or you have any neck, shoulder or back trouble (or want to prevent such trouble!), a **telephone headset** is the answer. Besides being more comfortable, a headset frees up your hands to take notes, handle paperwork or operate a keyboard. I always use a headset whenever I conduct interviews for articles or seminars or when I know I'll need to write or use a keyboard during the call. If you don't like the look or feel of a headset, at the very least use a **shoulder rest**, a device that attaches to your telephone handset and allows you hands-free movement. (One neurologist believes that cradling the phone for just three or four minutes a day while taking notes is enough to stress the neck and cause muscle spasms.)

Make sure your headset is compatible with your phone equipment. Some headsets will not work with all electronic phones. (If your phone has any of these typical features—speaker phone, memory dial—it's electronic.)

Where do you buy a headset? Radio Shack has headsets, as do many stores that sell telephones and other electronic equipment. Look for headsets in mail order catalogs, too, such as the Hello Direct catalog (800/444-3556 [CA] or **www.hellodirect.com**). Office machine dealers may have them, also. Again, I can't emphasize enough the importance of compatibility. Very often sales people will not be aware of compatibility problems, so either bring your phone to the store to check it out or if you order a headset, make sure it is completely refundable without any restocking or shipping/handling fee.

My favorite source for telephone equipment and accessories is the HelloDirect mail order catalog. Their service and support is excellent. I used them for my current telephone headset, the HelloSet Pro and the handy Touch-N-Talk handset on-off hook device. This quality business headset comes with a lifetime warranty. The amplifier is guaranteed to work with any phone (it's been field tested on more than 400 different phone terminals) and it has a handy mute button (great for private side conversations or when a sudden cough comes on). Contact Hello Direct at 800/444-3556 (CA) or **www.hellodirect.com**.

A **voice mail system** (or a telephone answering machine) is a must for most homes and small offices. There are many on the market today with a variety of features from which to choose. Here are some features that are nice to have:

- ability to pick up messages off site by dialing a code

• ability to change outgoing messages off site

• if you have two phone lines, a system that can answer either line

• voice mailboxes for multiple outgoing messages; in a voice mail system, each mailbox can be used for different announcements or for leaving messages for different individuals or departments

• if you use a telephone answering machine, get one with a computer chip instead of a tape—a computer chip provides better sound quality and lets you play back, repeat or skip messages instantly without having to wait for the tape to forward or rewind. Voices and messages are "digitized" on a microchip.

To maximize your telephone time, use a **clock** placed strategically in front of you. And if you frequently place calls to another time zone, use a second clock specifically for that time zone. A **countdown timer** (available through an electronics store or catalog) will help you consciously choose how much time you want to spend on each call (a simple cooking timer is a low-cost substitute).

Computer Accessories

Protect your eyes. Make sure your screen has an **antiglare filter** (as mentioned earlier). Purchase an antiglare filter at your local computer store or through one of the catalogs listed at the end of the chapter.

3M manufactures an excellent glass circular polarizing filter with antireflective coating to help relieve eyestrain associated with computer monitor use. (For names of dealers call **800/553-9215**.)

Set your monitor on a **tilt stand** if you need to adjust the proper angle of the screen to your eyes.

Avoid eyestrain by using at least a 17-inch monitor, which offers high resolution and lets you work more comfortably with more windows on your screen. Ideally, you should try out a monitor before you buy; computer expert Lawrence Magid suggests viewing small black type against a white background to judge overall resolution and quality.

Protect your floppy diskettes. Buy **plastic diskette boxes** with divider tabs to store programs, files and backups on disks.

Store CD-ROMs and DVDs in jewel cases or other protective containers.

To guard against the possibility of electrical power disturbances wiping out data, use a **surge protector**, also called a **surge suppressor**. Typically, you use a surge protector for computers and printers but it's also useful for copy machines, faxes and other equipment. Service calls fell by 51 percent at Arizona State University after surge protectors were installed on copy machines.

Adapt a desk return that's too shallow with a **keyboard extender** or a **key-**

board drawer that mounts under the desktop and conveniently pulls out. Another type of keyboard drawer is a stand usually made out of steel upon which you place your CPU (central processing unit) and monitor and there's space underneath to store a keyboard drawer, which pulls out when in use. A keyboard drawer is a space saver and depending on the type, can be a good accessory to lower a keyboard that's too high for comfortable typing. Eldon's Underdesk Keyboard & Mouse Superstation maximizes valuable desk space by holding large and odd-sized keyboards underneath a desk. The convenient mouse deck has built-in wrist rest, eliminating the need for bulky mouse attachments.

Articulating keyboard arms are similar to underdesk keyboard drawers but they usually have different adjustable positions.

Look for a keyboard drawer or arm that either has a wrist rest built in or can accommodate one. Look, too, for accessories that will position your mouse as close to the keyboard as possible so that if you're using a keyboard drawer or arm, you're not reaching for your mouse on the desktop. Eldon makes several such products: the Eldon Underdesk Mouse Tray that mounts under a desk, creating a 10-inch work and storage space, the Eldon Mouse Deck which provides mousing support at the same level as the keyboard (the sliding tray may be attached to a variety of keyboard drawers for right-and left-hand users) and the Eldon Underdesk Keyboard & Mouse Superstation (just discussed). Look, too, for a mouse pad that has a built-in wrist rest. Newell Office Products makes such a pad and calls it a Mouse Perch (800/487-0781 [WI] or **www.newelloffice.com**).

For lap users who prefer the keyboard and mouse all on the same plane, Fox Bay CarpalRest Wrist Support with Mouse Area combines a comfortable, padded fabric wrist rest with a platform to support your keyboard and mouse. (It's available through Daisy Wheel Ribbon Co., 800/266-5585 [CA] or **www.daisyw.com**.)

Speaking of the keyboard, if yours is located in a dusty or dirty area, protect it with a "keyskin," a special, thin, molded, plastic membrane that allows keys to be clearly visible, protected and usable. Also, be sure to cover your computer when it's not in use.

Straighten up your computer cables and wires—for aesthetics as well as safety—with cable management accessories. Velcro USA Inc. makes a "Wire Management" line of clips, ties and covers that will keep cables in their place.

APC's PowerManager (800/840-4272 [RI] or **www.apcc.com**) gives you power control, cord management and guaranteed surge protection for life. Lift the lid and you can neatly wrap the cords inside the unit. You can control up to five peripherals (six outlets total) directly from your desktop. Surge protection helps prevent hardware damage and data loss. The Pow6T model adds telephone protection that prevents spikes and surges from reaching your modem, fax, answering machine and telex equipment via phone lines.

Keeping Supplies in Order

Deciding what supplies to buy isn't as much a challenge as keeping your supplies organized and stocked. The following will help:

• Organize your supplies for easy access, keeping the most frequently used most accessible.

• Group supplies by type as well as by frequency of use.

• Label supply shelves, drawers or cabinets and/or use color coding.

• Replenish supplies regularly and systematically and have one person per work group in charge of the ordering process; you may want to use a special office supply order form (paper-based or online) that includes typical supplies to check off and pertinent time frames, e.g., when supplies are ordered and when they're needed.

• Place a re-order chart near supplies for people to indicate special requests or whenever a supply is getting low.

• Place re-order slips strategically close to the bottom of supply boxes: whoever gets a slip turns it in to the person who orders supplies.

• Prepare a "frequently ordered items" form for each vendor you use, listing items and stock or catalog numbers; refer to these forms to speed up the reordering process.

• If you use forms in your office, consider putting the master on an overhead transparency sheet and placing it on the bottom; that way no one will use the last form and the master is always within easy reach to make more copies.

With regard to printer paper and toner cartridge supplies, I'd like to recommend that you use recycled products but you should check with your printer manufacturer. Your printer warranty may not cover damage from a remanufactured cartridge or from using recycled paper. Two major printer manufacturers have instituted model programs for recycling used laser printer cartridges: Hewlett-Packard (800/527-3753) and Canon (800/962-2708).

As for paper, there is a definite move to switch to recycled paper. The entire California court system for one has mandated "the use of recycled paper for all original documents filed with California courts." Knowing that 50 percent recycled paper is less likely to jam than 100 percent may help but you should still ask your manufacturer(s) what is best for your printer as well as your copier.

Your Total Environment

How do you feel about your work space? Do you feel comfortable there? Is it you? Is there something about it that rubs you the wrong way (or the right way)?

Aesthetics, air, comfort, safety, lighting and privacy—these are some of the important environmental factors that affect how you feel about your work space. See how much you're aware of these and other factors and whether there are any you should modify.

Aesthetics

If you spend at least one third of every week day in your work space—that's at least eight hours a day—you deserve to have a working environment that's aesthetically pleasing.

Color

Many studies have revealed the "psychology of color," showing the effect of color on our emotions and state of mind. They have found, for example, that red excites us; in fact, when red is used in restaurants it is supposed to make us salivate! But used in moderation, red can be a great accent color, particularly for a sales or marketing office where you want an upbeat atmosphere.

Blue is perhaps the most universally pleasing color and is generally a calm color, depending on the shade, of course. Grays, browns and other neutrals are even more subdued. All three can work well in professional offices.

Burgundy and deep forest green are rich colors that can work well together or separately in professional offices, too. They can be used as main or accent colors.

Use of "trendy colors" can give a more contemporary feeling, which may be important for your type of office. You do run the risk, however, of having those colors go out of style more quickly. Use of more traditional colors and color schemes avoids this problem and may convey a more permanent, solid business environment. Base color decisions on the nature of your business, who comes into your office and your own particular preferences.

Choose light and dark colors to enhance your space. Lighter colors tend to open up space and work well in smaller offices. Darker colors make rooms feel smaller, cozier and more intimate. They work well in large office spaces that could otherwise appear too intimidating or sterile.

Don't ignore the impact of color. The question to ask is: What are the right colors for you?

Personalization

Color alone is not enough. Your office is not just a place to work. It should be a reflection of you. It needs to be personalized with objects you love.

In fact, why not have objects you love around you, such as art, photos or plants? Just remember, they should complement not clutter your work space.

If you've become bored with your office, consider moving personalized objects to different places. We all need variety; just moving things around or changing objects from time to time can make a big difference.

Air

What can you do about the air you breathe? First of all, be aware of it. Second, see if you can change any unpleasant atmospheric conditions or adapt to them.

Airborne Toxins

The most obvious toxin in the air is cigarette smoke. Some studies have shown that cigarette smoke is more harmful to someone nearby inhaling "secondary" smoke than the smoke inhaled by the actual smoker. If smoke is a problem for you, stay away from it!

Many cities and companies now specify that smokers must go outside or to other specially designated areas to smoke. If your city or company doesn't have such requirements, consider working toward establishing them. Sure it'll take some of your precious time, but isn't your health precious enough? At the very least, make sure that office workers who smoke have an air cleaner or purifier unit on their desk to remove at least some of the smoke.

As far as other toxic substances, such as asbestos, read your newspaper to stay current on new discoveries and legislation. Notice, too, whether you experience certain symptoms such as nausea and dizziness only in your office environment. Invisible toxic substances pose a real problem in detection and in identification but we're bound to see more research on this in the future.

One estimate put nearly a third of all new office buildings at risk of indoor air quality problems. Consider putting in some plants. A study by NASA found that plants can remove up to 87 percent of toxic indoor air within 24 hours.

Plants can absorb common office pollutants that include: formaldehyde (from particle board, wall paneling, plywood, furniture and carpeting); trichloroethylene (from some inks, paints and varnishes) and benzene (from tobacco smoke and some plastics, inks and oils). According to the book *50 Simple Things Your Business Can Do to Save the Earth*, use at least one four-to-five-foot plant per 100 square feet. Good plants to use with fluorescent lighting include: philodendrons, golden pothos, English Ivy, peace lily and mother-in-law's tongue. Spider plants and flowering plants such as azaleas and chrysanthemums work well with more light. Before purchasing plants, ask whether they are poisonous (small children may be in your office occasionally or more frequently).

If you're planning to move your office to a new location, consider the air quality there, too.

Temperature

Here's one of those factors that is far easier to adapt to than to change. I can't tell you how often I have complained to facilities managers about the temperature, which for me is almost always too cold in modern buildings, where you are at the mercy of a thermostat that either isn't working or is adjusted to somebody else's body!

I used to work for an aerospace company. Our department was on the same thermostat as the computer room. It was always "freeeezing" in the office. I kept a little portable heater on under my desk. (Fire regulations where you work may prohibit this solution.)

I've had offices where I've had to keep an extra sweater in the office at all times, particularly during the summer when the air conditioning tends toward the cool side. Another option is to close off most of the vents in your office in the summertime when the air conditioning is running fast and furiously. If your office is too hot, your only option may be to keep complaining or work at home if possible. But recognize that temperature is a factor in your productivity and your attitude toward your workplace.

Comfort And Safety

Fifty percent of disabling office accidents are the result of slips or falls—most of which could have been prevented.

Keep floors clear of cords, cables and other objects. Even a rubber band on the floor can be a hazard. One office worker slipped on a rubber band, breaking his arm in two places and crushing his elbow. He lost six weeks of work.

Our discussion of ergonomics in this chapter certainly relates to comfort and safety. Check out your chair and your equipment according to the ergonomics chart and criteria discussed earlier.

I recommend that whether you work for yourself or someone else you should become more responsible for your own safety. As of this writing, ergonomic regulations and programs are coming under less scrutiny by the government than in years past. Learn what you can to protect yourself. If an employer doesn't provide what you need, you may wish to provide it for yourself or look for another more ergonomic workplace.

Lighting

Lighting is related to comfort and safety, as well as aesthetics. Select the right **amount**, the right **kinds** and the right **direction** to make lighting work best for you.

Make sure you have enough light. Some offices are too dark and depressing. Interior offices usually need additional lighting. That one panel in the ceiling just won't do it.

Make sure you don't have too much of the wrong kind of lighting in the wrong places. If you're using a computer terminal, all those overhead fluorescent lights could be causing irritating glare. Better to use a lower level of overhead lighting combined with **task lighting**, localized sources of lighting for specific tasks or areas. An example of task lighting is a desk lamp that sheds light on desktop paperwork only and stays off the computer screen. Another possibility is to use filter tubes that fit over fluorescent bulbs.

Balance fluorescent lighting with either a natural light source (a window) or incandescent lighting. Fluorescent lighting by itself is very hard on the eyes.

In addition, some research studies indicate fluorescent lighting may be emitting harmful ultraviolet rays that cause such symptoms as fatigue and dizziness. Some retail stores are putting **ultraviolet shields** on their fluorescent lights. You may also consider replacing your fluorescent lighting with **full spectrum lights**, also called **health lights** or **Durolights**.

Noise

It's becoming more common for offices to have open plan layouts that don't have separate, walled offices. While this openness can save on rent and create an environment that encourages teamwork, it can also create a noisy environment. Here are a few tips to reduce the noise factor. Position telephones so co-workers don't face each other. Use ceiling tiles that are noise reduction efficient (they should have a reduction coefficient of at least .85). Have taller partitions (at least four to six feet high) to create barriers. Have sound-masking systems which produce a sound similar to moving air.

Privacy

The last environmental factor concerns the need for privacy in your office. Privacy usually comes from some sense of enclosure, which can include visual as well as sound barriers. Having some barriers, be they walls, movable panels, plants, bookcases or file cabinets, is important for most people.

For one thing, effective communication needs privacy. Studies have shown that employees who sit in an open, "bull pen" environment tend to communicate less freely. On the other hand, employees who have some measure of enclosure and privacy tend to communicate more freely and openly.

Privacy also can improve productivity. Most people need to have their own space to focus, concentrate and shut out some of the distractions. A smaller, more controlled environment is also less stressful for most people.

Energy Efficiency

Finally, there's one environmental factor that goes beyond your work space to affect others: energy.

Many people mistakenly believe that computers and other equipment will last longer if they are left on all the time. They not only will not last longer but they will also use up more energy. So, if you don't plan to use a computer, monitor or printer (especially older laser printers) for at least an hour, turn them off to save energy.

By the way, screen saver programs for your monitor do not save energy. If you don't want to turn your monitor off, see whether your operating system (e.g., Windows) has an energy-saving option on the Display icon.

Resource Guide

Furniture and Equipment

Whenever possible, see furniture and equipment "in person." At the very least, get color chips of finish or fabric or actual samples. Never buy a chair without sitting in it first. Suppliers are listed from different parts of the country; you can often save significantly on shipping when you order in a geographical area that's nearby.

National Business Furniture is a mail order catalog that has a substantial selection of furniture at discount prices with a guarantee for 15 years (except for normal upholstery wear). They offer thousands of products. 800/558-1010 (WI) or **www.nationalbizfurniture.com**.

Accessories And Supplies

Allsop Inc. manufactures a line of computer and office equipment accessories and supplies that include diskette cases and computer cleaning kits. 800/426-4303 (WA) or **www.allsop.com**

Curtis Manufacturing Company, Inc. (Rolodex) manufactures more than 100 computer and electronic accessory products, which are available through dealers. 800/955-5544 (NJ) or **www.curtis.com**

Daisy Wheel Ribbon Co. is an excellent direct mail source for computer supplies and accessories with great customer service. 800/266-5585 (CA) or **www.daisyw.com**

Hello Direct is an excellent catalog of telephone productivity tools that I have used and recommended. 800/444-3556 (CA) or **www.hellodirect.com**.

Inmac's award-winning mail order catalog offers one of the best selections of quality computers, supplies, accessories, furniture and data communications products at great prices. 800/547-5444 (NJ) or **www.warehouse.com**

The **Lillian Vernon Neat Ideas for an Organized Life** catalog offers a wide array of home office products. Check out their Web site, too. Lillian Vernon, 800/285-5555 or **www.lillianvernon.com**..

Reliable Home Office is a beautiful catalog that features many attractive desk and office accessories for your office at home as well as at work. 800/621-4344 (IL) or **www.reliable.com**

Secure-It, Inc. makes Kablit locks and cables to help you prevent the theft of valuable computers and peripherals. 800/451-7592 (MA) or **www.secure-it.com**

Books And Other Reading

Cumulative Trauma Disorders: A Manual for Musculoskeletal Diseases of the Upper Limbs (Bristol, PA: Taylor & Francis, 1988) was edited by Vern Putz-Anderson of the National Institute for Occupational Safety and Health and is considered to be one of the best books on RSI (Repetitive Stress Injuries).

How to Survive Your Computer Work Station (CRT Services, Inc., 1998) by Julia Lacey shows specifically how to prevent and eliminate physical, vision and stress problems related to computer use. It deals with office setup and solutions to existing problems. $16.95 plus $1 shipping. CRT Services, Inc., 800/256-4379 (TX) or **www.howtosurvive.com**.

9 to 5 Fact Sheets contain valuable information about good office design, particularly for computer workers. To get the fact sheets and a complete listing of other work-related books and reports contact the 9 to 5 National Association of Working Women at 800/669-0769 (GA) or **www.9to5.org**.

Working From Home, Fifth Edition: Everything You Need to Know About Living and Working Under the Same Roof by Paul and Sarah Edwards (New York: Putnam, 1999) has several excellent chapters on setting up and equipping a home office space. Paperback, $18.95. 800/788-6262

7

UP-TO-DATE
PAPER FILES
AND BEYOND

Quick Scan: They're out of sight, out of mind. Or so you'd like to think until one fateful day when you can't find that all important document. Or until your paper files are so full that it's physically dangerous to pry open files to slip in just one more paper. Find out how to organize your files so that they become an ally, not an enemy. Discover which filing supplies can make a world of difference. While the main emphasis is on your own personal filing system, this chapter also includes information useful for larger or special office filing systems.

For most people, paper files are like skeletons in the closet—bad secrets that no one likes to talk about. Who wants to admit that files are bulging with out-of-date papers, that they are difficult to handle and retrieve and that very often files are misplaced or even lost?

Then there are the *piles*—the papers that never make it into the files. They sit on desktops, in bookcases, on tables, on file cabinets, and yes, even on the floor.

The Three Filing Phobias

Besides these excuses, there are three fears people have when it comes to files and piles. I call these fears the "3-Ds" because they each start with the letter "D."

First, people are afraid of Decisions. If you don't know what to call papers, you'll end up calling them nothing. Papers then collect in unnamed stacks and piles, as well as in drawers and in-boxes.

Second, people are afraid of Discards. Heaven forbid you should throw anything out—you might need it someday.

Third, the fear of Disappearance haunts many. "Filing a paper in my system is like filing it in a black hole—never to be seen or heard from again," one new client told me.

Let's see how your files stack up.

How Do Your Files Stack Up?

Here's a quick quiz to rate the state of your filing system. Check "yes" or "no" after each question.

	YES	NO
1. Is filing a real chore?		
2. Would it take a long while to catch up on your filing?		
3. Do you often have trouble finding and retrieving papers —often enough to cause irritation?		
4. Do you keep many papers and/or publications "just in case" someday you may need them?		
5. Is your filing system characterized more by randomness than careful planning?		
6. Are your files inconveniently located?		
7. Do you frequently have trouble deciding what to name files or where to file papers?		
8. Is it difficult to tell what's in each file drawer without opening it up?		
9. Are you afraid to attempt retrieving a document from your files (or piles) while someone is waiting in your office or you're on the phone? (Would you prefer to look without the time pressure of "beat the clock"?)		
10. Are you copy machine happy—do you make unnecessary duplicates of papers?		
11. Are all your filing cabinets/drawers stuffed to the gills?		

If you have at least three "yes" responses, keep reading! Below are some typical reasons I hear from people who explain why their files are usually not as functional as they should be. See if you relate to any of the following:

- I don't have a secretary.
- I don't have time/I'm too busy putting out fires.
- Setting up a system is menial, clerical work.
- It's not my job.
- I don't know what to call things.
- I'm creative and my work style is "organized chaos."

Now that we've psychoanalyzed some filing phobias and quizzed you on the status of your filing system, here are some valid reasons for *making the time* to set up or revamp your deskside files. Check any that apply to you:

- You look and act more professional and competent when your information is organized.
- Organized information helps you plan your activities.
- It's easier to get work done.
- You feel better when you know where everything is. You have more control over your work.
- You save time looking for things.
- Accessible, fingertip information is a key resource for your productivity, professional image and peace of mind.
- Add some reasons of your own, making them relate specifically to your goals. What will a good filing system help you achieve or accomplish?

Five Easy Steps
to an Organized Filing System

Most people in the workplace are foggy when it comes to filing systems. They haven't been "office trained," a term coined by one of my seminar participants. They don't realize that the clerical work of filing is only a part of an organized filing system. The *mental*, conceptual work is the most important aspect of a good system.

Most people also don't know where to start. What follows is a blueprint to guide you in designing or revamping your system. Here are the five main steps I use with clients:

1. Categorize any existing files as "active" or "inactive" and pull inactive files from your existing filing system.

2. Write out your filing system categories and subcategories *on paper*. Get input from any others who'll be using the system.

3. Physically set up the system. Have all supplies on hand as you prepare file labels and purge, consolidate and arrange file folders.

4. Put the finishing touches on your system. Label drawers and prepare a file index or chart for yourself and any others who have access to the system. If others are involved, introduce the system at a special training meeting.

5. Maintain your system by sticking to a routine.

We'll go into more detail about these five steps after becoming more familiar with the thought process behind every good filing system.

A Closer Look at the Five-Step Process

There are three essential questions to answer about each paper or file:

1. **When** is it used? How many times a day, a week, a month or a year do you handle it?

2. **What** is it? Under what category(ies) does it belong?

3. **Where** should it go? Near your desk? In storage? In a filing cabinet? Which drawer? A notebook? The trash?

Steps One through Three will deal with these questions.

Step One: Active and Inactive

Files should be categorized on the basis of *frequency*, that is when or how often they are used. There are two basic types: **active** and **inactive**, sometimes also called **open** and **closed**.

Active (or open files) belong in your office because you will refer to each of them at least several times a year. You will either add to these files or retrieve something from them. Examples include your financial records for this year and active client or customer files.

Working files are active files that are used most often—daily or several times a week. They should be the most accessible to you at your desk or work station. They can go on a credenza, a side table next to your desk or inside the most accessible file drawer. The most active working files can be part of your daily paperwork system as described in Chapter 4.

Inactive, closed or storage files are used infrequently, if at all, and should usually be kept out of your office. If you opt to keep these files in your office, put them in the least accessible locations—in the rear of a file drawer, on a top shelf or in an area separate from your main work area. Whenever possible, remove files to someone else's office or to a designated storage area on or off site.

As you begin to sort through any existing files, be thinking of these two basic categories: active and inactive. Go through your existing files and weed out all the inactive ones and either discard or store them. By the way, this file sorting process should be done quickly by looking at file names only. *Do not sort through papers in files at this time.*

Now that you've sorted through your files, you're ready to tackle any piles of paper you may have accumulated. Go through these piles quickly, pulling active and/or important papers. Don't spend hours and hours going through piles, however, or you'll never create your filing system. These five steps will help you streamline the process:

1. Get yourself a countdown timer. (An egg timer is fine or you may prefer an

LCD countdown timer available at an electronics store such as Radio Shack.)

2. Quickly sort through piles using the timer. This is not the time for a thorough analysis of each and every paper. As my friend and colleague Maxine Ordesky says, "Separate the treasures from the trash." For our purposes here, "treasures" are any papers that will go into active files or any important documents that you *must* save and file. Set aside for now "semi-precious" papers that may go into storage. As far as what "trash" to toss at this time, apply my two **Discard Dilemmas** rules: a) when in doubt, *save* legal, tax information and b) when in doubt, *toss* resource information. (For more information on purging, see Chapter 5.)

3. Clear the decks. Put your "semi-precious" papers temporarily in records storage boxes with lids (such as Fellowes Bankers Boxes). Label the outside of the box "Inactive Papers" and add any specific description of the contents, unless they're just miscellaneous. Try to keep the filing area as clear as possible—that way you'll be able to think and work more clearly.

4. For your "treasured" papers, think about category and file names and jot a name on each paper in pencil. If any of these papers could go in existing file folders, file them now. If they need folders of their own, quickly put these papers in folders and jot a name on the file folder tab in pencil. Or use removable Post-it brand File Folder Labels for temporary labels. If you have no extra file folders on hand or there are too few papers for their own folder, then paper clip related papers together and jot a future file name down on the top paper or on a Post-it label in each grouping.

5. In summary: spend most of your time on *important* papers.

Step Two: The Name Game
Once you have the two most basic groupings of active and inactive, you are well on your way.

Now you're ready to identify what are the major areas or divisions of your work and/or your work-related information. Start thinking in terms of the largest, *broadest* categories for your active files.

Naming categories and then files is the most critical element to setting up an organized system because it will aid in the retrieval of information. Human beings are much better at storing information rather than retrieving it—whether it goes into our brains or our file cabinets. Just as our memory works best by connecting to related information, so, too, will a file naming system work when we make those connections.

One estate planning attorney who is a sole practitioner with a personal computer has designated four main areas of information: Clients, Business Operation, Estate Planning Information and Personal Computer Resources/References. A management consultant has these three categories: Business Administration (which includes client files), Resource Information (for seminars and articles) and Marketing/Business Development. A computer systems engineer has files for Communications, Software Applications and Hardware.

Here is a listing of general categories. Circle any that might apply to your work. Add your own at the end. Remember to select the *broadest subject areas* (not necessarily specific file names) that apply to you: Accounts; Background/ History; Business Administration; Clients or Patients; Communications (in company or organization); Contacts; Customers, Legislation; Management; Marketing; Products; Projects; Reference; Research; Resources; Samples; Staff; Support; and Volunteers.

To start breaking down these broad categories into subcategories and specific file names and to help you visualize their relationship to one another, do the following. Use **colored index cards** with one color for each of your major file categories. Put each file name on the appropriately colored card and put it with the other cards. Spread out the cards and arrange them alphabetically or by subject. You can use the cards later to make up your filing system labels and also right now as you design your system on paper.

Designing a System on Paper

A filing system on paper serves as a blueprint that charts out all category, subcategory and file names and shows how they all fit together.

If you have a computer, a word processing program would be helpful at this step. Besides being able to easily move words around, many word processing programs let you sort (arrange) words alphabetically.

Start with one of your major category areas. Use the File Chart shown in Figure 7-1 as a guide to help you easily list your own file categories and names and show how they are related. A File Chart is an outline of your filing system.

Look at your existing file folders as well as the paper-clipped groupings and new folders you created in Step One. See if file names suggest themselves to you. Look for patterns, groupings and combinations that go together. Be creative but don't create file names that you won't remember later. Don't try to think of every file name right now; this is not your final system—it's only the beginning.

Using a pencil (or your computer), write down a major work category from your filing system. Now complete what you think will be the main headings. Leave plenty of space between headings. Select names for headings that make sense to *you* (and anyone else using the system). Stick with unadorned nouns for headings, if possible. Next add some subheadings. Figure 7-1 shows an example for Resource Information with three headings and two levels of subheads.

As you chart out headings and subheads you'll start to see which names belong together and which ones need additional subheads. You're creating your own file design. Don't get too carried away with elaborate headings and subheads. Often one heading and one level of subheads is plenty. Keep your design simple!

Now complete your File Chart for one *major category only*. Then, when you're ready, do a chart for each of your other major categories in your filing system. Remember, nothing is etched in stone; your file chart is only a guide. If your file charts are on computer, you may now wish to alphabetize any headings or subheads that are actual names of clients, companies, vendors, etc., or you can wait to do it in Step Three.

Figure 7-1. SAMPLE FILE CHART

MAJOR CATEGORY (OR DRAWER NAME): Resource Info.

HEADING	SUBHEAD	SUBHEAD
Contacts	Stores Consultants Service	Answers on Computers
Manuals		
Products	Hardware Software	

Step Three: Putting It All Together

Where files will go in your system is a combination of what types of files they are, *who* uses them, *when* they are used and how much room you have. You should now know approximately how much room you have after having completed Steps One and Two because you've determined how often files will be used, purged your system of unnecessary inactive files and identified all your active file names.

One of the most important aspects of your filing system is location. Here are some guidelines to consider when deciding where to put your files:

• The more files are used, the closer they should be to your desk or main work area.

• Keep like files together. Group files by subject, type or frequency of use.

• Choose appropriate media to store your information—perhaps you want to use notebooks or boxes rather than file folders. Maybe you have large, bulky or odd-sized items that require special filing solutions.

• Security may be a factor; take any necessary precautions to secure confidential information.

• Select the appropriate cabinets or equipment.

With regard to cabinets, I suggest you start with what you have on hand. If you're starting from scratch, estimate the number of filing inches you now have and project, if you can, how much you'll need over the next several years. Look at your available floor space and your current or projected office layout to determine what will physically fit in your space (allowing space also for drawers to be pulled out).

Vertical cabinets will generally give you a few more filing inches per floor space than **lateral cabinets** but you need space into which you can extend the vertical cabinet drawers. Some people prefer the look of lateral cabinets along with being able to use the drawers either side-by-side or front-to-back. Whether you choose vertical or lateral, look for cabinets with high quality rolling or gliding mechanisms, built-in glides to accommodate hanging files and tilt-proof or nontip safety features.

You can almost triple the number of files in the same floor space if you choose **open shelf file cabinets**. Besides holding a large number of files, these cabinets give you easy access to files. I would recommend you get flip-front doors so you can close and lock cabinets. (Bindertek's Law Files described in Chapter 4, work great in an open shelf filing system.)

Now you're ready to physically set up your system—a time-consuming task that's nice to share with someone else, if you have such luxury.

Decide if you want to use **color coding** in your system. A simple color-coding scheme by drawer or by major category can be helpful, especially when you go to refile a folder. We use blue hanging folder tabs and file folder labels for our business and administrative files, for example, and yellow ones for our resource information files. You're less likely to misfile a folder in the wrong drawer with color coding. You can also see at a glance the type(s) of folders in a particular drawer. (For more elaborate color coding, see "Special Office Filing and Information Management Systems" near the end of the chapter Resource Guide.)

Make sure you have the right supplies on hand (also see the chapter Resource Guide). Here's a typical "shopping list" I suggest to clients, followed by comments describing why these items are important:

• One box of **hanging file folders** (generally 25 to a box); they come with or without tabs; get them without tabs if you're going to use color coding

• Hanging **box bottom file folders**, one-inch capacity, one box of 25, no tabs included

• Hanging box bottom file folders, two-inch capacity, one box of 25, no tabs

• Plastic tabs for any hanging folders that don't come with tabs; tabs come in two-inch or 3½-inch lengths—I prefer the 3½-inch size; if you're going to color code your files, get colored plastic tabs or buy colored plastic windows (to use with any clear plastic tabs you may already have on hand)

• Third-cut **interior folders** (100 per box); interior folders are cut lower than ordinary manila folders so that the folders sit inside the hanging folders without sticking up; they come in a variety of colors; third-cut folders work with the standard file folder labels you'll be getting; for more about "third-cut" and "fifth-cut" see page 124.

• Self-adhesive file folder labels; if you're color coding your files, buy the colored labels

To make full use of your headings and subheads, use hanging file folders, especially the one- and two-inch box bottom folders, which work great as your major headings. Inside each box bottom folder, place several interior folders, specially cut manila folders that can serve as subheads. If possible, avoid using only one interior folder per hanging folder; too many hanging folders will take up too much space and you also won't take advantage of the heading/subhead classification system, which adds to greater retrievability. (Check the Resource Guide for descriptions and pictures of these different folders.)

Pull out your File Chart (or your index cards, if you used them). Go through each heading and subhead and indicate which of the headings and subheads will take regular, one-inch or two-inch hanging folders. Put a "1" by any that you think will be up to one-inch thick and a "2" by any that will be up to two inches thick. Those with 1s will take one-inch box bottoms and those with 2s, two-inch box bottoms. Write "H" for any of the remaining headings or subheads that would take regular hanging folders; otherwise they would automatically get interior folders. (Most of your subheads will probably take interior folders.)

With your File Chart or index cards as a guide, type or print your hanging folder labels using all capital letters.

Colleague Beverly Clower of Office Overhaul uses a Kroy **lettering machine** to create large, legible labels. She uses 18- and 24-point size wheels in the Helvetica bold, all caps, font style. The 24-point size is for headings and the 18-point size is for major subheads. Kroy produces black lettering on clear (or white, if you prefer), self-adhesive strips cut to size. Each strip is then affixed to the white label insert. (For more ideas about labeling, see the Resource Guide section on "Labeling Systems.")

If you have access to a personal computer with some desktop publishing capabilities, you could prepare your label names with the font and style of your choice. Print them directly on an 8½-by-11-inch sheet of "crack 'n peel" (self-adhesive paper used for labels). Avery's LabelPro software program is helpful if you have a laser printer.

Or if your printer won't accommodate crack 'n peel, print onto your normal paper, which will become the master. Then use the master to photocopy onto the crack 'n peel (make sure your copier will accept crack 'n peel—most high speed copiers should).

You might also try photocopying onto "65 lb. card stock," a heavier grade of paper that you could use instead of the furnished white label inserts. (Check compatibility of card stock with your copier.)

Insert the labels into the hanging folder plastic tabs. Put in order the hanging folders as you had listed them on your File Chart. Insert the plastic tab on the inside front cover at the far left for headings. For hanging folders with subheads, you may wish to place the plastic tab a little over towards the right. Also note that you should stagger any tabs that would block other tabs. If your box bottom folders require you to insert cardboard reinforcement strips on the bottom, add them now. Set up your new hanging folders in a file drawer. Place existing file folders inside the new hanging folders.

Now type labels for new interior folders. Before you affix them on the interior folders, place the three types of folders in front of you: left-cut, center-cut and then right-cut (assuming you are using third-cut folders). Pull folders in order of left-cut, center-cut, and right-cut. Don't always start at the left every time you come to a new hanging folder; keep going where you left off. That way you won't end up with a lot of extra right- or center-cut folders when you're done. In addition, you will maintain good visibility in your system by staggering folders in this way. Now affix the labels.

For even greater visibility and versatility, consider MAGNIFILES, which are V-bottom or box-bottom hanging files that come with special 11-inch long transparent (colored or clear), durable, magnified plastic indexes that run the full length of the file. Besides greater file name visibility, these file indexes give you plenty of room for file titles—five times the space of conventional tabs. Index strips come in white, full color or color tip styles. MAGNIFILES are available from Abbot Office Systems, **800/631-2233** (NJ).

For interior folders that will be handled frequently and will risk dog-earing, cover the label area with either self-adhesive plastic that you'll have to cut to size or, better yet, use pre-cut label protectors such as the Smead Seal & View protectors.

Arranging Folders

You can arrange your file folders in a number of ways: alphabetically, numerically or by frequency of use. You might even arrange your folders in a combination of ways. For example, you might use a basically alphabetical setup but group frequently used folders in a special, accessible location, for example, in the front of your file drawer.

Certain kinds of information work better alphabetically. For example, client or customer name files work best in an alphabetical system.

On the other hand, subject files do not always have to be in strict alphabetical order. It may be more convenient to place files you use more often in a more accessible location, irrespective of alphabetical sequence. Frequently used subhead files, too, may be placed out of alphabetical order within their hanging folders.

Numerical filing is a better method if you need to arrange files by date (e.g, purchase orders) or by number (legislative bills). Numerical filing is also useful when you want to keep files more confidential (it's more difficult to tell what's in a numerical file). A file index may be needed, however, in order to readily locate material. The index should be kept in a different location apart from the files to ensure their security.

Whichever method(s) you select, place all your interior folders into their respective hanging folders. Put any remaining, unfiled papers left over from Step One into appropriate folders.

Fine Tuning

You may have noticed that your existing files haven't yet undergone a complete and thorough purge. There's a good reason for this. It's better to set up a *functional* system first and fine tune later. Do your fine tuning now.

Go carefully through each of your existing, *active* folders in your system. Do you really need this information? How accessible does it have to be? Could a folder be consolidated with another folder? Use a timer and allot a specified period of time, from 15 minutes to an hour and a half on a given day. Or try giving yourself a goal, say, five folders in fifteen minutes.

You may find you need to add new labels (or delete others). Add them to your File Chart in a different color. Don't take time out to type or print the labels right now. Jot down file names in pencil on new folders.

When you've completed the purge for one complete subject area, type or print any remaining labels and attach them to the new folders.

Step Four: Finishing Touches

Now that you've physically set up your system, make sure you can tell the types of files you have in each drawer without having to open them up. You need a summary of your file drawer contents. Such a summary could be as simple as labeling each drawer with main headings.

Beverly Clower makes a "key to the files," which is a map or diagram of file cabinets and drawers plus their contents.

A simple list on paper, such as your File Chart or a "file index," could suffice. Better yet, keep a list on your computer that can be easily updated. Be sure to print out at least one "hard copy" on paper. It's important to have computer listings for both active as well as inactive files in storage boxes. I have a computer document file called "storage" that lists all my inactive paper files by Box A, Box B, etc.

Train anyone who will be using your filing system. Have a special meeting or training session to introduce the system. Distribute a file index, file chart, key to the files or other listing. If appropriate, show how to borrow files by leaving a folder-size **out guide** in the place of the missing file.

Step Five: Maintenance

The trick to a productive filing system is a regular maintenance program by you or someone you designate. Your program should be fairly routine and involve only a minimal amount of time—famous last words! But let's see how it can be done.

Start by making some decisions in advance about your file maintenance program. Answer the following questions:

1. Who's going to do your filing?
2. Will you file some or all papers "as you go"? Which ones?
3. If you plan to file papers in batches, how often and when specifically will filing occur?
4. How many times a year will you purge files and transfer formerly active files into storage? During which months or quarters?

Too many professionals and offices have *no* filing maintenance guidelines. Don't wait until an emergency, crammed file cabinets or a move forces you to take stock. It may be too late or you may be in the middle of a top priority project that prevents you from devoting what will now require a large chunk of time.

Set up your own maintenance system. Decide how many minutes a day or a week you (or someone you designate) will spend on it. Which day(s) will you choose and which time(s)? Be specific. Until your system becomes routine, write down your maintenance tasks on your daily to-do list or in your planner. Take a look at the Quick Chart (Figure 7-2) for other ideas.

The longer you wait to either set up or implement your maintenance system the easier it is for paper to accumulate once again. Get tough on paper!

The hardest part of maintaining your filing system is maintaining enough incentive. You have to believe this is a top priority or you'll keep putting it off. Filing systems often get put on the proverbial back burner until you've run out of filing space or a crisis occurs. Don't let that happen to you.

Figure 7-2. QUICK CHART: FILE MAINTENANCE TIPS

Here are some tips to make filing easier:
- Immediately after you read a paper or an article you want to save and file, jot down the subject or file name in the top right corner. This will save you time, especially if the paper is not filed right away so that you or an assistant don't have to re-read the paper before it's filed.
- If the information in the article will probably be obsolete after a period of time, indicate a discard date in the top left corner. This will help you easily toss old papers without having to reread them.
- As an experiment, keep track of papers or files that you actually go back and refer to. Jot down an "R date"—the date you referred back to a paper or file for information. At the top of the paper or file write "R" followed by the date. If you start to see several R dates, maybe you need to move this information so that it's more accessible. On the other hand, seeing no R dates, you may decide to discard more papers and files. If nothing else, R dates may show you how often or little you actually refer to files.

Three Filing Tips for Every Manager

If you're a manager or you work for one, you need to help implement three key ideas relating to your coworkers and your office filing system.

First, **take your office filing system seriously**. Filing is not just clerical busy work. It's a vital database without which your office or department could not function.

Evaluate your current systems, including the central filing system as well as individual filing systems. Begin by using the five steps we've just discussed. See if there's any duplication of effort, e.g., is everyone keeping a copy of internal memos that could be filed in one central location?

When she was a manager, CEO Kathryn Johnson created the "vanguard system" in which each of her staff became a specialist in a particular subject area and maintained files on that subject. Because each staff member was "in the vanguard," filing became easier, reading loads were lighter and department morale was boosted. Johnson still uses the system today with her current staff.

Second, **reduce paper to be filed and stored through systematic records management/purging, paper reduction and recycling.**

One company has records management guidelines with retention schedules that culminate in an annual event called "Pack Rat Day." This event encourages all departments to review their records for storage or disposal according to the company guidelines. Each department tracks all "pack rat material" on a log sheet, which, along with records for storage or shredding, are turned in to the Records Systems department, the sponsor of the event. There is a Pack Rat Day celebration with refreshments, live music and departmental "Reformed Pack Rat Awards."

One aerospace company has had "Operation Roundfile" every year in which employees clean out their files and offices, tossing as much paper as possible. The company also has paper reduction programs throughout its divisions. One division came up with a motto, "Paper doesn't grow on trees—it is trees." This division set a goal of reducing photocopies by 20 percent, lines of computer print by 50 percent and mailing lists by 25 percent.

Smart managers are recognizing that it's more productive and profitable for their organizations as well as for the environment to cut down on paperwork and paper-generated communications in the first place. Look for ways to communicate using less paper, e.g., through e-mail, voice mail or routing one memo (instead of making copies of the memo).

Set up a policy to reduce paper in your office or organization. Adopt a **purge prevention policy** such as the one developed by one association executive who implemented what he called an "ongoing, self-policing, purge prevention policy" to limit office file cabinets to two lateral five-drawer units. He said, "It's so easy to become a walking encyclopedia of nonessential stuff. It's more time effective to go elsewhere for information, even if you have to wait 24 hours to get it than having to purge files every two to three years. It's a terrible waste of time to prune that stuff—it's better to deal with it the first time around."

Many organizations have instituted major recycling programs, not only to recycle paper that would ordinarily be thrown away, but also to buy paper products, such as file folders, made from recycled fibers. Esselte Pendaflex Corporation makes EarthWise, a complete line of filing supplies made from 100 percent recycled fiber, which should be available through your office supply dealer (or contact Esselte at 516/741-3200 or **www.esselte.com**). The Quill Corporation direct mail catalog features recycled products, including file folders (800/789-1331 [IA] or **www.quill.com**).

The third filing tip is **value the importance of training**. Smooth functioning office filing systems don't happen by accident. They take careful planning and training.

Whenever more than one person is using an office filing system, you need to set up at least one training session and preferably two. The first session introduces the logistics of the system—how files are named and arranged and how and when they are filed and by whom. This is a good time to introduce the file out guide and distribute a file index.

If you are at all concerned that there will be some resistance to the system, suggest that everyone "try it out" for the next couple of weeks and then meet again at a second meeting to discuss and evaluate the system. The more people are a part of any system, the more likely they are to accept it. You must, however, be open to their ideas.

If more managers would follow these simple tips, more offices would have better organized filing systems.

Resource Guide
Books and Booklets
Alphabetic Filing Rules published by the Association of Records Managers and Administrators (ARMA). This booklet provides guidelines for establishing a consistent, documented filing system, whether you have a manual or automated system. 800/422-2762 (KS) or **www.arma.org**.

Guide to Professional Resources lists the 150 publications available from the Association of Records Managers and Administrators (ARMA), 800/422-2762 (KS) or **www.arma.org**.

Guide to Record Retention Requirements published by Commerce Clearing House, Inc. This 432-page guide tells businesses and individuals that do business with government agencies exactly which records must be kept, by whom and for how long. 800/248-3248 or **www.cch.com**.

How to File Guide published by Esselte Pendaflex Corp. A great little full-color booklet with lots of photos, examples and information about filing tips, supplies and systems. 516/741-3200.

Filing Supplies
Folders
Hanging folders are the mainstay of frequently used paper filing systems. They provide easy access to paperwork, good visibility and an organized way to group files.

They are typically made of durable, two-tone green paper stock but many hanging folders also come in other colors and are made of other materials such as plastic or the more environmentally sound recycled fibers used in Esselte Pendaflex EarthWise folders, which contain the highest percentage of post-consumer content available today.

Special scoring in the middle of the flaps and on the bottom makes these folders more useful (see Figure 7-3). Scoring in the middle allows you to bend back the flaps so that the folder can be propped open in the file drawer until contents are reinserted. Scoring and folding at the bottom let you square off the v-shape bottom to increase the folder's storage capacity.

To really increase the capacity so that you can more easily use the hanging folder as a container for several file folders (or for catalogs), use a **box bottom folder**, which, depending on the manufacturer, comes in one- to four-inch capacity, letter or legal size, and two-inch capacity for computer printout size. Pendaflex box bottoms come in the standard green or in other colors. Special cardboard strips reinforce the "bottom" edge of box bottoms. On the Smead box bottom the strip is pre-installed. See Figure 7-3.

The Pendaflex Hanging Box File is a blue box bottom with sides that prevent papers and other materials from slipping out.

The Pendaflex Hanging File Jacket lets you file small items with standard-size papers so that they won't slip out.

Pendaflex hanging folders also come in a variety of different sizes to handle a variety of items, such as invoices, x-rays and computer printouts.

Interior folders are special file folders cut shorter to fit inside hanging folders without obscuring hanging folder tabs. Esselte Pendaflex Corp. makes them in two lines: the Pendaflex line, available in manila and ten two-tone colors

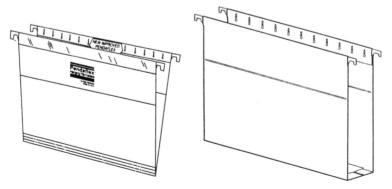

Figure 7-3. The classic Pendaflex hanging file folder (left) is reinforced along the top and bottom with a durable poly-laminate. The Smead Flex-I-Vision box bottom folder comes with sturdy reinforcement strips, which makes it the ideal folder for computer printouts, manuals, catalogs or telephone books.

to match Pendaflex hanging folders, and the EarthWise line, in five earth-tone colors.

For manila folders that are handled frequently and are used more outside the filing cabinet than inside, consider getting those with **reinforced** tabs or consider getting plastic file folders that are made in different colors and styles by JEFFCO, Inc. 800/248-3453 (AZ) or **www.jeffco.com**.

If you want papers you file to be more secure, less likely to fall out and easier to locate, consider two-hole punching papers in **fastener folders**. They're essential for important papers that have legal or tax implications where you just can't take a chance on losing any paper. Generally, you'll put papers in reverse chronological order—i.e., the most recent papers are on top. Hole-punched papers take up less space, which is particularly important in businesses where bulky files are the order of the day. You can buy folders with the fasteners already attached or buy the folders and fasteners separately, which is more economical.

Wherever you'd use several fastener folders for one client or project, the **partition folder** is great. The partition folder, also called a **classification folder**, is made of heavy duty pressboard, and lets you group related papers together in different sections of the folder by either attaching two-hole-punched papers to fasteners on either side of each partition and/or by placing unpunched papers in between the partitions. Different styles are available from different manufacturers. You can get from one to three partitions, some of which are pocket dividers. The Pendaflex Hanging Partition Folder is really two folders in one—a hanging folder and a partition folder. (See Figure 7-4).

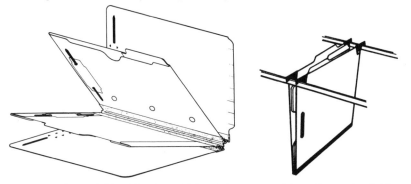

Figure 7-4. This Smead Classification Folder (left) comes with pocket style dividers ; on the right is the Pendaflex Hanging Partition Folder.

If you frequently pull files out of the filing cabinet and take them to different locations, you may want to use folders that have sides to protect the contents. The **file jacket** comes in two styles—flat or expansion (see Figure 7-5). File jackets can be used within your filing system or as part of the daily paperwork system discussed in Chapter 4. Oxford file jackets come in manila and in ten colors.

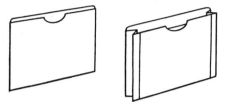

Figure 7-5. Oxford Manila File Jacket (left) and Expandable Manila File Jacket

Much sturdier than the file jacket, the **file pocket** in Figure 7-6 has accordion style sides called "gussets" that allow for more expansion and use. The file pocket can fit inside a file cabinet, on a shelf or in a metal collator (see Chapter 4). The file pocket will hold several related file folders together or other bulky materials, including catalogs and books.

The **expanding wallet** (also in Figure 7-6) is similar to the file pocket except it usually has a flap with a clasp, tie or an elastic cord. It is useful for carrying, transporting or storing records. Wallets come with or without internal dividers or "pockets." I use wallets with pockets to store my annual tax and business records.

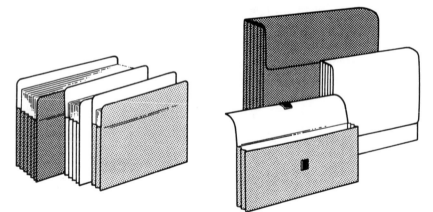

Figure 7-6. Wilson Jones ColorLife File Pockets (left) come in five bright colors. Wilson Jones ColorLife Expanding Wallets with single pocket and multiple pocket styles include easy-to-use "Gripper" Velcro closures.

The **expanding file** or **accordion file** is similar to the wallet in terms of construction, except it's larger and you can get it without a flap. The expanding file is a box-like, multi-pocket file with preprinted headings such as A-Z, 1-31 and Jan.-Dec. If you're looking for an extremely durable material for an expanding file, check out CaseGuard in the All-state catalog (800/222-0510 [NJ] or **www.aslegal.com**).

Check out the new Oxford Plus line of reinforced expanding products. These file pockets, expanding wallets and expanding files feature unique rip-proof gussets that are four times stronger plus they have special reinforcements at other critical wear points to prevent tearing, fraying and bursting.

Labeling Systems

Labeling systems are useful for file folders as well as a variety of other office applications.

Kroy, who pioneered labeling and lettering machines, has a range of systems from portable models to more sophisticated keyboarded desktop systems. You can make colored labels for not only filing systems but also for such items as maps, overhead transparencies and video disks.

Dymo creates labels on your PC (**www.dymo.com**). Casio has a hand-held label printer that works with or without a computer.

If you're going to be doing many file folder labels, look into Avery LabelPro Software. The software has over 200 pre-set layouts for Avery products including index dividers, card products and file folder labels. One layout, for example, lets you print 30 file folder labels on an 8½-by-11 sheet. Sample labels for file folders as well as for a variety of other uses (such as disks and mailing addresses) are included with the software and the manual. LabelPro by Avery Dennison is a real time-saver (800/462-8379 [CA] or **www.averydennison.com**).

And here are two simple tips to prevent label sheets from curling in your laser printer, which can cause faded and broken type on labels. Before printing, first pull each sheet firmly over the edge of a table, label side up, to create a curl in the opposite direction. Second, feed and print one sheet at a time.

Other Supplies

You'll need **hanging file frames** to support your hanging folders, unless your filing equipment already has them or glide rails built in. Traditionally such file frames come notched at half-inch intervals that you can break off to fit your drawer; but since most never break off easily, I recommend having your supplier cut them to size for you. Better yet, get the Pendaflex SpeedFrame that requires no tools, snaps together, easily adjusts to letter or legal size and fits all standard 24-to-27-inch file cabinets.

The Pendaflex Links is a useful accessory that will help you manage and separate your hanging file folders. Made of stainless steel, links fasten hanging folders together to prevent between-folder misfiles.

Smead makes **self-adhesive vinyl pockets** in seven different sizes which you can attach to the inside of file folders. These pockets can hold such items as business cards, computer disks, CD-ROMs, photos, or any loose items that need to be kept with the file.

Hanging folder **tabs** generally come "fifth-cut" or "third-cut." The "cut" refers to the width of the tab in relation to the folder. A third-cut tab, for example, is cut one-third the width of the folder, allowing the tabs of three folders filed back to back to be seen at one time. Since the tab is used for labeling, select the size that will best do the job. Use third-cut if you need a larger label surface.

Pendaflex Printed Label Inserts let you save labeling time. Inserts are printed A-Z for name, subject and alphanumeric filing; states for geographic files; and months (Jan.-Dec.) and daily (numbered 1-31) for follow-up, sequential or chronological filing.

You can also make the tab titles using your laser or ink jet printer or typewriter with Avery WorkSaver Inserts for Hanging File Folders. Just key in or type your titles, print, separate and insert them into the plastic tabs. A unique side-by-side folding format lets you print or type both sides at the same time.

Label protectors will help you keep file folder labels and tabs clean and resistent to wear and tear. Smead Seal & View Label Protectors, available in three sizes, are made of a transparent laminate and are available through office supply dealers.

You can also get label protectors by mail order from the Finance Business Forms catalog (800/621-2184 [VA]) or **www.financetabbies.com**) and the SYCOM catalog **(800/356-8141 [MA])**. If you only need a few and don't mind cutting them yourself, look under "Protectors" in an office supply catalog and then look for clear, self-adhesive, plastic sheets that you can cut to size.

Special Office Filing and Information Management Systems

If you're planning to design a filing system for a large office or an office with special information management needs, the products in this section could be helpful. Another place to look for local assistance with your filing or information needs is in the Yellow Pages under "Filing Equipment, Systems and Supplies," "Microfilming Service, Equipment and Supplies," "Optical Scanning Equipment," "Bar Code Scanning Equipment" and "Data Processing Equipment."

More on Color Coding

If your office is a medical office, for example, and has many, many files you'll probably select a more elaborate color-coded system that uses different combinations of colored, self-adhesive letters or numbers to quickly identify folders and prevent misfiles.

If you file patient files by their last name, for example, you would probably take the *first two letters* of their last name and put corresponding self-adhesive colored letters on the folders. Each letter of the alphabet in such a system has a color. For example all the "S's" are orange, the "I's" green and the "M's" purple. Take my last name, "Silver." My folder would have an "SI" on it where the "S" is orange and the "I" is green. When you file or retrieve the "Silver" folder, it's much faster to go directly to "SI" than to check through all the last names that begin with "S." If the next folder is "Smith," you'd see an orange "S" and a purple "M." Color coding file folders lets you find and file them more quickly.

There are other codes you can attach as well to folders, such as yearly codes or colors that signify a type of patient.

The following companies make a whole line of special color-coded tabs: Jeter Systems (800/321-8261 [OH] or **www.jetersystems.com**); Smead (612/437-4111 or **www.smead.com**); Tab Data File, **800/240-3453**); and TAB Products Co. (800/672-3109 [CA] or **www.tab.com**). Ask if there are local representatives to help you design your system.

Special Filing Equipment

High-density mobile filing systems equipment, consisting of heavy lateral filing units that usually run on mechanical floor tracks and all but eliminate wasted aisle space, are useful for large, centralized filing systems. Two manufacturers of these systems are: Kardex Systems, Inc. (800/848-9761 [OH] or **www.kardex.com**) and The Spacesaver Group (800/492-3434 [WI] or **www.spacesaver.com**). Jeter, Tab Products Co. and APW Wright Line (800/225-7348 [MA] or **www.wrightline.com**) also offer special filing equipment that can handle both small and large systems.

APW Wright Line is best known for its computer media filing accessories and equipment that store and organize items such as printouts, computer tape reels and diskettes.

Automated Filing Solutions

Because information continues to proliferate both in paper form and in computerized files, your office may need a **document management system** that includes software and possibly hardware components.

The term "document management" can refer to different types of systems and software, all of which involve use of a scanner. One type is focused more on scanning and storing *images* of documents, which you then index with keywords of your choice. With a stored image of a document you do not have editable text that you can word process.

Another type of system goes a few steps further. It takes the image and turns it into a text file (that you can edit) and also automatically indexes every word in the file. You can search these files for any words or phrases they contain (not just a few keywords). You can also turn the file back into the original image and print it out on paper. This way you don't have to store the original paper because it's stored in the computer either as a graphic image or as text (which may contain graphics).

For these types of systems you'll want to look for **document management software**, sometimes also called **document image management software**. Some of these programs also have workflow capabilities, such as document image routing, file creation tracking, editing and document sharing. (See also groupware in Chapter 11.) Take a look at PageKeeper by Caere Corp. (**800/535-7226** [CA] or **www.caere.com**) which has received good reviews.

When document management is more involved with keeping track of records and the use of bar coding, it moves into the area of **tracking software** or **records management software**. One major HMO uses customized records management software called Image-Trax from Document Control Systems, Inc. to track x-rays as they move from department to department and from desk to desk. We're talking about x-rays at more than ten medical centers and 50 medical offices with a patient base of several million. Contact Document Control Systems at 800/428-DOCS (CA) or **www.docsolutions.com**.

If you're serious about document management, you're going to need more than one of the low-priced, slow scanners discussed in Chapter 4. They're fine for occasional use or for desktop publishing needs but they aren't designed for heavy duty document management needs. Another caveat is make sure you have enough disk storage space for document management. Here's a tip: you can save space by deleting images after they've gone through OCR, provided you only need the text and not the image. Select a system that will grow with you because you won't want to change systems and waste time converting your system's files to another system.

Find out just how much time is involved with the various steps in the document management process—initial scanning, running an image through OCR, searches and printing. Determine whether the investment in time and money warrants your use of document management, to what degree and by whom. Do your homework—selecting a document management system takes some research and planning. And ask about references, current reviews or awards.

Here's another option. Since CD-ROMs can hold up to 650MB of data each, consider purchasing CD hardware to write data to your own CD-ROMs.

8

POWERFUL COMPUTING:
PC FILE ORGANIZATION,
HOUSEKEEPING
AND BACKUP

Quick Scan: Gain full value from your PC by discovering more effective, time-saving ways to organize your PC and its files so that you can work more easily, find files and information more quickly and safeguard your valuable work. Read this chapter, too, to learn how and when to back up your files. And if you want to protect yourself against computer disaster, because yes, it can happen to you, you'll learn important computer housekeeping, virus protection and recovery strategies.

One day, despite your computer's speed and all the space on your latest multi-gigabyte hard disk, you may discover you're having trouble getting around your computer hard drive. Files are hard to find. Naming, organizing and backing up all your files and folders just isn't as systematic as you know it should be.

Perhaps you thought your newest computer system would make everything easier and more automatic, certainly easier than dealing with all the paperwork on your desk and the files in your cabinets. But with a larger hard disk plus all those Internet and multimedia files and a workload that just won't quit—well, you just don't seem to have time to tweak your system (or you may be over-whelmed and not know where to begin).

The bad news is that just like paper files, your PC and its files need to be accessible, up-to-date, properly categorized and regularly maintained. You and your computer can slow down dramatically whenever computer file organization and maintenance is poor (or nonexistent).

But the good news is both you and your computer can function better when you better organize your folders and files, practice good computer housekeeping and use appropriate backup strategies.

PC File Organization Strategies

Assuming you're using Windows, there are several basic strategies to keep in mind.

Partition Your Hard Disk

Hard disks just keep getting bigger. If your hard disk isn't organized right, you'll waste time finding and backing up files (or you won't bother to back up files). Your computer probably contains thousands or possibly tens of thousands of software and data files.

The first step to organizing your hard disk is to divide it up into several **partitions** or sections.

Probably the best way to partition your hard disk is to use the top-rated partitioning program called PartitionMagic (PowerQuest Corp, 800/379-2566 [UT] or **www.partitionmagic.com**). A recent PartitionMagic ad compared a standard hard disk to "scrambled eggs"—actually the graphic showed a dozen raw, broken eggs with runny egg whites and yellow yolks. The copy read: "That's about the best description for your hard drive...all your data, applications and operating systems are mixed together in one big mess." The next image showed a dozen eggs all neatly lined up in a carton with the following caption: "This is your hard drive with PartitionMagic."

While placing files in folders is a computer organizing tool, having partitions on your hard disk makes organizing folders and files even easier.

Partitions allow you to separate your data (what you create) from 1) your operating system (such as Windows) and 2) the software programs you buy. Separating them makes is much easier to do backups since usually it's just your data files that you need to put on a regular backup routine. They're the files that are changing from day to day, week to week. If you're also constantly backing up your operating system and your software programs, that's a needless time drain and that extra time may keep you from doing backups at all.

Here's how partitioning works. The hard disk in your computer is automatically designated by the manufacturer and the operating system software as your "C drive." When you partition your hard disk, the C drive is divided up into partitions such as the C: partition, the D: partition and the E: partition. All of these partitions would be located on the one actual, physical hard drive (the C drive). The letters used for the partitions you create, besides the C: partition, will depend upon what other equipment you have in your computer such as a CD-ROM, DVD or a Zip drive. (Note that when you partition, the hard drive partitions get first claim on the letters C, D, E and F—your CD-ROM, DVD and/or ZIP drive may get a new letter after the partitioning.)

If you partition your hard disk into a C: partition and a D: partition, you could put your operating system and your other software on the C: partition. Then you could have all of the data files you create on the D: partition. To do your regular backups of your data, you would just select the D: partition. That really speeds up the backup process. Also, by having your data files in a separate place, it makes them more organized and easier to locate.

Hail the Hierarchy

Once you've organized your hard disk into partitions you're ready to take full advantage of your PC's **hierarchical folder system**. This system lets you create categories and subcategories into which you can put your application (program) files you buy and data (document) files you create. Using a hierarchical filing system helps you better manage the large numbers of files and folders that come with the increased hard disk storage that's now available.

Such a system lets you group files logically by categories called **folders** (also called **directories**). You can also create subcategories called **subfolders** (which are folders nested inside folders)—sometimes also called **subdirectories**.

Said another way, a PC hierarchical system gives you a way to graphically (visually) organize and see different levels and sublevels of the work you do. The big danger is not to get carried away and create too many levels of subfolders. **Limit the number of levels of subfolders.** Beware of creating too complex a system that takes too much time to use. In general, you don't want to go more than three levels deep.

You also want to make sure you don't accumulate too many documents or applications in any one folder or directory. When that happens, files can become difficult to find. That's when you may need to subdivide large folders or directories into smaller ones. But if you have too many small ones, your system can become too complex. It's all a matter of balance and good design.

To keep your system as simple and as accessible as possible, follow two guidelines. First, limit the number of documents or applications you keep in each folder, especially ones that you use frequently. One rule of thumb is to create a new folder or directory every time you accumulate more than 20 files in a folder.

The fewer files you have in a folder, the faster it is to find files—especially the files you use most often. And that's the secret: **keep folders you use most often, most accessible**. It slows you down if a folder is crowded with files you rarely use. Also get in the habit of moving old or rarely used files to archival or storage folders and disks.

Separate Your Software Programs and Your Data Files

As mentioned earlier, **keep programs and data separate.** Your software programs don't need to be backed up as often as your data files. Back up your software programs once and that's usually enough (unless you get upgrades). The files you create are another story. You are constantly creating new work product in your data files. Those need to be backed up regularly.

You want to avoid putting your programs and data together because it takes extra (unnecessary) time to back them both up on a regular basis. It's far easier and faster for your backup routine to back up only data files that change, not applications (software programs) that don't. Here's an easy way to separate and organize program and data files:

1. Put all of your programs in one folder such as "Programs" on one partition (such as the C: partition). Or, in that same partition, you could put each program file in its own separate folder or subdirectory (e.g., one for your word processing program and another for your disk utility/maintenance program).

2. Then in another partition (such as the D: partition), you could store *files in folders* in two main ways.

First, you could put your data files in separate folders (e.g., one for each client, project or type of work). Since most software programs are set up to store your data files right with the program files, you'll need to change the default setting to tell the programs (that are on the C: partition) that you want data files stored on another partition (such as the D: partition).

Second, you could use the "My Documents" folder in Windows or Microsoft Office. The default location for this folder is on the C drive. You may want to designate a different partition (such as the D: partition) for this folder to separate it out from your programs and operating system. Then your folders would be placed under "My Documents" in the D: partition. One consultant who is also a speaker and writer has folders under "My Documents" called "Write," "Consult" and "Speak" that are located not on the C: partition but on the D: partition.

If you share your computer with other people, it may make sense to have separate folders for each person's data.

It's All in a Name

Consistency and brevity are more important than creativity when it comes to personal computer file or folder names.

As an organizer, I recommend you create a good file naming system that uses simple names and consistent codes or abbreviations. I recommend that you begin each file name with a short, codified, abbreviated version that's followed by a clear descriptive phrase. It can save you time to use this kind of naming system.

I have used initials followed by a dash and an abbreviation for many of my file names. For example, in my system the "C-" prefix represents correspondence and the "H-" prefix stands for seminar handout materials.

You may also want to use a naming system that's parallel to your paper filing system. Mine are loosely parallel to one another. I generally prefer more subject-oriented naming schemes; I have a PR folder on my computer, for example, as well as a file drawer devoted to that subject. I also use alphabetical client files on paper and on computer. See if there's a way you can make your paper and computer systems more consistent with one other.

Speaking of file names, here's a tip that just could prevent a headache or two when using programs that give you a choice between "Save" and "Save As." Be sure to use "Save As" if you don't want to accidentally overwrite an old document with the same name as a new document. (Using "Save" automatically replaces the old document.)

Path Names

It may be helpful, too, to put the **path name** of a document at the bottom in very fine type so it will print out on a hard copy version. Later on, you'll know immediately where on your computer that document was created and stored. You may be able to have the path name automatically typed in a header or footer by selecting an option to include the path name.

Just like a person, each individual file has both a name and an address. A **path name** is the name and address of a computer file.

A name alone is not enough. Both a person and a file need more than a name to make them truly accessible. An address is necessary to locate a person as well as to distinguish one person from another. John Jones on Maple Street isn't the same person as John Jones on Elm Street. An address is a path to someone's door, starting with the state, going to the city, then to the street and number and finally to the individual.

A computer file needs an "address," too. A **path name** is the address for a computer file. Your computer locates a file by following a path first from the "drive" you're in (usually the C: or D: partition on your hard disk drive or it could be your "A" or "B" floppy drives), on next to the first folder level (and through any subfolder levels) and finally to the actual file name.

Generally it's easier to click your way through the path with a mouse to find the right file. If you prefer to type in the path name, here's how you'd do it: a) type the drive or partition letter followed by a colon and then by a back slash; b) type the names of the folders and subfolders in order containing the file, typing backslashes before each folder name; and c) finally type the name of the file with a backslash preceding the file name. Here's an example: D:\ABC Corp\proposals\#1.

Keep your organization simple by reducing the number of folder levels. That will keep your mouse clicking (or the time spent typing a path name) down to a minimum.

To repeat, build some consistency, rather than creativity, into your folder and file names. Try to make folders and subfolders parallel by using the same names and sequence of names. For example, if you have consulting clients, each client might get their own first level folder by their name with the following second level folder names: Proposals, Corresp (for correspondence) and Reports. Use consistency when naming files, too.

And just as there can be a John Jones who lives on Maple as well as one who lives on Elm, so, too, you can have the same file name (or the same file) in two different folders. The path name lets you locate the correct file at the correct address.

You can't have two folders at the first level with the same name. But with two different first level folders you could have two second level folders as well as files, with the same names.

Organizing Your Desktop

Unfortunately, clutter isn't limited to your desk; it can also accumulate on your computer **desktop**, the main staging area on your computer screen where you lay out your computer work using windows and **icons**. (For your info, it was Xerox who invented many of the graphic elements in today's "graphic user interface" [GUI] world, including icons, the little pictures that represent programs and files; and of course, Apple Computers was a real GUI pioneer with its Macintosh.)

Here are some ideas on how to better arrange your desktop so it's more functional for you.

First, check out your desktop's overall appearance. Is it too cluttered or busy for your taste? Can you find what you want easily? Do you have too many icons? Are they logically grouped together? You may want to avoid using "wallpaper" (the graphics that cover the background of your screen) because it can add to a more cluttered look.

Group your icons in alphabetical order or using some logical grouping. Play with the spacing between icons and eliminate any unnecessary space. Keep icon label names as short as possible. You can also customize the look of your icons and your desktop.

Group everyday programs and/or files together or use special features such as **shortcuts** that bring them up automatically. Shortcuts let you quickly open a program or data file or folder.

For programs or files you use constantly, put Shortcuts on your desktop. You can add Shortcuts to the My Documents folder or another folder where you store active documents. Make the Shortcuts you use most often the most accessible.

Another option is to use the Quick Launch toolbar in the task bar to give you quick access to the Windows desktop and to let you add icons to frequently-used programs, disks, folders and documents and shortcuts.

See the Resource Guide for utility programs that can help you further organize and customize your desktop and file management.

The Rewards of
Computer Housekeeping

Regular computer housekeeping, especially computer file maintenance, is essential to the health and performance of your computer. Not only will it be easier to find files, but you can improve the productivity and speed of your computer—particularly your hard disk.

What's more, if you never do maintenance and your hard disk fills up with files, you're just asking for a computer crash.

Bigger is Better, Right?

If you've ever been tempted to substitute a bigger hard disk for computer housekeeping chores, think again. You may have also been tempted at one time or another to buy another file cabinet for all your papers and files. Or perhaps you've bought a bigger house to accommodate all the "stuff" you've accumulated (you may remember the famous George Carlin routine).

If you're behind in your housekeeping, a bigger hard disk is just going to make matters worse. Just as with file cabinets, you can only tell how much space you need after you have purged your files. Once you've cleaned out your hard disk, see if you have 75 percent or more filled with current programs and files. If so, a larger or additional hard disk may be very appropriate.

By the way, when was the last time you cleaned out your hard disk? Have you ever cleaned it out? Since for most of us, out of sight means out of mind, it's particularly easy for computer files to accumulate. With the availability of larger and larger hard disks, this will continue to be a problem.

There are three reasons to take the time and trouble to clean out your hard disk:

1. to speed up your computer
2. to speed you up (locating files becomes difficult when your directories or folders are full of files that you aren't using)
3. to make more room on your hard disk.

A Squeaky Clean Hard Disk

The best computer file maintenance is done as you go—deleting duplicates and out-of-date files, storing inactive files on backup media and having a backup routine that you use regularly. But if you're like most people, you'll probably need to sit down once every six months to a year and do a thorough spring cleaning. Where do you begin and how do you proceed? Here are some useful steps:

• Before you do any "house cleaning," print a hard copy of your root directory ("C:\") so you can see at a glance all the names of your subdirectories or your first level folders (subdirectories).

• Go through each main folder or subdirectory and see if you recognize any files you created that you can delete. (Now's the time to remove those extra backups that your word processor may automatically make.) Use an uninstaller program to remove software programs—don't try to do that yourself.

• Look more closely. Are there any files you're no longer using but you'd like to keep in archival storage? If so, back these up on floppies, tape or whatever backup medium you're using. Or perhaps you have a backup device or program that can "tag" these specific files and back them up collectively. For files that are very important, make two archival copies that are kept in different locations.

• Consolidate any files you can—i.e., group separate, related files together in one new file or folder. For example, instead of having every letter in a separate file, group all the year 2002 letters together or all letters to a client together. A file is probably taking up more space (bytes) of your hard disk than you think. The size of a file in a directory listing doesn't tell you the whole story. Each file is allocated a certain minimum number of bytes on your hard disk, whether or not all of those bytes are actually used.

• Examine your largest files and decide how often you use them. Perhaps they can be stored elsewhere.

• Look for any folders or subdirectories that only contain a few data files. See if you can move these files elsewhere and delete these folders or subdirectories, which even by themselves take up space.

• Print a hard copy of your latest **catalog** (a listing of all the files in your folders or subdirectories) and keep them near your labeled backup media. If you back up your hard disk with a program that contains a catalog feature, print out the catalog when you complete your backup (I always do this after each full backup).

• Clean out your **cache** files if you surf the Web frequently. Cache files are like snapshots of pages you've visited so your browser can quickly recreate pages you've visited (to save you time). Unfortunately, all these files take up space on your hard disk. You can find your cache files through your browser.

Just as with manual systems, try to keep most accessible only the files you're regularly using. Only these files should be kept in your current folders or subdirectories. It's so easy to start stockpiling files that you never use. When you do, you'll soon discover you have trouble finding files that are needed.

Make sure you have the latest version of software programs by going to vendors' Web sites to check for upgrades. Many vendors provide free, downloadable updates (make sure you have an up-to-date virus program on your PC).

Defragmenting

After eliminating, transferring and consolidating files, your computer may appear neat and tidy, but chances are that many of the remaining files were and probably still are **fragmented**. Fragmented files have the file's information scattered in different places over your disk. When you save a file to a disk, the disk looks for the first available space (known as a **cluster**). If only part of a file fits there, that's where the first part goes. Then your disk looks for another place to store the balance of the file. As result, the more you use your hard disk, the slower it becomes because information for any one file may be in many places on your hard disk. The more scattered the stored information, the longer it takes for your computer to pull all the pieces together so you can work with the file. The way to fix this is to defragment your disk either using specialized software (such as The Norton Utilities (Symantec, 800/441-7234 or **www.symantec.com**) or looking for this feature under your operating system (Windows' Disk Defragmenter). Defragmenting (also called optimizing) your disk will restore your hard disk's original speed by consolidating file data together.

Experts suggest optimizing every one to two weeks. Optimizing not only keeps your access time from slowing down, but it also saves wear and tear on your computer. If your disk is optimized, your computer doesn't have to scramble around looking for all the clusters of a file and therefore, your computer doesn't have to work as hard. Check out Fix-It Utilities from Ontrack; it may be faster than Windows' Disk Defragmenter (800/645-3649 or **www.ontrack.com**).

Compression and Other Space and Time Savers

With regard to using **compression**, which removes any extra spaces much like concentrated orange juice removes most of the water, I generally recommend against using it to compress data files on your hard disk. It's generally fine, however, for backup, archiving, moving files and e-mailing.

Larger hard disks have also come way down in price, as have other media storage devices, making compression a much less needed option.

You can partition a large hard disk into smaller partitions (discussed earlier) to avoid wasting space on the hard disk (i.e., smaller partitions use smaller clusters—clusters may take up the same amount of space whether there is one word or 1,000 words in a file). So, smaller clusters can avoid having unused and unavailable space on your hard disk. Check to see if your hard disk uses the **FAT32 file system** rather than the older **FAT16**. FAT32 offers a smaller cluster size. To find out this information as well as a drive's free space, used space and total capacity, double-click on My Computer, right-click on the drive (or partition) you want to check and click on Properties. The General tab will show you this information. You may want to convert to the FAT32 file system.

You can look up when you last checked your disk for errors, backed it up or defragmented it.

If you're after a clean hard disk, you may want to remove unnecessary files that software programs have a habit of leaving around as well as those that accumulate from downloaded files (such as old .zip files and setup routines). Symantec's CleanSweep (**www.symantec.com**) may be the safest uninstall program with its built-in safety features (you can get this program separately or as part of Symnatec's Norton SystemWorks).

If you leave your computer on all the time in order that a) you won't waste time booting up and b) you'll save a little wear and tear on your computer from frequent startups, you might notice that some things aren't working well or work much more slowly. What's happening is programs are stealing memory (RAM) even after you close them—in technical terms, your computer is experiencing "memory leaks." Experts recommend that you should reboot (restart) at least every couple of days, which will restore your computer's full RAM. I recommend that you turn your computer off at night to save energy as well as to prevent "memory leaks." Or you can use an inexpensive program called MemTurbo by Silicon Prairie Software (**www.memturbo.com**) to prevent memory leaks.

Scanning

Scanning your hard disk is a good way to check for disk problems. Do it daily. You can use Windows' ScanDisk but turn off the "surface scan" option for a quicker scan. Keep it on when you do a more thorough scan every few weeks. Disk Doctor in Symantec's Norton Utilities by Symantec also performs disk scanning.

Viruses

With the widespread emergence of **viruses**, nasty computer programs that are inserted secretly and designed by "hackers" to cause great damage to data and/or computers, you need a good antivirus or virus detection program to protect yourself. Viruses are spreading because of the proliferation of computer networks and increased information sharing and online services. You might have a virus right now and not even know it because it can lurk for years until an event or date triggers its devastating consequences. You take a chance any time you insert a new floppy disk into your computer or download from the Web. Beware of e-mail attachments unless you know what they contain and who sent them to you. Unfortunately, new crops of viruses continue to appear and the e-mail attachment is one fast, quick way to spread viruses, as well as "worms" and "Trojan horses."

So what can you do? Get at least one good antivirus program (two would be better) and scan your hard disk initially and whenever you use any new files, programs or disks or before you open up attached e-mail files. Check out McAfee VirusScan by Network Associates (408/988-3832 or **www.mcafee.com**) and Norton AntiVirus by Symantec (800/441-7234 or **www.symantec.com**). Be sure to update your antivirus program at least once a month by using either the program's built-in update tool or getting updates off the vendor's Web site. Make sure you download the latest definition files monthly and scan your hard disk after updating those definitions. Also see GoBack on page 151.

Check out these **online antivirus sources** to keep up with the latest computer virus news and to check your computer with virus-scanning programs: **McAfee Anti-Virus Center** at **www.mcafee.com/centers/anti-virus**; **Symantec Anti-Virus Research Center** at **www.symantec.com/avcenter**; and **CERT Coordination Center Security Alerts** at **www.cert.org/nav/alerts.html**.

For extra protection there are also the following free Web-based scanning services: Trend Micro's HouseCall (**http://housecall.antivirus.com**) or Network Associates' McAfee Clinic (**www.mcafee.com/centers/clinic**).

To check for virus hoaxes (and to stop circulating those false-alarm e-mails) go to the following Lawrence Livermore Web site: **http://ciac.llnl.gov**.

Other Disk Maintenance Tools

Check the chapter Resource Guide under "Hard Disk/Data Maintenance and Recovery" if you're serious about keeping your hard disk humming. Consider regularly using full-featured hard disk maintenance utilities such as The Norton Utilities by Symantec (800/441-7234 [CA] or **www.symantec.com**) or Gibson Research's SpinRite (800/736-0637 [CA] or **www.spinrite.com**), which can test and repair a host of maladies.

Floppy Organization

Most of our discussion about computer file organization has focused on your hard disk. But chances are good you'll still be using floppy diskettes (also called floppies, diskettes or simply disks) from time to time because the floppy is not dead yet. In fact, it's a very handy backup device especially for current files you're working on. It's also a very stable storage medium. Unlike a backup tape, whose data can decay in two to ten years (check with the manufacturer), a floppy may last longer (once again, check with the manufacturer). Here are some tips to prevent you from floundering in floppies, as well as tips to save you time and aggravation.

As a general rule, separate program files from your data files. This can save you time during backup by letting you easily exclude program files (which don't change once you've installed them—if you do upgrade to a later version, backup the upgrade). Group data files together by subject, task or client or by a common folder or subdirectory name. Normally you'll just use floppy disks for small backup jobs.

Keep floppies in plastic storage cases specially designed for floppy disks. Get the kind with plastic dividers and stick-on labels to group different types of files. For extra security, buy cases with locks and keys.

Keep a set of up-to-date, printed **directories** for all your floppies. As used here, a directory is a table of contents for your floppy. It's a good idea to keep a set of printed directories in a nearby notebook or folder. Hard-copy directories can save you the time of inserting floppies and scanning the contents when you want to see what's on them. At the very least, use a handwritten label to describe floppy contents.

If you have hundreds of files, you may want to consider color coding. You can use colored diskette labels or buy diskettes that come in colors.

Whenever you label a diskette, always date it. In fact, anytime you work on a disk, write the date of that work session on the label. Use a thin, permanent felt-tip marker, such as a Sharpie pen, which works well.

Keep your floppies away from heat and magnetic fields. Avoid leaving floppy disks in your car or on top of your TV, monitor, modem or windowsill. Keep them away from telephones, stereos, headphones, magnetic paper clip holders, magnetic copy holders, metal paper clips, electric pencil sharpeners, electric cables and cords and all other devices that could have magnetic fields.

Worried about x-ray machines at airports? You don't have to be but avoid the walk-through security devices, which have damaging magnetic fields. Whatever you do, be careful about handing disks to a security guard, who may be standing at the back of the metal detector where there are magnetic fields that could cause damage to data.

If you use floppies often, consider using a floppy disk drive cleaning kit that cleans the drive heads. Don't use it too often, however; twice a year should be sufficient in most cases.

Remember, all disks can wear out from normal use. Never rely on only one disk to hold important information indefinitely—always have another copy.

And finally, when you buy diskettes, buy the best. You don't have to buy the most expensive, but whatever you do, avoid generic, dirt-cheap disks, that carry no manufacturer's name. These disks are said to have high failure rates—as high as 20 percent. High quality disks have no more than a one percent failure rate.

CD-ROM/DVD Organization

Chances are your CD-ROMs are proliferating with all the information available on CD-ROM disks and the use of CD-ROMs by software publishers. And you may also be using **CD-Rs** (recordable CD-ROMs), **CD-RWs** (rewritable CDs) or **DVDs** that are useful for general and special purpose backups (such as distributing databases throughout a company or keeping several different versions of a lengthy document all together but off of your hard disk).

To increase the number of CD-ROM disks that are physically available on your computer, you'll want to get a **CD-ROM changer**. Pioneer New Media Technologies (800/444-6784 [CA] or **www.pioneerusa.com**) is the "pioneer" in this product line. They make a six-, 100- and 700-disk CD-ROM changers. The disk changer uses a plastic **magazine**, a caddy with swing-out trays (six for the six-disk changer and a 50-disk magazine for the 100- and 700-disk changer). And here's a way to store and organize your CD-ROMs: you can get several magazines and use a different one for each category or subject matter of disks, for example, one for business data and another for entertainment.

Besides organizing your CD-ROM disks, such magazines also reduce handling. A simple fingerprint, not to mention a scratch, on the data side of a CD can mar the data and make it operate poorly. The data is on the shiny side, not the label side. If you ever have to put a CD down on a table, put it label-side down.

Always hold a CD by its edges. Never stack unprotected CDs.

Always store a CD in something—be it the plastic jewel case or cardboard sleeve it came in, a special CD-ROM storage wallet (available through computer outlets and music stores) or even extra Tyvek disk sleeves or vinyl holders from old 5¼-inch disks (you can also buy these inexpensive sleeves separately). You should label sleeves with a felt-tip pen if you can't see what's printed on the CD.

If the CD isn't preprinted, label it, too, with a permanent felt pen—but one that's expressly for that purpose because an ordinary, pungent-smelling, alcohol pen can destroy CD-Recordable disks. (And never write on a CD with a sharp pen, which can go right through the CD's thin coating.) Don't put a label on the CD. Here's another organization tip: paste a copy of each program's serial number to its CD jewel case or use a marker to write the number on the label side.

Also look for CD organizers from Allsop Inc. (800/426-4303 [WA] or **www.allsop.com**), Case Logic (800/925-8111 [CO] or **www.caselogic.com**) and Kensington (650/572-2700 [CA] or **www.kensington.com**).

If you do need to clean a CD, only use soft, lint-free material or cleaning pads, which you can buy at music and stereo stores (cleaning materials for audio CDs will work for data CDs).

And if you should ever insert a CD or DVD in a drive and see an error message that says it's unreadable, you can try a couple of things. First, give it a quick cleaning by wiping gently on the data (nonlabel) side of the disc in a straight line from its center to its edge using a lint-free cloth that's been moistened with a few drops of water. After it has dried thoroughly, reinsert it and try again. If it still doesn't read, the disc may have a scratch, in which case try using one of these two products: CD/DVD Scratch Repair Kit by Memorex (800/636-8352 or **www.memorex.com**) or **WipeOut** by Esprit Development (562/997-3806 [CA] or **www.cdrepair.com**).

A Clean Mouse

A clean mouse is a happy, well-functioning mouse. Whenever your mouse starts acting a little quirky, it probably needs a good cleaning. First, check to see if there's any grime on the bottom of your mouse; if so, clean it off with a little rubbing alcohol. That may, in fact, be all you need to do. If more effort is needed, check with the manufacturer of your mouse before taking the following steps.

If the mouse still doesn't work right, then turn off your computer and disconnect your mouse. Turn the retaining ring counter clockwise to the left ("lefty loosey, righty tighty") and remove the ball. Use a toothpick to scrape the gunk off the rollers and finish up with a foam-tipped swab moistened with alcohol or window cleaner. Blow out any loose particles on the inside with a can of compressed air. Wash the ball in barely soapy water and dry completely. Reassemble your mouse, tightening the ring to the right.

More PC Housecleaning

Since you're so adept now with that can of compressed air, you may be ready to use it at least twice a year on the inside of your PC (but first check with your computer manufacturer). Don't hold the can upside down, however, or you'll release refrigerant instead of air. Without opening up your PC, periodically spray air on the fan in the back (you can see the fan through a grid in the rear of your PC case). "Airing out" your PC should help prevent dust from wreaking havoc on sensitive electronic parts. (Again, double check with your manufacturer.)

Other PC Housekeeping Tips

Be aware for security reasons that when you delete files from a disk or computer, those confidential files may not in fact be gone. It's often possible to restore those so-called "deleted files."

To permanently delete files, you could use Symantec's CleanSweep. Or, if you're recycling disks, try GreenDisk, an award-winning company described in Chapter 5's resource guide that recycles disks after first removing all sensitive information.

As for all of that old computer hardware and software that keeps piling up, check out Chapter 5 to see where you can donate out-of-date equipment to better deal with the mounting "e-waste" problem that we all face. Estimates are that within a few years there will be 315 million obsolete computers in the U.S. alone.

Disaster Prevention

Good organization, computer housekeeping and backup can help prevent some disasters. Here are a few other tips that can help.

1. Before you upgrade your operating system, **check out the compatibility** of everything you intend to run. After you upgrade your system, avoid, if possible, adding more than one thing at a time. Most importantly, wait until whatever you add, be it a new software program or some new hardware, works well for you. Adding anything new can create problems and it becomes difficult trying to un-scramble problems and affix any responsibility to a particular product (or a company). **Never do an operating system upgrade without first having a full, complete backup of all programs and data files**. Also make sure you have all your installation CDs for all your software as well as for the previous operating system.

2. It's a good idea to do a backup before you install *any* new software.

3. During a power outage, don't just turn off your PC; unplug it and all the attachments.

4. Never reformat your drive without first testing your backup files.

5. Be careful about movement. Don't move or bump a drive while it's in operation. Carefully transport a removable drive in a padded case to prevent harmful movement.

6. To protect your files from unauthorized use (just as you wouldn't give a house key to just anyone), you might want to limit access to your computer files. In an office situation, you could set up password protection through different programs. If you have a computer in your home office and you want to limit access to your kids, Edmark's KidDesk (800/426-0856 or **www.edmark.com**) may be just the answer.

7. As for computer theft, there's a popular security software program that lets your stolen PC (via modem) silently report the thief's phone number and address. Called CompuTrace, it's available from Absolute Software, 800/220-0733 or **www.computrace.com**. CyberAngel from Computer Sentry Software works in much the same way (800/501-4344 or **www.sentryinc.com**). Mike Hogan wrote in *PC World* that you should have an OWNER file (or maybe one called LOST & FOUND) in your notebook and desktop computer and perhaps you should add the offer of a reward if your computer is "found."

8. Consider a personal **firewall** to protect your computer from hackers if you have a cable modem or a DSL line. You'll need such protection because a "broadband," high-speed connection requires your computer to always be on (and thus an easier target for hackers). Check out Symantec's Norton Internet Security (800/441-7234 [CA] or **www.symantec.com**).

Back It Up!

You can't talk about computer organization without talking about backups. For our discussion here, a backup is a duplicate copy of computer data (the files you create as well as the software programs on your computer) that is stored on another medium besides the primary one you're using. There are two parts to making backups: establishing a **backup routine** and selecting a **backup device**. The backup device or medium you select is only as good as the regular routine you actually use to perform backups.

Why Bother?

You never backed up your filing cabinet; why should you back up your computer files? First, the chances of wiping out your computer data are much greater than losing your hard data. Second, it's so easy today to back up. (And why tempt fate anyway?)

Backups are insurance for valuable, current data that would either require more than an hour to re-enter or would be next to impossible to re-create exactly as inputted the first time. Whenever I'm producing original, creative material, I not only save it on my hard disk, I save it on a special backup floppy or Zip disk as well.

Besides making additional copies of important information, backups can serve as **archival storage** for less important information that is not being used and is taking up too much space on your hard disk. Once you've backed up this archival information, then you can delete it from your hard disk (always test that the backup worked before you start deleting from your disk). Make two archival backup copies if the information is very important and keep the copies in separate locations—for example, at home and at the office.

Good backups will let you conduct business as usual even if your hard disk crashes or your entire computer is in for repair. Don't wait until a crash to get serious about backing up. As writer Wes Nihei observed in *PC World*, "Backing up files is a lot like dental hygiene: by the time you get serious about flossing and brushing, it's usually too late."

How Often, How Much?

Your backup routine depends on how often your files change, the number of files you modify a day, the kind of information or applications you use and how easy your backup device is to use. It may also depend upon whether you keep any hard copy that would enable you to re-create computer files. Based on these criteria, **check any of the following you think would apply to your situation:**

• Each day back up any data, folders or applications you have modified that day.

• Have two rotating sets of complete backups where the most current set is off site (at home, for example, if your office is not in your home). As soon as you make your most up-to-date backup, take it off site and bring back the older backup set.

• Do a full backup of your data every day.

• Do a full backup of your data every week.

• Do a full backup of your data every month.

• Do a full backup every time you install software, if possible.

• Have three complete sets of programs and data: one you're working with on your primary computer and two current backups—one on site and an additional backup kept off site.

• Do a full backup of your active program files (as compared to your data files) at least every six months and store it off site. If all of your program files are grouped together, it's faster to back up them up from that one location.

• Do a complete backup of your hard disk every two weeks with a backup tape overnight (one tape's capacity should equal or exceed that of your hard disk).

• Check for reliability before you need it by trying to restore once a month at least a few files from a backup.

• If you use tape backup, use more than one tape, preferably four, that you rotate and make at least one full backup that you store off site. By the way, tapes last longer when rotated (tapes are typically good for 150-200 uses—call or e-mail the manufacturer of your tapes to find out about the life of your tapes).

• If you're a corporate user and you're on a network, ask your network manager if personal data will be backed up or if you'll need to do your own private backup; also find out if there are any corporate policies regarding transporting any backup data to and from home.

Data processing departments generally keep daily files Monday through Thursday, make a weekly backup on Friday and do a monthly backup every fourth week. Copies of weekly and monthly backups are kept off site as well as on site. My general recommendation is **always have at least one complete, current backup off site**.

Types of Backup

Your backup routine should include **selective** as well as **complete** or **full** backups. Complete or "full" backups are used to copy the entire contents of your hard disk and would be useful if you had a system failure and you had to restore the data on your hard disk. Backup devices do complete backups in one of two ways: **file-by-file** or **image**. File-by-file backups are more common.

Image backups (also called "disk-mirroring") that make a mirror-image copy of your hard disk may require special software that doesn't come with the backup device. And, you might not be able to restore an image backup to a different hard disk other than the original. (If, for example, your hard disk crashes and can't be repaired, you may possibly be unable to transfer your image backup to a new hard disk.)

File-by-file backups, while generally slower than image backups, don't have that problem. Not only are they more reliable, they also make it easier to find backed-up files. You can also restore individual files without having to restore the entire hard disk. New technology is aiming for faster, file-by-file backups. File-by-file backups can be used for selective as well as complete backups.

Selective or partial backups are used to copy individual files, programs or data. An **incremental** backup is a type of selective backup that copies only files that have changed since your last backup. If your backup device can do incremental backups, you will save time—keep this feature in mind when you select a backup device. A **differential** backup is like an incremental backup except it will overwrite a previous version on your backup medium.

You would make incremental backups if you needed to save each version of a file because you might need to refer to one of these versions or you need an audit trail. If you don't need to see old versions, but only the current, most up-to-date version, use differential backups. Use differential backups if you work with the same files over and over again and only need to see the latest versions. Differential backups can save time and space.

Additional Tips for a Better Backup Routine
Following these simple backup tips can save you many headaches down the long haul. **Check off all the ones you already do; circle those you will incorporate into your routine after reading this section:**

• Keep a backup log of when and what you back up. Printed directories are useful, too.

• Always back up newly installed software, particularly if you made any special installation procedures. Keep a hard copy record of the answers you gave to installation questions in case you need to reinstall the program.

• Make copies of your customization files, Registry and application configuration files.

• Make sure you have a backup of your backup software so you'll be able to restore files after a crash.

• Make emergency floppy disks called **emergency boot floppies** to get you up and running again on your existing computer or another computer (some utilities such as antivirus products create their own emergency boot floppies). Make up-to-date Windows start-up disks (Control Panel, Add/Remove Programs and Startup Disk) as well as copies of all your device drivers. "Write-protect" all emergency floppies (so the files cannot be erased or replaced) and store them in a safe place. (To make a basic emergency boot disk, insert a floppy; then click on

Start; select Settings and then Control Panel; double-click Add/Remove Programs; click the Startup Disk tab; and click the Create Disk button (and have your Windows CD-ROM handy).

• Make a backup of files that change every day. Make the backup as you go. After saving a file to your hard disk, copy it to a floppy or other backup device. Or make your backups at the end of the day from a daily, written list of modified files.

• Carefully date and label all backup media with a soft tip pen; use color coding if necessary. If you make daily backups on floppies, use a different color label or diskette for each day of the week, for example, red for Monday's disk, orange for Tuesday's, etc.

• When you install a backup device, test it out with some junk files before betting your life on it.

• Use hard copy as important backup.

• Have at least two current sets of all important work—one should be off site.

• To check if a backup was successful, randomly restore a few files from the start, middle and end of your backup set.

• Try to select a backup program that can also be run from a floppy and keep the floppy with one set of backup disks. That way you won't have to reinstall the program before restoring files.

• Whenever possible, exclude unnecessary files such as README, BAK or TMP files from your hard disk.

• Store your user names, IDs and passwords on paper and keep them in a safe but convenient place that you'll remember—convenient because you should be changing your passwords frequently for security reasons. (If you asked Windows to remember a password but can't remember it yourself, use the freeware Revelation utility from SnadBoy Software at **www.snadboy.com**. If you store passwords on computer and your computer is stolen, you may have a bigger headache than just a lost computer.)

• Clean tape drive heads after about 20 uses and retension tapes periodically.

• Store backup tapes and disks in cases or caddies away from magnetic fields (such as power supplies, telephones and monitors) that could corrupt them.

Backup and Storage Devices

Backup devices are generally one of two main types, **disk** or **tape**. There are many kinds of disk devices and they all have their pros and cons. In general, disk devices are generally faster in terms of backup speed than tape devices. It's also easier and faster to locate backed-up data on a disk. But disks often cost more and sometimes hold less data than tapes (which are ideal for full backups that need to store large amounts of information).

Many people are using low-cost **CD-Rs** (readable CDs) and **CD-RWs** (readable/writable/erasable) to do partial backups, say for data files, or even full backups. CDs can hold up about 650MB—which is more than ample for most people's data files. Since a full backup won't fit on one CD, you may be able to use Adaptec's EasyCD Creator 4 Deluxe program, which lets you back up your hard disk to multiple CDs (800/442-7274 or **www.adaptec.com**). Most people prefer the CD-RW because it can be used over and over again. But if you need a backup to be nonerasable (for example, for archival purposes) you may prefer CD-R. There are some compatibility issues, however: some CD-ROM drives can't read CD-RWs and most DVD drives can't read CD-Rs. On the up side, DVD drives can read all CD-RWs.

Remember, though, you need a CD drive that's a **recorder** or **burner**. An ordinary CD-ROM drive just reads CDs; it doesn't "burn" or record data or music.

A CD-RW drive is a great device for backing data files. You can update files you've already saved to the CD or you can erase and reuse the disk. (A CD-RW disk can generally be overwritten up to 1000 times—check with the manufacturer.) For more information about choosing a CD-RW drive go to Andy McFadden's CD-Recordable FAQ at **www.fadden.com/cdrfaq**.

Let's look at something that's even better than CD-RW, although it costs more: **DVD-RAM**. As of this writing, DVD-RAM disks can hold 5.2GB. If you don't already own a tape backup device, you should probably seriously consider the DVD-RAM option. If you don't need this much capacity and you need an easy way to distribute information to others, then a CD-RW drive may be your best choice.

What about Iomega Zip drives? The current Zip disks holds only 100MB or 250MB, which may be fine for data files but it's not for large amounts of data or full backups. Then there are Iomega Jazz drives that hold one or more gigabytes.

Some experts recommend a second hard disk (external or internal) for backups. The disadvantage is if that's your only backup, in case of fire or other disaster, you'll have no off-site protection. But it would certainly let you get up and running again very quickly if your main hard disk crashes. Besides offering large capacity, an external hard drive may be able to be used with different PCs, including laptops.

Many experts still recommend good, old-fashioned tape backup because it offers a reliable alternative that's easy to set up and manage and comes in a wide range of capacities, speeds, formats and prices. The most popular format for individual or small business use is DAT (digital audio tape).

As for backup software, you may want to use the backup program that comes with Windows. Unless you have Windows 2000 or a special backup utility program, however, you won't have a scheduler to perform unattended backups say, in the middle of the night. A "storage management package" could be what you need. Three leading packages are Computer Associates' ARCserveIT and also Cheyenne Backup (800/424-3936 or **www.cheyenne.com**), Stac Replica Tape and Veritas Backup Exec (**www.veritas.com**).

If you've ever wondered how long magnetic media lasts here are some interesting estimates: 10 to 20 years for magnetic disks and two to 100 years for CD-R/RW disks, depending on the quality of the brand (always check with the manufacturers).

Compared to other magnetic disks, CD-R/RW disks (sometimes called "optical disks") are also more resistant to damage from magnetic fields, dust, temperature extremes and shock. They are also inexpensive. They are, however, slower than other magnetic disks.

As for laptop computer users, consider the CMS Automatic Backup System (ABS) for Notebooks. It consists of a Type II PC Card interface that slides into an available slot and can back up hard disks of different sizes (CMS Peripherals Inc., 800/327-5773 [CA] or **www.cmsproducts.com**).

Selection Criteria

Before you select a backup device, consider the following criteria:

• ease of use and convenience (if it's not easy to learn and use, you won't bother with it)

• speed—how much of your time will it take; how fast is it in different modes of operation—with or without compression, with or without verification (error checking)?

• ability to share with others (e.g., do your customers have the same type of device such as a Zip drive?) or for you to take on the road or use at home

• capacity (be sure to match the capacity of your hard disk with the size of your backup tape or other device; how much do you need now and in the foreseeable future?)

• internal vs. external

• portability/physical size (are you going to be removing and transporting the device frequently and if so, how far?)

- operator monitored (or does it "run in the background" by itself?)
- compatibility (with other office computers and/or your network)
- security
- performance
- reliability/verification (what kind of "error checking" does it have?)
- additional hardware required (the cost factor aside, what kind of space do you have for more hardware?)
- file-by-file or image backup
- cost of the device and backup media

Go back and check off all the criteria you must have and compare them to your budget and your information needs to determine the price you're willing to pay. Be aware that even as you read this page, new and updated backup and storage technologies and devices are emerging.

Web Backup and Storage

These days numerous Web sites offer storage space, some for free. Unfortunately, most of the free sites don't give you much space (as of this writing, only 25-30 megabytes). Some will let you *pay* for more space or will give you X amount of space for each new person you bring on board their site.

Make sure the Web storage site you're considering has a secure connection. Look for two signs of security: 1) a small lock icon that appears at the bottom of a secure page and 2) if the Web address of the page you're viewing starts with **https://** (the "s" stands for "secure").

Find out about the catch(es) and the hidden costs. Nothing's really free; your Web storage site may display banner ads or worse, may monitor your surfing habits. Check out the cost of phone charges, too (which could be significant because file transfer rates tend to be slow). See if you need to periodically click a banner ad or navigational button in order to stay connected. Never give out a credit card number. Read any usage agreement carefully before signing up for a "free" service.

There are also Internet storage services that charge a fee for you to back up larger files at offline servers and let you schedule automatic, unattended backups at night. Some will even send you your data on CD-ROM. One such company and service is @Backup (**619/455-3500** [CA] or **www.atbackup.com**). Other popular services include Atrieva Service through Atrieva Corp. (800/287-4382 [WA] or **www.atrieva.com**); Connected Online Backup (**www.connected.com**);

Personal Vault through Network Associates (800/332-9966 [CA] or **www.mcafee.com**); and SafeGuard Interactive (412/415-5200 [PA] or **www.sgii.com**).

Online backup services are great if any of the following apply: a) you have an always-on cable modem or DSL line, b) you don't regularly back up your data, c) you travel frequently and want to be able to retrieve a file from any location at any time or d) you want a backup offsite. (By the way, privacy shouldn't be an issue because good companies encrypt and compress the data you back up but of course, check to make sure).

Resource Guide

Note: Always check with vendors for the latest version of software products and the compatibility with your existing hardware and software. Many of the software products are widely available through computer dealers, software stores, the Internet or can be ordered directly by calling the listed number. See this chapter and the index for other products.

Disk and File Management Programs

The following utilities will help you better manage your personal computer files and enhance functions and features in your operating system or environment. They have had excellent recent reviews in major publications and/or have received awards.

DiskJockey is a Windows file management software program that computer guru John C. Dvorak touted highly and compared to DOS's X-tree (a program I personally had used as well as recommended in earlier editions of this book). DiskJockey lets you view the contents of all types of files. Clear & Simple, 860/658-1204 or **www.clear-simple.com**.

Drag and File is an easy-to-use File Manager replacement and viewer with some additional utilities. Canyon Software, 800/280-3691 (CA) or **www.canyonsw.com**.

DragStrip is an inexpensive, shareware utility to help you organize applications, documents, projects and Web pages into a tabbed, book-like icon that sits neatly on your computer desktop. Aladdin Systems, **www.aladdinsys.com**.

Enfish Tracker is an indexing program that lets you find any file, e-mail message or book-marked Web site in seconds. Enfish Technologies, 888/222-3634 or **www.enfish.com**

File Ferret 32 is a low-cost program downloadable from the Web that lets you search by size, date or text strings to find anything on your disk. Fineware Systems, **www.fineware.com**

Jasc Media Center Plus allows you to organize your multimedia files by creating albums. Files within each album may be arranged in a variety of ways. Albums can even be merged together. This program also lets you catalog your multimedia files using keywords and comments. The program keeps track of file locations on removable disks such as floppies and CD-ROMs. JASC, Inc., 800/622-2793 (MN) or **www.jasc.com**.

PartitionMagic by Power Quest Corp. is a top-rated partitioning software program that allows you to partition your hard disk without moving or losing data. 800/379-2566 (UT) or **www.powerquest.com**

PowerDesk Utilities is an award-winning file manager that let you easily create custom toolbars to give you better access to your files and programs. Ontrack, 800/645-3649 or **www.ontrack.com**

Quickview Plus is an award-winning file viewer utility and file manager that integrates well with standard e-mail systems. You can view, copy and print over 200 formats. Jasc Software, 800/333-1395 (MN) or **www.jasc.com**

WinZip is the leading compression/expansion tool that assists with compressed downloaded files. Nico Mak Computing, **www.winzip.com**

Hard Disk/Data Maintenance and Recovery

A number of specialized programs and services can help you keep your hard disk clean and correct specific file and data problems you may encounter on your computer. Software listed here has received great reviews and/or awards and includes antivirus, diagnostic and uninstaller programs. (See this chapter itself for other products.)

BlackIce Defender is personal firewall software that protects a PC that connects constantly to the Internet via a cable modem or DSL line. Network Ice, **www.networkice.com.**

GoBack allows you to revert your PC back in time, repairing problems created by software, accidental changes or viruses. Wild File, Inc., **888/945-3345** (MN) or **www.goback.com**

Guard Dog provides Internet users privacy as well as antivirus and hard disk protection. Network Associates, 408/988-3832 (CA) or **www.mcafee.com**

Norton SystemWorks includes five utilities in one suite (you can buy them separately if you prefer): **Norton Utilities** is the industry leader in detecting, repairing and preventing hardware and software problems; **Norton AntiVirus** has powerful antivirus capabilities; **Norton CleanSweep** is an outstanding uninstaller that removes unneeded programs (including newly installed ones) and files; **Norton CrashGuard** protects against system crashes and screen freezes; and **Norton Web Services** helps keep your system up to date with the most current software patches, virus definitions and hardware drivers

Ontrack Data Recovery Inc. provides a data recovery service that generally takes two to five days. 800/752-1333 (MN) or **www.ontrack.com**

Windows includes its own built-in utilities that may be good enough for you: **Disk Defragmenter**, **ScanDisk** and **Disk Cleanup** (which were discussed earlier) and **Maintenance Wizard,** which lets you set up a schedule for running Disk Defragmenter, ScanDisk and Disk Cleanup. To call them up begin at Start and go to Programs, Accessories and System Tools.

Reading, Reference & Resource Info

Association of Personal Computer User Groups (APCUG) has more than 400 groups that help you keep up with the changes in computer technology and if you choose, to also get involved with community service such as providing used computers and computer expertise to schools and other organizations. (I've been able to donate used computer hardware to one group.) Groups break down into many special-interest sections. Go to the web site at **www.apcug.org**.

Larry's World is the Web page for one of my favorite computer columnists, Lawrence J. Magid (**www.larrysworld.com**).

PC Magazine, The Independent Guide to Personal Computing, comes out every two weeks and features in-depth product reviews and industry trends. The "Editor's Choice" designation helps you quickly spot winning products and programs. 800/289-0429 (CO) or **www.pcmagazine.com** or **www.pcmag.com**

PC WORLD is a user-friendly monthly publication that features more practical (rather than technical) PC product reviews and articles. 800/234-3498 (CA) or **www.pcworld.com**

Personal Technology Web site (through *The Wall Street Journal*) includes past computer columns, free of charge, by one of my favorite columnists, Walter S. Mossberg. **http://ptech.wsj.com**

9

MORE WAYS
TO MANAGE YOUR
WORK, PROJECTS
AND INFORMATION

Quick Scan: Discover specific tools and systems to keep track of the detailed information related to work, projects, people, resources and records. If just too many of your office details are slipping through the proverbial cracks, you could profit from a simple system or two. Here are some ideas that can help.

L et's face it. Life keeps getting more and more complicated each day. So many details to take care of and so much information to manage. How do you stay on top of it all?

Some people are lucky. They can delegate the details to someone else. But whether you can delegate or not, you still need sound organizational tools and systems to manage your high-demand work load.

Why? If you're like most people, you probably do or supervise plenty of paperwork, record keeping and follow-up activities in your work, all of which generate many layers of information. When you can manage information effectively, you'll make a professional, lasting impression on people. It says you care about **quality** and **service**. It says you *care enough to follow up and follow through*—which is quite a feat in the midst of an ongoing information explosion that we all face each day.

Effective follow-up and follow-through require *systems* to organize details and see the big picture, too. Systems can be manual or computerized. Generally, it's best to start out using manual systems first (even if you have a computer).

While complexity may necessitate a computerized system later on, start first with a manual one. The trick is to keep systems *simple*—as simple as possible.

And should you happen to be fortunate enough to have an assistant, remember this: **when you have a good system in place, delegating is easy.**

Remember, too, a computer will not get you organized. Start planning logically and systematically on paper and then if necessary find a computer solution that conforms to you, not the other way around.

One technique I advise is **manage your "info flow."** Analyze all information sources and media and determine: a) the purpose b) the people who need to know (including yourself) and c) the next steps. See if there are ways to reduce or simplify your info flow as well as that of your work group. One study revealed that 50% of U.S. professionals get repeat messages that say the same thing.

Work and Project Management Shortcuts

Where most people get into trouble is trying to keep everything in their head. And then they get upset with themselves when they forget something using the infallible "mental note system."

The other ploy that has equally bad results is relying on countless written slips of paper on your desk, in your wallet and on your wall. The problem with paper slips is that they create clutter and stress in your life. They also tend to "slip" through the cracks and get lost—which is probably why they're called "slips" in the first place.

Forms, Checklists and Charts

It has been said that one person's form is another person's red tape. But a *well-designed* form is a clear, concise and useful summary of information at a glance. And contrary to popular belief, forms can actually help you *reduce* paperwork.

A good form *consolidates* information that is repetitive or might otherwise be scattered in many different places in your office or computer (or someone else's). A good form saves you time flipping through many pieces of paper (or through many different computer screens). Use forms to track such things as work flow, projects, responsibilities, schedules and personnel. Use forms to simplify communication.

A clean, well-designed form is not only pleasing to the eye but is more likely to insure a quicker response. Form phobia really sets in when clutter meets the eye or when poorly-designed forms keep asking for the same information over and over again.

We use the **program tracking form** in Figure 9-1 to record and consolidate important information and activities for each speaking engagement.

Positively Organized!®

PROGRAM TRACKING FORM   Today's Date:

Date/#_____ Time_____ Title_____

Type of PO! Program_____ Type of Mtg_____#____

Fee/Contract Terms_____

Name of **Organization**_____

Key Contact/Title_____

Off #   Home #

Address_____

Other Contacts/Numbers_____

Location of Prog/Mtg_____Mgr/#_____

Hotel Reservations at_____By Org____GLA_____

Nearest Airport_____Distance to Mtg/Hotel_____

Ground Transp._____

Travel: Drive/Fly Booked on_____w/_____

Departure Date	From City to City	At	ETA	Airline	#

Departure Date	From City to City	At	ETA	Airline	#

Departure Date	From City to City	At	ETA	Airline	#

Deadline for Ticketing_____ Receive Tickets by_____ Fare $_____

<u>Program Checklist</u>

Sent to Client

				Requested from Client	**Date Rec'd**
_____	Contract	_____	Intro	Signed Contract	
_____	Photo	_____	Invoice	Deposit of $_____	
_____	Bio	_____	TU Note	Hotel Confirmation	
_____	Blurb			Mtg brochure/map	
_____	AV/Setup			Mtg agenda	
_____	Handout for dup.			Trade pubs/bkg	
_____	PR			Pre-program ques	
_____	Pre-program Ques.			Fee/reim	
				Letter of Rec.	
				Referral	

To Be Done   **By Date**   **Date Completed**

Write program_____

Prepare handout_____

Prepare/organize audio-visuals_____

Confirm a-v, setup, handouts one week before_____

Contact introducer/confirm has intro_____

Packout list/pack_____Wardrobe _____

Figure 9-1. Program Tracking form

Create your own forms files in your file cabinet or on your computer. Collect samples of forms you like and those you often use. Make up a form to inventory all the forms you have in your office and when they're used. My husband designed such a form when he worked as a summer intern for the federal government. You may discover there are forms you should modify or eliminate altogether. We keep most forms and form letters on computer. Our software programs let us easily create a special form letter called a **mail merge letter**, which merges information we select such as names and addresses or key phrases into our form letters.

Speaking of computers, watch as they continue to make paper forms obsolete. Electronic forms give you more control over and flexibility with information, are more responsive to our fast-changing business environment and are environmentally-friendly. Paper forms are costly and wasteful; organizations have been spending $6 billion a year on preprinted forms, one-third of which end up being thrown away before they're even used.

If you like and use forms, consider getting a **forms software** package. Forms software includes a variety of different programs. One type helps you design your own forms on screen and print them out on your printer. Another type helps you fill in preprinted forms that you use all the time, such as Federal Express forms, so that the information lines up correctly. More sophisticated forms software programs give you many options, including designing your own forms on screen, scanning an existing form into your computer, filling out preprinted forms and linking your databases with your forms. (See the Resource Guide for examples of popular products.)

The **checklist** is an example of a form. Checklists are old standbys that insure you won't forget something and often can be kept and referred to repeatedly. I have travel and seminar packing checklists that I use year after year, for instance.

Use a standardized checklist form to help you remember the repetitive tasks involved in similar projects. My program tracking form has a checklist at the bottom.

Charts provide the added dimension of a diagram or graph that shows relationships between different components. It is more of a visual picture of information, almost like a map.

The chart is a two-dimensional form that shows relationships visually and graphically. The chart maps out details and the big picture at the same time. It summarizes information at a glance. Sometimes a chart is large enough to go on a wall (as you'll soon see) or small enough to fit on a form.

Charts are also good at showing numerical information, which, according to research, helps produce quicker, easier decisions. When information is expressed in numbers rather than words, complex decisions can be made 20 percent faster. It's also easier to evaluate many more factors and options with numbers than with words. There's an added strain when making decisions with words alone.

In working with clients who have many ongoing projects where each project has most of the same tasks, I have developed the **checklist chart**. Figure 9-2 shows an example of the checklist chart I helped design for the office of professional speaker Danny Cox. The chart is a preprinted, 8½-by-11-inch form kept in a transparent plastic sleeve that sits conveniently on the desk of Tedi Patton, who uses it to coordinate all upcoming program details on a daily basis.

Since Cox travels so extensively, his office also uses a map of the United States that is dotted with his engagement locations. Self-adhesive dots indicate not only the location but the engagement dates. The map is a useful planning tool when the office gets calls from around the country asking when Cox will be "in their neighborhood."

Calendar or scheduling charts are a good way to show the relationship between periods of time and people, tasks or projects. Some scheduling charts list the months and weeks of the year. Such a chart can easily be turned into a **Gantt chart** or timeline that shows task start dates and deadlines and responsibilities. (Henry Gantt invented this useful chart while working for the government during World War I.) Day-Timers makes a variety of scheduling charts and forms that adapt elements from highly acclaimed project management tools such as Gantt charts, PERT charts (*P*erformance *E*valuation and *R*eview *T*echnique) and CPM (*C*ritical *P*ath *M*ethod). These tools show the steps and sequence that must occur for a project to be completed. Figure 9-3 shows a portion of a Gantt chart.

If you're comparing prices and features for products (such as computers) or services from suppliers (such as print shops) consider developing a simple chart so you can record the information as you go. It's a lot easier than whipping out all those notes later on. Your chart keeps you on track by reminding you to ask the same questions of everyone. Leave some blank spaces for additional questions that come up as you do your research.

Use **quadrille** or **graph paper** to make your own charts. The "non-repro blue" lines will not photocopy but they will guide you in drawing your own lines. They come in many different styles and are available from your office supply store or catalog as well as a number of personal organizer companies, such as Day-Timers, Inc., Geodex and Time/Design (see Chapter 2 or the index).

PROGRAMS IN PROGRESS

CLIENT NAME	PROGRAM DATE	AGREEMENT SENT	AGREEMENT RETURNED	DEPOSIT RECEIVED	INTRO.	ROOM SET-UP	PHOTO	HANDOUT	AIRLINE RESERVATIONS	FINAL PROG. C/L	MONTH-OUT CHECK	TAPES PACKED / SENT	

Figure 9-2. A checklist chart I helped design for the office of Danny Cox

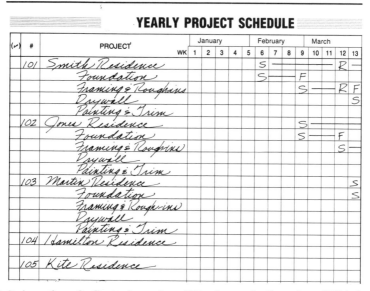

Figure 9-3. A portion of a Gantt chart where "S" refers to the Start time, "R" is for Review and "F" is for Finish.

If you need to track projects or personnel visually in such a way that you and/ or other people can easily see the information, use **wall charts**. Also called **scheduling** or **visual control boards**, wall charts provide visibility to keep you on target. They're not the most attractive things in the world but if you have a work room or don't have to impress anyone with aesthetics, they are very functional.

Wall charts have an advantage over other systems because they crystallize your ideas, intentions and plans and make them visible. A wall chart gives you a visible game plan and very little escape. It's staring you straight in the face. Color coding works great for wall charts. You can code people, types of activities, progress and deadlines.

Use wall charts to track one complex project, several simultaneous projects, a production schedule, your master calendar, personnel schedules and marketing or fund-raising campaigns. They come in many different sizes, styles, configurations and materials. **Magnetic** wall charts have different components that you can move around. See Figure 9-4.

Some people prefer the flexibility of a homemade chart such as the **action board** that was used by psychiatrist and author Dr. David Viscott. With his system, you create the action board by putting up six or seven index cards on a wall or bulletin board. Each card stands for a different project and includes a key contact. Under each project card put another card that lists the next project step to

Figure 9-4. Magna Visual Work/Plan Visual Organizer Kit

be taken. Each project relates directly to your most important life goals.

If your work could benefit from charts that show either a process (such as a flowchart that maps out work flow or the steps needed to complete a project) or *structure* (such as an organization chart), consider using **diagramming software**. With single purpose or multipurpose diagramming software packages you can create such diagrams as flowcharts, process charts, organization (org) charts, floor plans and space plans. (See the Resource Guide for some examples.)

Don't let forms, checklists or charts scare you. They aren't straitjackets; rather they're guideposts to help you work through the maze of details in your office and your head.

Turn to the "Forms, Checklists and Charts" section in the chapter Resource Guide for more examples of tools and systems you can use.

Capturing and Harnessing Creative Ideas

There are many exciting ways to capture and harness all those creative ideas you (and others) may have in your head. One way is to chart them out.

Let me share with you one of the greatest and simplest tools I use to chart ideas whenever I begin a project or a writing task. It's called a **Mind Map** and it was originally developed in 1970 by Tony Buzan of the Brain Foundation in

England. I first heard about it at a professional communications meeting devoted to "writer's block."

The Mind Map is an effective way to free up your mind and let your ideas flow. It's a combination brainstorming and outlining tool where you can see your ideas and thought patterns more graphically. The Mind Map is a great organizing tool for writing, speaking, project planning, meetings, training, negotiating, learning, memorizing and thinking. To learn more about Mind Mapping techniques and products contact The Buzan Centre of the Great Lakes at 734/451-1146 or **www.buzancentre.com**.

I've also used **Clusters**, another idea organization tool. Clusters are described by Gabriele Rico in his book, *Writing the Natural Way*. See Figure 9-5.

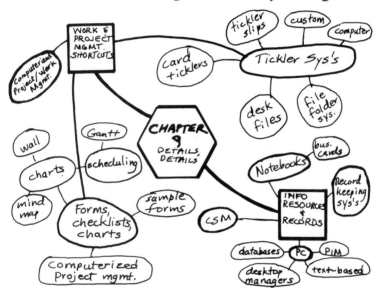

Figure 9-5. A Cluster outline I did before I wrote Chapter 9 (as it looked in the second edition of my book)

The versatile SCAN/PLAN Instant Information Scan System (as discussed in Chapter 2) is a great knowledge management tool to physically manipulate, categorize and organize either handwritten or computer-generated ideas using colored index cards or special laser cards. Contact SCAN/PLAN, Inc. at 800/ SCANPLAN (800/722-6752 in CA) or **www.scanplan.com**.

Idea software programs offer more ways to brainstorm and organize your thoughts and ideas. MindManager by Michael Jetter combines the power of Mind Mapping with your PC and has integrated Internet conferencing. It's available through The Buzan Centre of the Great Lakes (which was just described).

Inspiration (see Figure 9-6) is a visual idea development tool that combines diagramming with outlining and can take you from idea generation to final document. It's useful for brainstorming, planning and writing. Both PC and network versions are available from Inspiration Software, 800/872-4292 (OR) or **www.inspiration.com**.

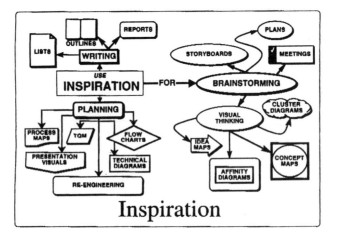

Figure 9-6. Here's an idea map that shows what Inspiration software can do.

Computerized Project and Work Management

Think of computerized solutions as ways to extend your brain, giving you at once greater control, creativity and flexibility over your work and projects.

For project planning and scheduling, consider **project management software programs** for the personal computer. What differentiates project management from time management programs with reminder and tickler features is the use of more graphic charts that let you more easily see progress and spot delays as well as better manage resources.

These programs combine charts and reports that let you see project information in a variety of ways. You can easily make changes such as automatically updating schedules. Reports are easy to generate and distribute. And it's easy to store completed projects and schedules for reference later on—which means less reinventing of the wheel down the road.

Look for these features when you select a project management program: ease of learning (does it take a Ph.D. in computer sciences to grasp it?); ease of use; good reviews by experts and/or people you know; an easy-to-use tutorial; and the ability to use it on the Internet. It's also a plus if the program can do both Gantt and PERT charts.

And here's a project planning tip: at the end of recurring projects summarize any steps or ideas that worked really well and any that didn't. Use the most recent summary as you begin planning the recurring project.

Management software, also called **MBA-ware** or **decision support software**, uses business theory and management expertise to help with problem solving and making complex decisions. The software analyzes and advises, helping decision makers create uniform criteria and options. It's particularly helpful for making personnel decisions.

Process management software is aimed at supporting the worldwide drive to improve business processes and help organizations remain competitive through programs such as Business Re-engineering, Business Process Improvement and Total Quality Management (TQM).

Such software helps you document process steps and estimate the duration of each step; define the information and materials that flow through the whole process; identify the people and materials used by the process; assign people and materials to each step in the process; and calculate the process performance via quantitative measures or simulation. The following are typical questions such software will help you ask and answer: 1) How long does the process take?, 2) Who needs to work on the process?, 3) How much does the process cost? and 4) Are there any bottlenecks? Process Version is an example of process management software—see the Resource Guide.

Popular project management, decision support and process management programs are listed in the chapter Resource Guide under "Project and Work Management Software."

Top Tools and Systems to Manage
Information Resources and Records

Each day you're bombarded with more pieces of information. It becomes a real challenge to organize all this information. Fortunately, you have many options.

Database Programs

A **database management program** is one of the best ways to gain control over and access to many records and resources. A database program lets you not only store but sort and call up information based on criteria that you select. It's the sorting capability of a computerized database that provides real information power.

There are basically two different types of database management programs: **structured** and **unstructured** (also called **free-form**), although sometimes you can have a combination. In a structured database program, one **file** may contain hundreds or thousands of **records**. Each record is an entry consisting of different items or **fields** of information. Let's suppose you create a file of all your clients.

Each client would be a different record in the file. The client's name, address, phone number are three different fields in the record. The blank form that appears on your computer screen showing the different fields before they're completed is a **data-entry form**, because you use it to *enter data* or information for each field.

The simplest database programs function basically as computerized address books. Some come with PIMs (discussed in Chapter 2). Their functions include the storage of names, addresses and phone numbers and they may also print mailing labels.

This type of program is often called a **flat file database**. Features and capabilities may include sorting, searching, reporting and **mail merge** (using your own word processor or a built-in word processor that prints form letters).

Contact management programs or **contact managers** are easy-to-use flat file database programs that were designed originally for those in sales but now are used universally by anyone who needs to stay in touch with 50 to thousands of people on a regular basis. Such programs let you schedule and track calls, remind you with alarms when to do follow-up calls, encourage you to keep notes on calls and meetings with contacts and usually have an autodialer. It may also have other features such as scheduling, text search and mail merge. Goldmine and ACT! are examples of a contact manager.

Since the term "contact manager" has become more popular, you may see it used for simple address book style programs. You'll also see it used to describe programs that either are PIMs or have many PIM features. In other words, the line between contact managers and PIMs is blurring more and more.

Sales and telemarketing programs are specialized contact managers that are ideal for anyone who is managing a client database and/or is marketing products or services and wants to track these marketing efforts. Many of these programs combine features from other software such as database management, word processing, telecommunications and built-in follow-up. With strong workgroup capabilities, they let you easily manage personal and group calendars and schedules on and off the Web. Consider these programs if you're in real estate, insurance, inside or outside sales, consulting, financial services, association management, direct mail marketing, to name a few areas.

The most sophisticated database management programs are the **relational databases**. Most of them are difficult to learn, some require a programmer and they tend to be expensive. What sets them apart besides these negatives, however, is their ability to work with more than one file at the same time. Relational databases can share related information between two or more files, keeping files up to date with just one entry of data. Relational databases are great for inventory control and billing, for example.

Many file managers are adopting the more sophisticated features of "high-end" relational database programs, while still being easy to learn and use.

Don't confuse databases that come on **CD-ROM**, such as PhoneDisc, with database *programs*. CD-ROM databases are for playing or reference only; you can not manipulate or add any data to them as you can to a hard disk or a floppy disk. CD-ROM stands for Compact Disk Read-Only Memory and each 4¾-inch plastic CD-ROM disk can store more than 600 megabytes of data, the equivalent of more than 250,000 pages of text or hundreds or up to thousands of images. It can also store sound, in CD format, just like your CD music disk, from whose technology the CD-ROM developed.

According to most sources, PhoneDisc CD-ROM telephone directories provide the most complete and accurate listings available. (Don't expect 100 percent accuracy; actually, PhoneDisc advertises 93 percent.) If you call directory assistance a lot for phone numbers or if you're involved in telemarketing, consider one of the PhoneDisc directories. Two of the most popular are PhoneDisc Business Mailing List which contains 15 million U.S. businesses and PhoneDisc PowerFinder which integrates 95 million residential and business listings with full reverse searching. PhoneDisc directories come with fast, search software to let you find information in a variety of ways. Contact InfoUSA, 800/284-8353 (NE) or **www.datadiscusa.com**.

When the resource information you want to store on computer isn't as structured as database records, you may prefer to use an **unstructured** or **free-form** database program, also called a **text-based management system** or a **text-based program**. Such a program is much more *free-form* in nature, generally without predefined fields and records, and includes **free-form text databases** and **outliners**. A text-based program may be ideal if the information you're managing resides in long documents.

Text-based programs give you more flexibility, although frequently less speed. You don't have to make your information conform to a database configuration. Search features are varied; some programs have you search on key words, others can search for "strings" of words or phrases.

Some Organization Tips for Designing Structured Databases

I have use structured database files with fields for years. I spent time up front designing the data entry screens, thinking about the naming and placement of field names. Careful design has helped speed up searches to find information.

I have found **codes** to be very useful. Let me give you an example. I have a field in most of my database files called "contact," in which I place codes that indicate the type of contact. I use the letter "c" for a consulting contact, the letter "s" for a speaking contact, "p" for professional and "f" for friend. I can then sort or do a report for all of my professional contacts, for example, or all of my speaking and consulting contacts.

Don't be afraid to reorganize database files. You may decide to split a large one into several smaller files. Conversely, you may decide to put several together in order to be able to sort by zip code. In either case, it will be easier if you've designed the fields in each file uniformly so that they have a one-to-one correspondence between the fields. Ideally, if you use two street address fields in one file, you'll not use three in another, especially if you ever plan to merge the files together at some time in the future.

Data Access and Search Tools

Accessing the information you need is becoming more challenging with increasingly larger and larger databases of information that you can store on your computer as well as those that are on-line. Fortunately, there are some products that can help. Most of these products focus on **keyword** searches and a handful focus on the underlying **concepts** or the linkages between data rather than on just keywords or phrases actually contained in the data.

PageKeeper automatically organizes and finds scanned documents, word processing files, Web pages and spreadsheets in any file format. It also lets you annotate anything with Post-it Software Notes from 3M.

PageKeeper works like a search engine and instantly retrieves what you need using powerful search capabilities including content and keyword searches, Boolean operators, fuzzy searches, relevancy ranking, similar document search and other methods. Contact Caere Corp. at 800/535-SCAN (CA) or **www.caere.com**.

If you need to keep up on the news, particularly news on certain topics, you can get your own personalized "newspaper" via a number of online Web sites, many of which are free. Functioning much like your own personal clipping service, these sites can provide customized news delivered daily to via e-mail. Some also have links to the full stories. The following sites have received some noteworthy attention: **www.infobeat.com**, **www.nt.excite.com** (NewsTracker by a company called Excite) and **www.totalnews.com**.

There are also some handy Web sites that function like online telephone directories. If you ever get "return to sender" pieces of mail or you just want to look up the address, phone number or e-mail address of a person or business, try using **www.switchboard.com**. (For more on Web searching, see Chapter 13.)

Record Keeping Systems

Beyond the programs and products we've already discussed, a couple of other systems can help you track record keeping details.

If you work with different clients or projects, the All-state Legal catalog has an easy manual system to keep track of billable time or expenses for clients or projects. No longer will you have to spend hours searching through your files, calendar, receipts and notes at billing time. (Although designed for attorneys, this system easily adapts to other professionals, such as consultants and writers.)

The system comes in two main styles: a time and service record system called Time Record and a system that tracks costs and expenses called Expense Record. Both are "one-write" systems that are designed to be used "as you go" (which is the ideal way to use a system anyway). Call 800/222-0510 (NJ) or log on to **www.aslegal.com** for more information.

The Time Record works the same way as the Expense Record. Some of my clients have selected one or the other, depending upon the type of records they need to keep the most. Others like having the two different systems.

For a builder/contractor client of mine, I recommended the Time Record to keep track of time and materials on building job sites. The Time Record form is attached to his clipboard, making for a convenient and portable system that's with him all the time.

Another "one-write" record keeping system that I recommend is the Safeguard bookkeeping system (available in 200 formats). This is a simple-to-use manual system that is great for an entrepreneur or professional in private practice.

The system comes with a "pegboard" or accounting board, imprinted checks in duplicate, journal sheets and sometimes special ledger sheets (depending on the style of system you select). First you set up your journal sheet (which is similar to an itemized check register).

When you write a check, the information is automatically transferred in one-write fashion to the duplicate check as well as the journal underneath. Then you simply write the amount of the check under the appropriate column. At the end of a monthly cycle (or when the journal fills up) use a calculator with a tape to add up all the columns vertically and horizontally to make sure you're in balance (Attach each copy of a check to the corresponding paid bill).

If you select a different one-write system, make sure the checks don't have a black carbon strip on the back, which can interfere with endorsements. Use one-write checks that provide high quality transfer of written information to journals, ledgers or duplicate copies beneath checks.

Don't underestimate simple, small, spiral-bound, record keeping books for tracking mileage, car and travel expenses as well as personal records, assets and information. Such books are available through most office supply sources.

If you use a loose-leaf-style organizer that you carry with you, you could both track expense records as you go and store receipts in special expense envelopes that come with your system.

If you're a PDA user, you may already have built-in software or be able to get software to track time and expenses. Tucows Network has a Web site where you can download PDA software (**www.tucows.com**).

Resource Guide

Note: See this chapter as well as Chapters 2 and 11 and the index for other products.

Forms, Checklists and Charts

Day-Timers, Inc. offers a great selection of planning and scheduling forms as well as Marking Time dry-erase wall scheduling charts. Day-Timers, Inc., 800/225-5005 (PA) or **www.daytimer.com**.

FastTrack Schedule lets you create and update presentation-quality Gantt chart schedules quickly and easily. AEC Software, 800/346-9413 (VA) or **www.acesoft.com**.

iGraphics Professional is an award-winning program that enables business people to clearly and quickly communicate ideas and information with ready-to-use diagrams such as flowcharts, timelines and network diagrams. This full-featured flowcharting program helps you graphically depict process flows in order to quickly analyze inefficiencies and bottlenecks in a process. Its breadth of diagramming functionality, along with its rich environment for customized application development, sets it apart from other diagramming tools. Micro-grafx, 800/676-3110 (TX) or **www.micrografx.com**.

Magna Chart is a magnetic visual control board system that comes in different styles. Magna Visual, Inc., 800/843-3399 (MO) or **www.magnavisual.com**.

Magnetic Concepts visual control charts come in a dozen different models, all of which have a rotating sleeve that never runs out of space and allows for continuous scheduling. Charts are available to meet different scheduling needs. Magnetic Concepts Corp., 800/824-0212 (CA) or **www.bigboards.com**.

Memindex Wall Planning Guides are write-on/wipe-off planners that come in a wide selection of styles. Memindex, Inc., 800/828-5885 (NY) or **www.memindex.com**.

Office Depot has an Office Solutions section on its Web site that provides downloadable forms, sample letters, contracts and spreadsheets.

www.officedepot.com

PLANIT Board Systems Inc. makes a good selection of dry marker white boards. PLANIT Board Systems, Inc., **800/222-7539** (CO).

Post-it brand Printed Notes by 3M are handy forms that eliminate the need to write and rewrite requests for action. (You can also design and print your own custom messages at your printer.) Look, too, for the Post-it Designer Note Organizer to keep your Post-it Notes handy, as well as your floppy disks.

The Timewise catalog offers a good selection of wall planning charts and boards. Timewise 800/523-8060 (NY) or **www.timewiseboards.com**.

TopDown Flowcharter is a highly-rated, easy-to-use, flexible program that creates flowcharts for a variety of business planning and documentation uses, including process flow and matrix diagrams, office procedure charts and network diagrams. Kaetron Software Corp., 800/938-8900 (TX) or **www.kaetron.com**.

Visio is an award-winning, multipurpose, enterprise-wide business drawing and technical diagramming program that lets you easily create flowcharts, org charts, network diagrams, software and database diagrams, technical schematics and more. 800/248-4746 (WA) or **www.microsoft.com\office\visio**

Project and Work Management Software

ActionWorks Process Builder helps managers see and understand how work gets done, how long it takes, what it costs and who is involved. Managers can perform "what if" modeling by graphically mapping how the process works and making changes on screen to create alternatives. Through this process, they can see and evaluate the impact of changes before implementing them, saving time and money. **ActionWorks Metro** is a Web-based workflow solution. Featuring collaborative design, it's a process design tool, a built-in forms designer and more. **ActionWorks eBRM2000** is for teams to use. Action Technologies, 800/967-5356 (CA) or **www.actiontech.com**.

Business Insight is an MBA-ware, expert-system program that assists in developing and evaluating marketing strategies. It gathers information about the various factors in your business, your prospects, your product or service and your competition and then uses the knowledge of over 40 business and marketing experts to evaluate both product-based and service-based businesses. Business Resource Software, Inc., 800/423-1228 (TX) or **www.brs-inc.com**.

DATA is a decision analysis program for analyzing, structuring and reporting on real-life business problems using graphical decisions trees and multi-attribute analysis. TreeAge, 800/254-1911 (MA) or **www.treeage.com**.

Details is a project-oriented specialized database that allows you to schedule, organize and track project information and produce user-definable customized reports. AEC Software, 800/346-9413 (VA) or **www.acesoft.com**.

Microsoft Project is a sophisticated, yet easy-to-use, award-winning program that has workgroup capabilities and tight integration with other Microsoft products. It is a Web-enabled project management program. Look also at its companion program, **Project Central**. Microsoft Corp., 800/426-9400 (WA) or **www.microsoft.com\project**.

Process Version is "the flowcharter with brains"—both a flowcharting and process analysis tool. It's simple and flexible as a flowcharting package, yet will provide you with the intelligence you need to fully analyze your business processes. It will help you develop business process solutions. Scitor Corp., 800/549-9876 (CA) or **www.scitor.com**.

Project KickStart is a project brainstorming and planning tool that asks key questions to help you conceptualize and organize a project from scratch. It links with major project management software programs. Experience in Software, 800/678-7008 (CA) or **www.projectkickstart.com**.

Project Scheduler is a good project management program that has its own graphical user interface, is easy to learn and use and gets high marks from computer magazine reviewers. Scitor Corp., 800/549-9876 (CA) or **www.scitor.com**.

SureTrak Project Manager is particularly good for those who are new to project management. Primavera Systems Inc., 800/973-1335 (PA) or **www.suretrak.com** or **www.primavera.com**.

TeamFlow provides an easy way for any manager or team leader to keep track of all the steps of a project as it relates (is "deployed") to members of the team. Worksheets can be multi-layered and as detailed as desired. Flowcharts can be easily edited. It includes Gantt and org charts and works over the Internet. CFM Inc., 800/647-1708 (MA) or **www.teamflow.com**.

Other Work Management Tools

DAZzle Plus is an award-winning, easy-to-use envelope and label printing program that works with Act! and Goldmine. The envelope manager has its own database capability. You can design and print mail pieces with graphics, text messages and barcodes using any Windows printer. It has a patented ZIP Code look-up feature you use with a modem that finds ZIP+4 codes and corrects addresses. It is CASS certified for bulk mailings. PSI Systems, 800/576-3279 (CA) or **www.envmgr.com**.

SCAN/PLAN's patented "QuickScan" technology using 3-by-5 or 5-by-8 cards plus 8½-by-11 pages allows the user to access information almost instantly. The system is perfect for organizing any information or activity, including projects, goals, records and tasks, as well as learning facts and skills. Other applications include writing, outlining speeches, notetaking and even creating company manuals. SCAN/PLAN, Inc., 800/SCANPLAN (CA) or **www.scanplan.com**.

3M dispensers for Post-it Pop-up notes are handy dispensers that permit easy, one-hand dispensing of Post-it notes so you'll always know where your notes are.

3M Laser/Copier Labels, product number 7701, has one 8½-by-11-inch yellow label per sheet, which I use for presentations. The labels use repositionable adhesive. I print out presentation comments of any length, which were inputted in my computer, onto the label sheets. Then I cut up the comments and affix to them my presentation notes. I have the convenience of making my own customized, removable notes that can be moved easily from one presentation to the next. They're available in 25 label sheets per package from most office supply dealers.

3M tape products I couldn't live without: Post-it brand Labeling and Cover-up Tape and Scotch brand Removable Magic Tape. Post-it Tape is a removable, opaque white tape for clean and quick copy blockout when making photocopies. Scotch brand Removable Tape is transparent, attaches papers temporarily and removes easily without causing damage and you can write on it with ink, pencil or marker. Both tape products come in a variety of different widths.

ZIP+4 Diskette Coding is a one-time mailing list clean-up service offered by the U.S. Post Office. You can send up to 50,000 names from a mailing list on a diskette and they will convert the list to standard format, complete with nine-digit zip codes and corrected street and city names. Call **800/238-3150** and ask for the "ZIP+4 Diskette Coding" program.

Database Programs and Contact Managers

ACT! is a powerful, award-winning, easy-to-use contact management program designed for sales and mobile professionals. It offers a tightly integrated database, activities scheduler, word processor and report generator. Interact Commerce Corp., 888/265-1885 (AZ) or **www.actsoftware.com**.

askSam is a highly-rated free-form database that combines database, text-retrieval and word processing functions to manage both structured and free-form information. You can import information from a variety of sources including e-mail and the Internet or online research and communications. You can easily search for any word or phrase and generate database reports. Any OCR will work with it. Network and electronic publishing versions let you share and distribute information respectively. askSam Systems, 800/800-1997 (FL) or **www.asksam.com**.

GoldMine is an award-winning, comprehensive contact manager for networks and remote users. This powerful enterprise-wide business tool lets you automate common repetitive office tasks with its "Automated Processes." Features include calendaring, e-mail, mail merge letters, telemarketing, sales forecasting, lead tracking, fax/merge, wireless data synchronization, communication server capability, sophisticated security, "remote transfer synchronization," report generator, user definable screens and fields and unlimited additional contacts. Goldmine Software, 800/654-3526 (CA) or **www.goldmine.com**.

INFO SELECT is an award-winning, fast way to deal with notes, ideas, plans, contacts and all your random information. It's a personal information manager that is a free-form text database that lets you make miscellaneous notes on computer (instead of on paper slips) and search for them instantaneously. If you keep a lot of miscellaneous notes or ideas that are unrelated to each other or to particular projects or people, this could be a handy program. Micro Logic Corp., 800/342-5930 (NJ) or **www.miclog.com**.

Microsoft Access is an easy-to-use, fast relational database management system that's good for beginners, experienced users and even developers. Workgroup features enable you to share information with others with or without intranets. Microsoft Corp. 800/426-9400 (WA) or **www.microsoft.com**.

Record Keeping Systems And Software

Acroprint Time Recorder Co. offers automated time keeping systems that can tie into your computer for tracking and printing reports on time-and-attendance, labor distribution, job costing, payroll, overtime, tardiness, shift summaries and more. Acroprint, 800/334-1790 (NC) or **www.acroprint.com**.

Safeguard One-Write Bookkeeping System (available in 200 formats) is great for a private practice or a small office. With Safeguard, you keep a check journal and your tax records as you go. Safeguard also has computer forms and laser forms. Safeguard Business Systems, Inc. (PA) 800/523-2422 or **www.safeguard.com**.

Timeslips is a top-rated time and billing system that helps any size company account for its time and expenses, produce customized billing and generate reports. TIMESLIPS Corporation, 800/285-0999 (TX) or **www.timeslips.com**.

10

WORKING
WITH OTHERS

Quick Scan: If you have customers, coworkers or both, you need to read this chapter. Mastering the other chapters without mastering this one will leave you organized, but working in a vacuum. The real purpose of organization in today's competitive marketplace is to find better ways of working with others. The other chapters focused largely on you as an individual peppered with a few workgroup solutions. In this chapter you'll discover more ways to bring others into the fold by building a more human, caring work environment while you're building quality, innovation, service and teamwork.

The first nine chapters focused largely on what you as an individual can do in the work place. As a consultant and a trainer, I have found this is generally the best place to start. But for dramatic results, you need to spread the word so that everyone with whom you work has a chance to be their best and make exciting contributions toward helping your organization—whether it be your office, work group/team, department, supplier base or company—reach its goals.

Why Everyone You Work with
Is Your Customer

You have probably heard about the importance of customer service and customer satisfaction. You may not, however, realize the extent to which it applies to you and your work. The point is, no matter what kind of work you do or organization you work for, customer focus needs to be the bottom line.

To compete and be profitable in today's world economy, your organization can no longer be doing "business as usual." The old maxim, "if it ain't broke, don't fix it," isn't true any more. Change is the name of the game and to stay competitive in business, you need to **improve and innovate** in order to **provide quality goods or services for your customers**.

Notice I've highlighted several key words. "Customers" need to be your primary focus. There are two kinds of customers for every organization: **external** and **internal**. Some consider external customers to be the most important. They're the ones who are paying for your goods or services. They're the ones you need to satisfy first to stay in business.

Even the federal government now has customers. A friend of mine who works for Social Security showed me a report called "From Red Tape to Results: Creating a Government That Works Better and Costs Less" and the following words appear: "...we are going to make the federal government customer friendly. A lot of people don't realize that the federal government has customers. We have customers. The American people."

Internal customers are the team members with whom you work to provide the goods or services for your external customers. They could be office coworkers, contacts in another department or division or part of your supplier base.

For many, internal customers, are a close second. That's not so, however, for Hal Rosenbluth, CEO of the third largest travel management company in the world, Rosenbluth International, which was featured in *INC. Magazine* and was a Tom Peters Service Company of the Year award winner. Rosenbluth, who calls his internal customers "associates," says, "We don't believe our customers can come first unless our associates come first. If we have happy people here, then they're free to concentrate only on our clients." Stated another way, if your internal customers aren't happy, chances are good your external customers won't be either.

Ralph Stayer, CEO for Johnsonville Foods Inc. in Sheboygan, Wisconsin, talks about employee happiness as a starting point.

> At Johnsonville, we want people to be happy, but never satisfied. We want people to see themselves becoming something. People should be continuously learning and striving to make something bigger and better of themselves. We try to make sure that happens. We aren't making just sausage here. I use the business to make great people. I don't use people to make a great business. If everyone is moving forward and working together, then the sausage will take care of itself.

So in a very real sense *everyone* with whom you work or interact is your customer (and vice versa). Even if you're a sole proprietor, you simply don't work in a vacuum. Once you recognize that we're "all in this together," you start to appreciate the importance of teamwork, service and quality.

"We are in the Quality Revolution and it's every bit as critical as the Industrial Revolution," so said Lloyd Dobyns, writer/narrator of the PBS program "Quality...or Else."

Even 99.9 percent quality isn't good enough; the following would result if organizations in the U.S. abided by only 99.9 percent quality: 1,314 phone calls would be misplaced in the next minute; 22,000 checks would be deducted from the wrong bank accounts in the next hour; 20,000 prescriptions would be written incorrectly this year; and 315 entries in *Webster's Third New International Dictionary* would be misspelled.

Focusing on quality products and/or services leads to and will increase customer satisfaction—external as well as internal. To be on a quality team gives you a sense of pride and accomplishment, which is sometimes all too elusive in today's fast-paced work world.

Quality is more than a buzz word or a fad; it's a way of doing business that permeates every aspect of a business **by focusing on the customer and the work process.**

To **focus on the customer** means to provide service and quality *as the customer sees them.* You stay close to your customers (both external and internal) by listening to them, asking them questions and working diligently to meet their needs. Customer focus means following through, doing what you say—which all involves good organizational skills and systems.

Oddly enough, some companies seem to provide just the opposite of customer service and satisfaction, especially if a "problem" arises. My husband just bought a new computer system by mail order through a company he'd happily done business with before. It seems they've grown a bit too much and aren't customer responsive anymore. The company made a mistake in fulfilling the order and my husband was the one who had to pay for it in wasted time trying to get the mistake corrected. The person who took the order claimed he was unable, "given the way things work at this company," to resolve it, and so my husband was left scrambling to fix it himself. (I'm sure tempted to tell you the name of the company, as so many angry customers will often do.)

What galled my husband even more was that not one person at the company even empathized with an apology. "Service is Sometimes Saying You're Sorry" is the apt title of a consumer affairs article that I had clipped when researching this chapter. Not admitting any wrongdoing coupled with no apology and no attempt to resolve the problem is a good way to lose new and old customers.

And that brings us to the importance of **customer retention**. It costs six times as much to attract new customers as to retain existing ones. A study cited in the *Harvard Business Review* said that customer retention has a substantial impact on profitability, with the increase in dollar value of repeat customers ranging from 25 to 85 percent. Customer retention may, in fact, account for the biggest source of future sales growth.

By the way, only 30 percent of customers with problems complain (they just take their business elsewhere) and only two to five percent of complaints ever get voiced to the headquarters level. I, for one, have faxed the prior page to the president of the computer company my husband just dealt with.

I like the sign at Ed Debevic's Restaurant in Los Angeles that reads: "At Ed's, we promise Friendly and Courteous Service at Reasonable Prices. If for any reason we fail to live up to this promise—please don't tell anyone."

Focus on the work process is the means by which you provide customer service. It's examining the effectiveness of your organizational skills, tools and systems to check whether they're the best means for providing goods and services on time, within budget and to the customer's satisfaction. Work process has been the main focus of this book.

My goal in faxing the computer company president was not to affix blame on anyone but rather to encourage the company to get to the root cause of the problem. The question the company needs to ask is, "What is it about the system (or the company) that allows this kind of problem to be handled in this fashion?"

Identify and eliminate inefficient work processes, especially those that stick out like a sore thumb. I remember many years ago standing endlessly in a hotel checkout line, while the woman ahead of me noticed one particularly inefficient hotel clerk. She commented, "He never gets anything right. And it takes him a long time to get it wrong." There has to be a better way of doing things such as hotel checkout (and of course, many hotels have innovated "express checkout" systems that save valuable customer time—both the internal and external customers' time). And as someone once said anonymously, "It takes less time to do something right than it takes to explain why you did it wrong."

Make sure you evaluate your existing work process. There may be steps that shouldn't be done at all. Get involved with **work simplification** if possible. For example, one major American auto maker developed an automated system to track sales, inventory and production because of a complex system that gave consumers options in some 40,000 possible combinations. A foreign manufacturer, on the other hand, didn't need such a complex automated system, because it created only 32 possible combinations. Try to eliminate the problems that require a complex automated system in the first place.

But what about customer service? Some might argue that 40,000 combinations give the customer more choice; others would argue that having too many choices overwhelms most people. Look, too, for a balance between serving the external and internal customers.

A quality work process depends on the genuine commitment by everyone in an organization, especially those at the top, to quality, innovation, customer service and internal customer support. An openness to change and continuous quality improvement is evident at all levels of such an organization. In a quality-conscious organization you'll see a driving emphasis on training, communication, innovation, flexibility, employee involvement and teamwork.

And according to a two-year Labor Department study, companies that train workers, involve them in decisions and give them a stake in the business are more profitable than those that do not. The Secretary of Labor said the study shows the "surest way to profits and productivity is to treat employees as assets to be developed rather than costs to be cut."

It's good to see the emphasis shifting more to "human capital"—the worth of individuals and how to maximize it in a very human sense. To that end, we're seeing a greater emphasis on what people need in the work place (and their lives) to help them thrive and ultimately contribute more in terms of the quality and quantity of their work.

We're seeing work places offering more to meet the needs of their people. "Family-friendly" programs are springing up everywhere. Flexible schedules, telecommuting and special nonmonetary rewards and perks acknowledge that people have a life outside of work.

At the same time, people are working harder and longer than ever. But when they're working in collaborative, high-functioning teams to develop a quality product or service, they are experiencing a sense of belonging, purpose and meaning.

Look at where you work. See if there's at least a spark of caring about quality, service and the external/internal customers. If so, you should be able to use at least a few of the ideas in the following sections to help develop your organization.

Challenging, Changing Times Present Opportunities

Change and innovation is the name of the game today against a backdrop of fast-paced, instant communications and demanding workloads. Fortunately, we have the tools and the know-how to address these challenging times.

Now more than ever we must get things done and eliminate unnecessary steps, tasks, activities and projects. Doing some serious work flow analysis is essential (refer to Chapter 9's Resource Guide for some flowcharting products that may help you). And the progressive companies, the ones that are surviving and thriving, are doing it in cross-functional teams and in the "flattened hierarchies" that Tom Peters has been preaching for years.

A flattened hierarchy brings internal and external customers closer together as problems come into the foreground faster and demand immediate attention. If you have team players around who accept change and are interested in solving problems, your organization will most likely thrive.

A flattened hierarchy only happens, however, if your organization has a pervasive, empowered work climate that fosters trust, teamwork and recognition—a climate that famous humanist psychologist Abraham Maslow termed "enlightened management." He also used the term "synergy" to describe the cooperation that such a climate creates.

Not many people know that Maslow, who brought us the "hierarchy of needs" and "self-actualization" we learned about in our college Psyche 101 class, also wrote about business management and economics in the early 60s. He had a chance one summer to observe close-up one company that had high performing work teams and was so inspired by what he saw that he tape recorded his thoughts and later wrote a journal he called "Summer Notes."

He informally distributed mimeographed copies of the journal to colleagues—including prominent university dean and business theorist Warren Bennis, who encouraged him to publish it. It had several small printings in the 70s under an awkward title; nevertheless it did come to the attention of leading management guru Peter Drucker who said it had a big impact on him. You can now find the journal in a collection of Maslow's previously unpublished papers called *Future Visions* edited by Maslow's biographer, Edward Hoffman.

Maslow also wrote about the importance of "continual improvement" at work where everything functioned as a "web" of interrelated parts.

He observed what happens when you give freely of yourself and your resources in a such a synergistic environment. He wrote that "generosity can increase wealth rather than decrease it" and "the more influence and power you give to someone else in the team situation, the more you have yourself."

Redefining Work

The notion of "it's not my job" goes completely out the window today, along with the concept of a "job" itself. The term "work" is replacing the term "job," which harkens back to the Industrial Revolution, where work was much more narrowly defined. So, you'll need to change your perception of your work—which, now will provide you more variety, less clarity and more opportunities than you may have time for!

In addition, many people today have what author William Bridges terms "portfolio careers," which consist of a mixture of part-time jobs or a full-time position supplemented with freelance work or self-employment.

Partly because of portfolio careers and partly because of our demanding times, people are working harder than ever putting in long work weeks. Do, however, avoid pointless "face time," the assumption that you should sit at your desk or be at work for longer hours, sometimes before, as well as, after work. Face time also assumes in some businesses that you would never leave the office before a certain time, say, 8:00 p.m. Face time can be devastating to not only one's personal life but to productivity as well. Remember that you should be paid for the results you produce, not for face time.

Surefire Ways to Increase Quality and Teamwork Whether or Not You're the Boss

One *Wall Street Journal* story said it concisely: "Teamwork is in." The story described a study focused on 4,000-plus teams in more than 500 companies and found that performance and advancement were being measured not only by individual achievements but also by the ability to be a team player.

There's no great mystery to producing a winning team that offers quality goods or services. It takes a consistent, organized approach that addresses three key areas: communication, employee involvement and training.

Underlying these areas, however, should be a genuine foundation of *caring about people*. Without this foundation, many of the ideas in this section could be perceived as insincere and manipulative. It doesn't matter how many great, innovative ideas you introduce into your organization if an uncaring attitude exists. As the saying goes, "People don't care how much you know until they know how much you care."

Communicate with Internal and External Customers

People in the work place often take communication for granted and assume that enough of it goes on. There's plenty of talking, voice mail and e-mail. But the sheer quantity of communication that takes place doesn't insure quality nor caring in the communication.

Quality communication is a two-way street. First, **keep people informed**. As Thomas Jefferson observed, "When you don't keep people informed, you get one of three things: rumor, apathy or revolution." (And he ought to know.)

You'd be surprised how frequently people in work groups really don't communicate with each other to keep one another informed—even of their simple comings and goings. It's especially important to keep a receptionist, assistant or office manager informed, particularly if they have any dealings with external customers. Lack of basic, up-to-date information about the availability of key personnel can create a credibility gap in the organization. Decide who needs to know what as well as how and when they will get that information.

Some groupware programs have electronic in/out boards or a simple in/out wall chart may do the trick for a small office or a home office; whichever tool you choose for keeping tabs on people's whereabouts, use it consistently. Dedicated "in-and-out board programs" are also available; take a look at OfficeHours for Windows (TEAmaker Corp., 503/520-5050 [OR] or **www.teamaker.com**) and StatusView (IDP Corp., 919/878-0204 or **www.idpcorp.com**).

For any team that works closely together, such as a manager and an assistant, I almost always recommend a five- or ten-minute daily morning meeting. Sometimes it's not always possible to meet every day to go over priorities such as the day's or week's calendar, key projects, mail and messages but if the team makes a commitment to meet and does so more than half the time, there's all that much more communication taking place.

Communicate clearly, concisely and positively, whenever possible. Ask yourself as you begin any communication, what's the key question, its deadline and/or time frame—and be as specific as possible. Try to use numbers to add clarity to convey how much time you have ("I have three minutes to talk"), how much time you'll need, how many things you want to discuss, etc.

Don't forget to compliment key colleagues you work with, ideally at least once a day. But of course, you must be sincere. The power of a compliment can help transform a working (or personal) relationship. I have seen it happen in my consulting work.

Be positive and open about possibilities rather than negative and close-minded. Instead of saying, "I don't know" and leaving it at that, you might add, "But I'll find out." Instead of saying, "We can't do that" or "we never have done it that way," try "Let's see what we can do."

There may be times when you'll need to give some "constructive criticism" but even then, you can approach it positively as a way to help someone else grow and develop. Become aware, too, of different communication styles and preferences. Communications research indicates that people like to receive communication in the way they're most likely to deliver it. Male/female communication styles are useful to study and apply; Deborah Tannen has done some excellent work in this area (see her books/cassettes *Talking From 9 to 5* and *You Just Don't Understand*).

Use multiple channels of communication but limit them, if possible. Multiple channels can make communication more interesting and less likely to fall prey to distortion or bias from information that's conveyed through only one channel or source. Such channels can include any of the following: e-mail, telephone calls, meetings, memos, faxes, company publications, coworkers, higher-ups, the "grapevine" and customers.

Include at least one personal channel of communication such as the phone or face-to-face meetings, especially if you're relying heavily on a less personal channel, such as e-mail. This is especially important for team members or customers who are scattered all over geographically. Remember, the purpose of communication includes not only the sharing of information but also the development of relationships.

Be on the lookout, also, for communication channels that are innovative, creative or humorous. Use color-coding whenever possible to flag or categorize messages. Even one U.S. president used color-coding on a "message calendar" to highlight key topics to discuss with his aides; he had different colored bars on each of the calendar's days, for example, purple for foreign policy, orange for the economy, blue for social policy and green for government reform.

To avoid information overload, **beware of using too many channels or communication tools**. Most of my bigger corporate clients provide each employee with several means by which they can communicate with others inside and outside the company. The problem is workers spend a lot of time checking *all* of these communication channels several times a day (and night). They may also spend time finding out the communication channel preferred by the receiver. It gets very complicated and time-consuming. I developed a survey for a large corporate client in which I had all members of one department indicate their preferences, both when sending and receiving communications. Then I charted them all out so everyone could see one another's preferences. You could do such a survey within your workgroup, maybe even agreeing to reduce or eliminate certain communication channels.

Keeping people informed is only half of the communication story. To complete the story, **ask people what they think**. This needs to happen regularly for both internal and external customers. Be prepared, however, that once you ask people what they think, you must really *listen*, take the information seriously and *act on it*.

Conducting a survey, such as the one I just described, is an excellent way to see what's on people's minds. Keep surveys as simple as possible. Design a major benefit into the survey—why should anyone want to take the time to complete it? Tell survey participants *what's in it for them*.

Companies are surveying both their external and internal customers. Some companies are involved in a "360-degree feedback" process to see how they're doing, which may include surveys by external customers, employee performance appraisals, "upward appraisals" (subordinates' evaluations of their superiors) and "peer appraisals." The latter are more typical of companies with a leaner, flattened hierarchical structure.

Insurance agent Don Gambrell uses a clever, two-sided, Farmers Insurance form/response letter to encourage customers to renew their policy and/or communicate with him about why they haven't done so. On the left half of the page is a brief, friendly letter called "This is My Side" asking for the customer to respond to the other half, called "This is Your Side," which has six different quick responses to check off. An SASE is also enclosed. He's used this form for over 20 years because it works.

"The President's Luncheon" is one way a federal credit union asks employees what they think. Every month, six or seven employees are chosen at random to have lunch with the president and discuss any topics they feel are important to them, to the credit union or to management.

One CEO has a dedicated phone line for employees to call him. The line rings directly in his office and isn't screened by anyone. Whenever it rings, the CEO picks up the phone and speaks openly and confidentially with employees.

Another company set up a toll-free number for employees to leave messages, which are then transcribed anonymously by an outside company.

The suggestion box can be a good way to get feedback but one department discovered a new twist. This was a busy mail and phone department, where phones rang off the hook and ten disgruntled employees didn't work well together. The department replaced the suggestion box with a "Gripe Box," and employees completed "Gripes and Complaints" cards anonymously. Though the Gripe Box sounds negative, it worked because it reflected how people were feeling and gave them a chance to vent those feelings. Gripes and complaints were handled openly but anonymously at department meetings, solutions were generated and today everyone gets along very well.

One organization asks employees to bring one to two suggestions to improve the work process every time they go to a meeting. Ideas are later evaluated and rewarded.

One small business owner I know of offers an open dialogue for her employees every other month over pizza. She takes them out for pizza and then they meet for two hours. The first hour is an open gripes session about anything and anybody, including management. The second hour is spent on positive comments and solutions to gripes.

Just staying close to your customers and having your eyes and ears open can be a very effective way to find out what people think; convey that information back to your customers and you have real two-way communication. That's just what a local caterer-restaurant owner did. Zabie Vourvoulis published a beautiful, two-color brochure for her customers, in which she affirmed her "commitment to quality" and acknowledged customers' contributions.

> We struggle constantly with the issue of service and how best to fill your
> needs. Many times, small suggestions or comments from you have led
> to big changes (paper biodegradable disposables for instance). We've
> also purchased new, more comfortable and sturdier stools, and we've
> developed an interesting, reasonably priced dinner menu...Your support
> has been wonderful. It's encouraging to know that effort and caring
> have a place in this fast-paced world of ours. We certainly appreciate
> yours and we hope that ours shows every day.

Many businesses are using e-mail to stay in touch with customers. You can do a lot of market research this way, although e-mail customers, who are often shrouded in some anonymity, can be rather blunt. Some businesses are using e-mail for their internal customers as well; one company lets employees disguise their identity and posts replies daily on an electronic bulletin board.

Standardize communication routines, whenever possible. See if you have any specific routines you're currently using in your own office, your workgroup and/or your company concerning communications—e.g, how the phone is answered, by whom and when calls are returned; how visitors are greeted and by whom; how faxes are handled and how often e-mail is checked. Do you have any procedures in writing? If not, now's a good time to start! Perhaps one person could put a draft on computer and the workgroup team members could modify it as necessary.

Develop and practice good listening skills. Listening is crucial to good communication skills and customer service. Yet recent studies show that 75 percent of what we hear is heard incorrectly and of the remaining 25 percent, we forget 75 percent of it within weeks or days. The average listener has an immediate retention level of only 50 percent; within 24 to 48 hours, the retention level drops to 25 percent.

It's not easy to listen. It takes great concentration, in large part because we hear four to five times faster than we can speak. We may become bored and think about other things to fill in the gaps when someone else is talking or even worse, interrupt people to complete their thoughts. To be an "active listener," which is the most effective kind of listener, requires the ability to slow down and concentrate, absorb information, put yourself in someone else's shoes, restate accurately what you've heard, ask clarifying questions and evaluate the whole process objectively. Listening is a skill to be learned and practiced, a skill especially hampered by our fast-paced world.

Personalize your communication, whenever possible. There are certain words people can't hear enough: their own names and "thank you." Take time to thank people for their thoughtfulness, hard work or good ideas. Sitting down to write a thank-you note is such a simple, but very powerful method of communication. It shows that the recipient is worth your time and you're organized enough to make time for it.

Writing quick, two- or three-sentence notes on personalized note cards (also called "correspondence cards") can be accomplished easily during spare moments, such as waiting in a doctor's office or sitting on a plane. (By the way, it's more effective to send a note right away but better to send a note late than not at all.)

Since writing thank-you notes is becoming something of a lost art, you can really make an impression on coworkers, customers and your boss. It's a really tangible form of communication. If you thank customers or others who complain, you also have a chance to turn around a bad situation.

Learning and using people's names can have a big impact on opening up communication. I had a dramatic example of seeing that it's "all in a name." Around 4:30 every afternoon, a postal carrier makes the last pick-up at several boxes near our office. Occasionally, I will go out to the boxes right at 4:30, when the postal truck arrives and hand my final mail to the carrier.

Over the years, there have been several carriers, each of whom was very friendly. When a new carrier assumed the route he seemed very different. He was very serious and wouldn't look up when you handed him mail. He appeared almost upset that you were breaking his routine. He seemed, in a word, antisocial. Normally, I would have introduced myself and made small talk but I figured that was a real waste of time with this guy.

Weeks went by and I avoided making any contact with the carrier. Being normally a very outgoing individual, I decided one day to simply introduce myself. Much to my surprise, when I told him my name and learned his was Richard, he really lit up and began to talk. Every time I see him now, he calls me by name and has something pleasant to say.

Richard is an internal customer who is part of my supplier base. The service he provides makes it possible for me to be of service to my external customers. Because he's a part of my team, it's important to be able to communicate with him.

Actively Involve Employees

Once you've begun implementing effective communication strategies, you've opened the door to employee involvement, the secret to quality and teamwork. Research indicates a direct correlation between high employee involvement and motivation, quality, productivity and profitability. Let's look at some ways for you and all employees to get involved.

Start by zeroing in on the **mission of your company or organization**. Everybody should have a copy of the company mission statement, as well as the company's guiding values. Mission and values statements are often buried in long-range planning documents that the upper management team may have generated. Progressive companies distribute copies of these statements to all employees, reprint them in company publications and may even make special posters that appear around the company. You should also share your mission and values with external customers. See Figure 10-1 for an example of the mission statement and guiding values for one personnel agency.

Figure 10-1. MISSION AND VALUES

Mission:

We serve the business community in a sincere and thorough manner by providing timely, cost effective results in meeting their regular, temporary and long-term staffing needs. We continually invest our talents to establish and maintain long-term relationships with both our clients and employees. Through innovation and education we strive to maintain the competitive edge.

Values:

Heritage of Excellence—We maintain the highest levels of professionalism to be the best we can.

Customer Service—We provide all of our customers with quality personnel services by treating each of their staffing needs as if it were our own.

Employee Responsiveness—We treat people in all positions with fairness and dignity. We provide opportunities for earned growth to reach their potential both inside and outside the organization. Our people are proud of their high standards and are equitably rewarded.

Civic Spirit—The community benefits from both our individual and company commitments to continually participate in the community's growth. Our people are educated and enriched through community involvement.

Adaptability—We test and try new concepts and services. We understand that one key strength in maintaining the competitive edge is our ability to identify and benefit from change.

Teamwork—We communicate openly and with trust in mutually pursuing opportunities and meeting challenges. Each person plays an integral role in the success of the PDQ team.

If your company has no written mission statement or guiding values, suggest that a committee or action team be formed to develop them. This group could have representatives from all different levels or departments in the company. This is a great way to build participation in the company and co-ownership of the mission statement and values. And ideally, the mission statement and guiding values will include the importance of employee involvement.

Managers as Team Leaders

If you're a manager or you work for one, recognize that the role of the manager today will be changing more and more to that of **team leader, teacher and coach** who facilitates employee participation and teamwork. Old, autocratic, traditional management styles of "do it my way" no longer work. As team leaders today, managers are *facilitating the process* much more than managing people.

According to foremost management expert Peter Drucker, the term "manager" isn't particularly useful anymore because in today's progressive organizations, managers increasingly work with "colleagues," rather than dominate "subordinates."

Interesting enough, a recent study showed that women more naturally exhibit the kind of nontraditional traits needed in today's new, enlightened managers— the ability to share information and power, encourage employee participation and demonstrate how both individual, personal goals may be reached while attaining organizational goals.

Today's managers and leaders would do well to embrace the following statement by John McDonnell of McDonnell Douglas about operating with a "fundamental belief that everyone wants to do a good job and that overall performance will be greatly enhanced if people are assisted, coached, trained and supported rather than controlled."

According to management consultant and author Lee Cheaney, today's managers should also "manage on the behavior of 95 percent of employees and not on the five percent who cause problems." He suggests dealing with that five percent promptly and fairly, spending the bulk of your time developing your team.

To develop the 95 percent, today's manager needs to help form work teams that have real authority to make decisions and to act. When one General Mills cereal plant gave such authority to its work teams, it realized a 40 percent higher productivity rate compared with traditionally managed groups.

We're seeing this kind of shift taking place in manufacturing circles as well as in service areas and in the office. Research indicates that workers are happier, too, with more involvement. Studies indicate that workers want much more than a paycheck and when ranking job factors, "money" comes after such things as honesty and ethical behavior of management, open communications, the opportunity to develop skills, being able to contribute, the nature of the work, the desire to have their work and innovative contributions recognized, work schedule flexibility and the effect of the job on one's personal/family life.

Managers today have the opportunity to address these factors through open communications and a participatory management style that gives more responsibility to workers and work teams.

Participatory managers encourage their people to make decisions and come up with solutions of their own. Sun Microsystems CEO Scott G. McNealy jokes, "When our people have difficulty making a decision, then I threaten to make the decision. That notion gets people scared enough to make the right decision themselves."

When I presented a seminar to a credit union group in Portland, one manager shared his policy, "Don't come to me with a problem unless you have at least two solutions."

In today's business climate, effective managers need to become leaders. They need to be proactive, embrace change and innovation, be passionate about their work, provide training and development opportunities and genuinely care about their people.

We need leaders who roll up their sleeves and work collaboratively *with* other team members in a highly charged, optimistic, pioneering spirit. Teams who work collaboratively can experience meaning, purpose and even joy as they pull their know-how and ideas together and discover that in the words of playwright Noel Coward, "work can be more fun than fun."

Team Meetings

Traditional meetings, as someone once put it, are all too often a place where minutes are taken and hours are lost. They've also been a place where, according to one survey, many participants feel uncomfortable freely sharing their opinions and believe that most meetings are dominated by hidden agendas.

Participatory team meetings on the other hand are an important way for workers to develop their skills and make innovative contributions. They're also important for dealing with problems, making decisions by consensus, promoting communication, developing leadership, building commitment, sharing information, setting goals and improving operations.

Unfortunately, many meetings aren't as productive as they could be. Some professionals spend between 25% to 60% of their time in meetings. Many meeting-goers feel that up to 50% of meeting time is unproductive.

To improve your meetings, why not have a meeting on meetings? Have your work team come prepared to share at least one idea on how to make more productive, participatory meetings.

Consider having a training session on meetings. I conduct such sessions and like to use an entertaining, informative video called "Meetings, Bloody Meetings" starring English actor/comedian John Cleese (available from Coastal Training Technology, 800/553-0091 or **www.coastal.com**).

In a nutshell, here are the ten tips I teach about effective meetings:

1. **Every meeting should have a stated purpose or goal** that is determined in advance of the meeting and that is defined in a **prepared agenda** to which participants have had a chance to contribute. The agenda should be distributed far enough in advance so participants can prepare (at least one day's notice, preferably more time). Each agenda item should be as specific as possible; should ideally include the individual who's introducing it and should cite the purpose of the item at the meeting, e.g, "For Discussion," "For Information" or "For Decision"; and should have a time limit.

One company I know distributes a memo/survey before each staff meeting that solicits two agenda items. It reads in part, "Please write down two things that you would like to hear talked about, questions that need answering, topics of interest, etc.," and participants are asked to leave the completed sheet in a specific person's in-box.

2. **Limit the size of the group.** Include only those who need to be there. Four to seven people is an ideal number of people for a planning or problem-solving meeting. (A training session or informational meeting could handle many more.)

3. Ideally **arrange participants in a circle to encourage more participation** and provide refreshments to set a more informal atmosphere.

4. **List start and end times for the meeting on the agenda and stick to them.** It may be helpful to use a countdown timer to stay on schedule or have a clock in your meeting room.

5. Each meeting should **have a facilitator who keeps the meeting moving**, clarifies and summarizes key points, acknowledges contributions of participants by name and ends the meeting on time. The facilitator can provide a quick verbal summary at the end, reviewing the goals of the meeting and how participants contributed to reaching those goals. To build leadership, use a "rotating facilitator," a different person from the work team to lead each meeting.

6. **Have a scribe take minutes** that reflect key points, decisions, action items and the responsible participants. Minutes should be prepared and distributed to attendees within a few days of the meeting. Underline or boldface action items, deadlines and names of responsible individuals so that they stand out. Have a different scribe at each meeting.

7. **Use visuals**. Have either the facilitator or someone else use a flip chart, overhead projector or a computer with a large screen to record key ideas and make them visible to everyone at the meeting. Such an ongoing record serves as a

"group memory," is useful reference for the scribe when preparing minutes and can be used at future meetings. Visual tools also can help improve retention of the information by 50 percent. **Drawing** simple cluster or Mind Maps (as described in Chapter 9) along with simple images can perk up on-the-fly visuals. (See *Beyond Words: A Guide to Drawing Out Ideas* by Milly Sonneman.) Post-it Easel Pads by 3M offer all the benefits of Post-it Notes in a large size that lets you easily and safely post and remove these sheets; this product also doubles as a flip chart pad that attaches to most easel stands and transports easily with a convenient built-in handle. The Paper Direct catalog (**800/A-PAPERS**) has some handy meeting and presentation tools and accessories for visuals. Also check out the affordable Ibid electronic whiteboard that connects to your computer, which can save whiteboard notes digitally and let you print them out through your printer (MicroTouch Systems, Inc., 800/642-7686, **www.microtouch.com**).

8. Include **follow-up** during and after each meeting. Send **minutes** after every meeting summarizing **key decisions, delegations and action items**. Several **standing agenda items** should appear on each regular meeting agenda. Action items, decisions and delegations listed in the minutes should be brought forward to appear on the next meeting's agenda for a status report follow-up. Always include time on the agenda for **successes and accomplishments** that have occurred since the last meeting as well as an opportunity to present **suggestions and ideas**.

9. **Be flexible and creative** with your meetings and **use different formats** that are appropriate. For manager/assistant teams I recommend **short, but frequent daily meetings** that take no more than five to ten minutes. Certainly a formal agenda for such meetings would be inappropriate but a "standing agenda," that covers routine items, such as the day's schedule, e-mails and other correspondence, telephone calls and certain ongoing clients, would be a good way to standardize and streamline this business meeting.

10. **Keep meetings confidential.** Confidentiality breeds trust and encourages participants to open up more fully.

To solve problems, identify solutions and build teamwork, **use "Quality Circle" meetings**, also called "brainstorming sessions" and "Nominal Group Technique." Such meetings (and parts within meetings) involve ideally four to 12 participants, have a facilitator, have a time limit and typically include four parts: 1) identification and definition of the challenge or problem (because as Charles Kettering once said, "A problem well-stated is a problem half-solved"); 2) in round-robin fashion, contribution by each participant of brainstorming suggestions, alternatives and solutions without discussion; 3) discussion and evaluation of the brainstormed ideas; and 4) selection of one to three ideas for implementation. Number 4 can be done by a simple show of hands but a more effective way is to use a preprinted voting card that includes a place to indicate your choice, as well as your priority ranking or the weight you assign to your choice. For example, you might vote for idea D and give it a priority ranking of only 2 (on a scale of 1 to 5, where 5 is high) because you don't feel so strongly about this particular idea.

Another way to do a problem-solving meeting is to have each participant zero in on one key problem area and generate some solutions *before* the meeting. Use a simple survey with three questions: 1) In the coming year (or any other designated period of time), what would you most like to see changed here at this company (or substitute department or other workgroup designation)?; 2) Describe how that change can come about by listing specific solutions and steps that need to be taken; and 3) How much time will you contribute to make this change happen and what exactly will you do to help bring about this change?

A solutions-orientation to any meeting keeps the energy on a more positive and focused level. You may even want to avoid using the word "problem," substituting instead the word "item," "idea" or "challenge." Try to encourage participants to state comments, ideas or questions as positively as possible and discourage negativity or criticism. It's an effective way to run a meeting.

Consider using graphics whenever possible in your meetings. One Wharton School of Business study showed that the average business meeting with graphics was 28 percent shorter than those without graphics. Maybe a picture is indeed worth a thousand words.

As a professional speaker, I pay close attention to meeting room logistics. I avoid long, narrow rooms and cavernous rooms. I love well-lit spaces. I always find out where the heating and air-conditioning controls are in advance (or who is responsible for controlling them). Whenever possible I place myself opposite the entrance to the room. I prefer a round table but if I get stuck with a long, rectangular one, I place myself at the head if I wish to present more of an authoritarian, expert position and in the middle on one side, if it's a more informal, participatory meeting.

Other Employee Involvement Programs

Many companies today have a whole variety of **employee incentive** or **employee recognition programs** that encourage and reward employee-generated, innovative, cost-saving ideas; a superior work effort; surpassed performance goals; and employee longevity.

Forms of recognition vary widely from certificates of appreciation (University of California, San Diego Medical Center has a Pride-O-Gram) to cash and prize incentive awards. After 61 years of offering cash incentives to employees for cost-saving ideas, Florida Power & Light (FPL) discovered employees overwhelmingly preferred premiums (special gifts); a staggering 52 percent of FPL's 15,000 employees participated in its new premium program the first year compared to a two percent participation rate while using cash incentives.

Increasingly we're seeing a shift toward time-based incentives. One company offered sales people who met certain sales goals the reward of leaving at 2 p.m. for a month; as a result, all sales records were broken.

There is a difference between "recognition" and "incentive" programs and the types of items that are given to employees. An incentive program is designed specifically to motivate employees, whereas a recognition program shows appreciation and recognizes achievement after the fact. In your organization, it may be more appropriate to use one type of program alone or to use a combination.

Some companies, one newspaper story reported, are rewarding employee risk-taking even to the extent of doing things wrong. Why you ask? Such companies are encouraging employees to think innovatively for themselves, to question the status quo and to try to solve company problems. Esso Resources Canada has an "Order of the Duck" award consisting of a wooden duck's head mounted on a plunger; the duck's head symbolizes vision and the plunger represents sticking your neck out. The award goes to an employee who challenges management or does something without the boss's approval.

Some employee recognition programs are more successful than others. The sincerity and caring on behalf of management may have much to do with how these programs are perceived and hence, their success. In addition, the programs should reflect the mission and values of the company.

These programs need to be spiced up from time to time as they can become old hat in a hurry. And what works well in one company may not work well in yours.

Survey employees to see what they think of such programs and the program awards and what changes they'd like to make. (You may find, for example, that employees rate a trip to Hawaii for two as a much greater incentive than an equivalent cash award.)

Performance management in which employees set and evaluate their own performance objectives is an important way to involve employees. Be sure to build in recognition and reward for good and/or improved performance.

As a part of their performance management process, one company has each employee complete a thought-provoking, two-page, self-evaluation form for past and future performance. The form asks employees to list their performance objectives for the coming 12 months, any necessary behavior changes they'll need to make and significant achievements during the past 12 months. In addition, employees are asked to "stretch" themselves—to make a special effort to accomplish something in the next 12 months and identify what that effort will be. There is also a chart for listing strengths, weaknesses, problems and opportunities.

Finally, beware of too much employee involvement, especially during the cold and flu season. One story in *The Wall Street Journal* had this humorous title, "Boss, You Look Ill (What We Mean Is: Beat It, Phlegm Boy)," which was about sick workaholic bosses who won't stay home and instead help spread illness at the office. It's no laughing matter that "office buildings can be incubators for infectious disease," according to occupational medicine expert Rupert Burtan. He suggests telling ill workaholics that it's simply "inefficient" for everyone in the office to get sick.

The Benefits of Camaraderie

Building camaraderie is a fun way to encourage employee participation, teamwork and creativity. Many companies are finding that the group that plays together, stays together. Odetics, Inc., an electronics company in Anaheim, California, that was featured in the book *The 100 Best Companies to Work for in America*, even has a "Fun Committee." Joel Slutzky, Odetics chairman and CEO, notes that since people spend more time at work than anywhere else, it makes sense to encourage them to look forward to coming to work. Besides low absenteeism, his company has a very low turnover rate and low medical costs for his industry. He also believes his employees are more innovative.

Slutzky emphasizes that fun events don't have to cost a lot but should be creative and different and go beyond the typical company picnic. Past events have included a 50s party; a "couch potato" contest that included miniature golf and paper airplane activities for employees "who wanted to get into fitness without working up a sweat"; plays put on by the company repertoire theater; a surprise bash to celebrate the company's 20th birthday; and a Secretaries Day celebration that had managers dress up as waiters and serve lunch to company secretaries in the cafeteria.

Every year, one company invites employees' children in for a visit. The children play games, have lunch with their parents and watch their parents work. A side benefit is that employees get to discover something personal about their coworkers.

You may spend at least eight hours a day at work, yet know very little about your coworkers. One organization has a voluntary Employee Profile form that asks about such areas as hobbies, outside interests and children. These forms are compiled and published periodically in an employee directory that helps employees become better acquainted.

I developed my own profile form when I was president of a professional association. It was a useful tool for board members to get to know one another. I included such items as, "family members or significant others," "pets," "education/Alma Mater(s)," "activities, hobbies, interests, charities, etc." and "special goals, dreams, aspirations." I encouraged my board members to answer any of the items that felt comfortable or appropriate for them.

Train to See a Real Gain

To maintain a quality-oriented team that focuses on continuous improvement and innovation, you'll need an ongoing, quality training program that provides team building, work process and group dynamics training and coaching, too.

Such training also requires the support of top management and should reflect a continuous-improvement, growth philosophy of your company. Unfortunately, in all too many businesses, training is perceived as an unnecessary frill. But top companies that seek to attain and maintain the competitive edge recognize that training is an integral, essential part.

Get involved in your own training. Assess areas where you could use some additional training. Progressive companies frequently conduct needs assessment surveys for employees and their managers to identify training areas. Some training departments have identified and organized skill areas by category and by level or position and invite all employees to evaluate their own skill strengths and weaknesses. Training programs and materials are developed or brought in-house, based on these identified needs.

Notice whenever you feel uncomfortable in doing new work or taking on a new responsibility. Don't pretend you know something when you don't. Don't worry about feeling inadequate. Let it be a signal that it's time for you to learn something new, and whenever you do, there's usually some feeling of discomfort that's natural.

This feeling often occurs when someone delegates something new to you. You may remember the four steps to delegation discussed in Chapter 3. The second one had to do with training. It's your responsibility to make sure you get the necessary training to do the delegated task. In a larger sense, it's your responsibility to make sure you get the necessary training to do all your work. Of course, it's easier in a corporate culture that actively supports training. But it's still your responsibility.

Remember training pays off. One economist found that even short-term, company-sponsored training brought higher wages and better performance reviews.

Capitalize on Cross Training

One way to get training, aside from a formal training department, is to take advantage of **cross training**. This kind of training lets you see, and in some cases lets you do, other people's jobs. There are many advantages to this kind of training. First, you have a chance to learn new skills or new aspects of your company. Learning additional skills could add to your marketing and career potential. Second, it can be helpful from an operations standpoint to have someone else fill in for you if you're out sick or on vacation.

Third, when you can see what procedures are followed by other people or departments, you have a chance to see why these procedures are necessary. You may be more cooperative when you're asked to fill out a form, for example, because you've seen firsthand, just how important it is to another department.

Building a real sense of cooperation is a major reason to cross train. One major company has a chart that reads:

~~Y~~OUR PROBLEM
Cooperation is spelled with two letters: "WE."

Cross-functional teams are a variation on the cross-training idea. A cross-functional team is when people from different departments or those who perform different functions work together as a team on a specific project or problem. Such teamwork breaks down barriers between people who work in different work groups, departments and even different companies. More and more teams and "partnerships" are flourishing than ever before and creating some impressive collaborative efforts.

Describe What You Do and How You Do It

Your department or office should develop its own **training manual** that describes all of the different positions and responsibilities in detail. Everyone should write a description of their responsibilities, functions and processes. All of the information should be checked, tested and updated from time to time. Writing the manual on a computer makes updates easy.

Normally, training for a new position is handled by one other person, often a predecessor. When the training isn't in some written format, vital items can become omitted.

It's important to document in a manual all that you do in your position. Such documentation might even justify why you need an assistant (or a raise!). Plus it's a real help when you train someone else to do your work—temporarily, when you go on vacation, or permanently, when you get that promotion.

How to Organize Others

A question I'm often asked by well-organized individuals is how they can organize a boss or a coworker. Impossible as it may seem, there are a number of steps you can take.

Broaden your definition of "organize." Make sure it goes well beyond clean desks to incorporate the importance of goal setting, prioritizing, working more effectively and the notion of process improvement. Make sure it also complements your "corporate culture" or the philosophy and mission of your organization as a whole.

In addition, recognize that organizing others is a communication issue and a training issue. The communication issue focuses on how to *motivate* someone to *want* to be better organized. The main way to motivate anyone is to ask yourself, "What's in it for them?" Remember the acronym for that all important question: WIIFT. There have to be real benefits for them in terms of power, prestige, profits or whatever is a real motivator *for them*. They have to clearly see a connection between getting organized and any benefits that are motivators.

Once you can show a positive connection, you have a good shot at helping them begin the organizing training process. As with most training, this is a process that takes place over time. There are skills to learn and habits to practice. If you yourself are organized and are a patient teacher who acknowledges and reinforces small successes, you have a chance to see some exciting results. If you're a team player, not a dictator, you could even transform your entire organization.

But even after all your efforts, you may at times need to recognize the limitations of certain individuals who just can't seem to grasp certain "basic" organizational skills. In those situations, you may just need to take more control, insist on a daily meeting (in person or by phone) and intercept certain details or papers that simply shouldn't end up in that person's office.

Let's see how Linda was able to apply these techniques to solve a paper organization problem that she faced with coworkers.

Preventing the Dump-It-on-the-Desk Syndrome

Linda, an administrative assistant for a small, paper-intensive public relations firm, had a problem. Everyone would feed work to her by dumping it in the middle of her desk. They also had the habit of interrupting her from other work to explain what they wanted done.

Together Linda and I devised a special daily paperwork system that helps Linda better control interruptions and incoming paperwork. She now uses colored, two-pocket presentation folders, a different color for each person. She puts mail in the right-hand pocket and staff members feed back work to her in the left-hand pocket once a day. If a special project or deadline comes up during the day, she has a red folder on her desk to handle these top priorities. (If Linda were more of an e-mail kind of person, she could have suggested an e-mail-based work management system.)

Designing the system was only half the story, since her system involved the other staff members who needed to "buy into it." So I suggested she make a presentation at a staff meeting to introduce the system and ask for everyone's support in *trying it out* for a week. Then everyone was to get together at the following week's meeting to evaluate their new *office* system (not Linda's system). The system is still working well several years later.

It's very important to get everyone's agreement and support whenever one person introduces a new system. Otherwise, the office staff may be resistent to a system that appears to be imposed upon them.

When introducing a system such as Linda's presentation folders, remember that good communication and training skills come into play here. First, communicate the benefits to everyone. Second, clearly train people in how you see the system functioning. Be open to reasonable modifications. Encourage people to be involved in this initial discussion (which is really a training session). Give up ownership of the system—it's no longer "my" system, it's "ours."

Managing Multiple Bosses, Projects or Priorities

It's a real challenge trying to work with multiple bosses or coworkers and juggle different projects and priorities. The key word here is "priorities" because that's where you'll need to start.

Begin by setting up a work priority system. First, define priority levels, get agreement on these levels from coworkers and bosses and incorporate these levels onto a work priority slip (you could have these levels printed onto Post-it Notes). Here are some suggested priorities that may work for you:

A-1 Drop everything—this requires immediate attention!
A-2 This is a hot priority to be done ASAP.
A-3 Handle this by the end of the day.
B-1 Complete by the end of the next work day.
B-2 Complete by a specified day, from two to seven days out.
B-3 This is an important but long-term project, due in more than a week's time up to several months.

Note that priorities can and will change; what was a B-1 yesterday may become an A-3 today, unless, of course, the task is reprioritized.

You also need to set up some guidelines along with any agreed-upon priorities. One guideline could be to work on all urgent priorities before going on to the next level. Another should offer suggestions on how to handle conflicting priorities (it's best to do this before the actual conflicts arise). Still another should provide for setting aside set blocks of time every day or week to work on long-term projects. Ideally, work as much out on paper (or computer) as possible and then have your team meet and work out the final details.

You could use different colored preprinted Post-it Notes or Flags by 3M for different paperwork priorities. Color has a way of really jumping out, especially with some of the new, bright colors that are now available. Another alternative to keep track of multiple projects you delegate is to use one of the tickler systems described in Chapter 2.

The Team with a Temp

At some point in time you may have the opportunity to either select and/or work with a "temp." If the temp reports to you, these ideas may be particularly useful.

I've found most temps to be friendly and interested in doing a good job. For some, the temporary position is a foot in the door of a company and they end up being hired for full-time employment. For others, they enjoy the ability to do a good job and not get caught up in office politics. Often, it's a good mutual "test" to see if the chemistry is there for something more permanent.

Consequently, the attitude is usually open and receptive, which is a good place to start, because you'll need to do some important training. Here are some guidelines I recommend:

• Take all of these suggestions, and any others you think of, and write them down (preferably on computer so you can more easily make revisions) and keep your list in front of you as you go over each item. (Or at the very least, photocopy the items here in my book.)

• Give temps an overview of your position, your responsibilities and your priorities, as well as a tour of the office and any other key facilities. Introduce key people with whom they may interact frequently.

• Provide an overview of temp priorities and responsibilities.

• Since communications most likely will be a good part of temp responsibilities, go into some detail about your phone system, voice mail, e-mail, fax machine and copier; train on both the mechanics as well as the policies and procedures you follow. Emphasize attention to detail, e.g., correct phone numbers and spelling of names.

• Encourage open, two-way communication with you and indicate the best times and methods you like to communicate—ask temps if they have any preferences; encourage questions.

• Keep assignments or projects small in number and complexity, especially at first; be sure to detail all the necessary steps.

• Never assume anything and communicate that you don't assume anything and to please excuse you for going over anything that is rudimentary.

• Carefully evaluate delegated tasks in terms of training time required, how long the temp will be with you, a temp's skill level; in other words, is the return on investment of time and energy worth it to you for any given delegation?

• Communicate any things you don't want your temp to do.

• At the very least, have five- to 10-minute, daily morning meetings.

• Communicate clearly, concisely and positively.

• Observe newly-trained temps or assigned tasks and provide immediate feedback.

Training and Leading by Organizing

As an organized member of your work group, you have a special ability to lead, if you are excited about organization and can train others in this vital area. Another way to say it is, "As you organize, so shall you lead."

As an organized person, you're a doer but you can also be a leader if you master the art of delegation, which has an important training and coaching component. (Review Chapter 3 for a discussion of delegation.) When you're organized, *Positively Organized!*, you have a good view of both the macro and the micro—the big picture as well as the details. You can see more clearly what needs to be done, when and how.

Getting involved in training others requires you to look for and apply a variety of approaches, depending on the needs of the individuals involved. Look, too, for books, videos, cassettes, training classes and seminars and consultants to teach organizational skills and processes. In some cases, you can be the trainer yourself if you take various tasks and activities, write out the steps involved ahead of time and then teach those steps to someone else.

Review this chapter, as well as the rest of the book. Look for ways to improve how you and your coworkers can get things done. Sometimes it's the little things that can make a big difference. I suggest, for example, that a manager/assistant team take five to 10 minutes daily to meet and discuss the day's schedule, projects and priorities. Or use a well-designed work request form to help organize and prioritize work flow. Such a form should have a checklist section for routine work, the time frame or deadline for completion (see the work priority slip discussion earlier in this chapter) and a "special instructions" area for writing additional comments, requirements or notes.

If you're not in management, don't be afraid you won't have enough impact. An organized person with vision, creativity and drive can accomplish miracles. But don't do it alone. Look for other like-minded individuals who are open to change, quality improvement and innovation.

If you are in management, you have a special responsibility to influence and inspire others. That does not mean, however, having others do it your way. It means facilitating change, teamwork and an exchange of ideas and information.

The Bigger Picture

See if you're working for an organization that shares your values. Look how people are treated where you work, throughout the organization. Is there an attitude of caring?

See what the prevailing attitude is concerning social responsibility, too. Perhaps your organization is a member of Business for Social Responsibility (BSR). Founded in 1992, BSR helps member companies of all sizes be commercially successful in ways that demonstrate respect for ethical values, people, communities and the environment. BSR can be reached at 415/537-0888 (CA) or **www.bsr.org**.

Responsible Recycling

One easy way to gauge your organization's attitude toward social responsibility is to see what recycling programs are in place.

Implementing a recycling program where you work is a way to demonstrate caring beyond your organization to your community, country and indeed, the world. It involves everyone, is an "easy sell" because of all the publicity on recycling, offers financial rewards for companies and makes people feel good about participating. It's a real "win-win" kind of operation, where the benefits are plainly visible.

The following are sample actions to take and products to use in your recycling program (see how many you're already doing or using):

• Whenever possible, avoid disposable cups, plates, utensils; Americans supposedly toss out enough of this stuff to circle the equator 300 times. (Once would be too much.) Let's go back to using ceramic mugs.

• Whenever possible, try to buy and use **recycled** and **recyclable** products. Recycled products contain a certain percentage of used materials (for example, recycled office paper has to have at least 50 percent recovered material). Recyclable means the product has the potential to be recycled.

• Cut the copier and printer habit, whenever possible, or if you must do so, try to copy or print on both sides and use scratch paper for drafts; if each copier in the U.S. used five fewer copies every business day, we could save up to 17.5 million reams of paper, which would save lots of trees and landfill space. (Check with your copier and printer manufacturers to see if it's safe to use recycled paper in your machines.)

• Form a recycling committee and designate a coordinator in your office, department or better yet, company.

• Design a recycling program that: identifies which materials will be recycled and which recycled materials will be purchased; provides a collection and storage system; offers ways to deal with confidential material; and develops an employee education and suggestion program.

• Consider using a nonprofit organization to help you with your recycling program. Datco, a division of the Autistic Treatment Center, received the Environmental Vision Award from the city of Dallas for its model program.

• Consider recycling these materials: aluminum cans, glass containers, paper (computer paper is the most valuable), envelopes and cardboard.

• Try to reuse items such as file folders and boxes.

• Use paper clips instead of staples. Paper clips can be reused and staples may interfere with paper recycling.

• Use paper shredders not only for controlling access to sensitive material but also to help you in your recycling program. Shredded paper makes great packing material or you can sell shredded paper directly to recycling houses.

• Use specially marked recycling containers.

Resource Guide
Reading And Reference

American Productivity & Quality Center is a nonprofit organization that works with business, labor, government and academia to improve productivity, quality and quality of work life. It issues a variety of publications, conducts courses and conferences and offers research, reference and individualized services. 800/776-9676 (TX) or **www.apqc.org**

Conquering Chaos at Work: Strategies for Managing Disorganization and the People Who Cause It by Harriet Schechter (Fireside, 2000). This wonderful book offers help, hope and humor for people in all different work places.

50 Simple Things Your Business Can Do to Save the Earth by Earthworks Group. Like its predecessor bestseller, this book includes some great, easy-to-apply reusing and recycling ideas with some convincing rationales for doing so.

The HUMOResources catalog is filled with books, videos, audiotapes, games, software and other items dealing with humor and creativity in the work place (as well as in your personal life). The Humor Project, Inc., 800/225-0300 (NY) or **www.humorproject.com**.

Out of the Crisis by W. Edwards Deming (MIT Center for Advanced Engineering Study, 1986). This is Deming's famous textbook on quality.

Quality is Free (Mentor Books, 1992) and **Quality Without Tears** (McGraw-Hill, 1995) by Philip Crosby. These books by quality guru Crosby are important resources for your quality library.

Quality Press is the publishing arm of the American Society for Quality Control and has a complete catalog of their publications as well as those by other publishers, all dealing with quality principles and processes. 800/952-6587.

The Training Store is a catalog for trainers and other human resource professionals. It features resources such as full training programs, books, videos, slides and accessories—all under $500 and most under $100. 800/222-9909 (PA) or **www.trcinteractive.com**

Trash to Cash: How Businesses Can Save Money and Increase Profits by Fran Berman (1996) is an implementation guide to an effective ongoing corporate paper recycling and waste reduction program.

Special Products for Special Needs

Abledata is an ADA (Americans with Disabilities Act) database of assistive devices. **800/227-0216**

Goodwill Industries contract services divisions recruit and train disabled or economically disadvantaged people, providing them with job skills and experience while also helping local business owners. Contact your local Goodwill office.

Job Accommodation Network is a free ADA consulting service for employers and disabled employees. **800/526-7234**

Office Systems for the Visually or Physically Impaired is a resource of technology resellers and consultants. **800/253-4391**

11

USING COMPUTERS AND TECHNOLOGY TO IMPROVE COMMUNICATIONS AND QUALITY

Quick Scan: Read this chapter if you want to tackle information/technology overload especially e-mail, voice mail and faxes. Discover also some workgroup computing solutions in order to better integrate your communications and to improve: a) your effectiveness working with other people and b) ultimately, your products or services. You'll find specific computer and technology tips and tools throughout the chapter as well as in the chapter resource guide.

Technology is here to stay. The trick today is to make the most of it and to control the barrage of information that is undoubtedly coming your way.

A Pitney Bowes study revealed that the average worker receives 201 messages a day, which includes e-mails, faxes, conventional and cell phone calls, voice mail and letters. How many on average do you receive daily? You know technology has taken over your life when your business card: a) has no white space, b) lists numbers for phone, fax, cell phone and pager, c) has at least two e-mail addresses, d) has a Web site and e) spreads across the front and back of your card.

Along with all this technology comes a sense of urgency and a expectancy of working quickly. We have instant communications that are leaving many people breathless. One *Wall Street Journal* story was entitled "Pushing the Pace: The Latest Big Thing at Many Companies is Speed, Speed, Speed" and another story outlined the "multitasking" occupational hazards that Type A personalities develop in using technology—they're using several different communication tools at the same time. As a consultant, I'm terribly concerned about these aspects of technology that are producing a pressure-cooker workplace. That's why it's so important to select technological tools carefully and conservatively and to identify and use specific guidelines and habits that spell out how and when to use these tools.

Control Your E-mail

Chances are you're having a love-hate relationship with your e-mail.

I attribute the popularity of e-mail (trillions of messages are sent every year) to several factors. First, it's easy to use. Second, it's an effective communication tool that can be quicker and/or clearer than other methods. Third, it's versatile and flexible—you can send a message to one or more individuals, with or without a document attached; you can do it whether you're in the office or on the road; you can easily reply to a message; and you can often confirm that a recipient actually read your message. Fourth, it's usually less expensive to use e-mail to communicate with people in other time zones (if you use an online service, it will cost you a local call). Fifth, there is greater connectivity now than ever before between e-mail users of all types—those on corporate networks, commercial online services and the Internet.

E-mail has also become the foundation for all kinds of workgroup computing products—document sharing, group scheduling, electronic-forms routing, workflow automation and discussion databases to name a few. E-mail is central to how many of us now work and communicate.

How to Deal with the Downside of E-mail

Unfortunately, all is not rosy with e-mail. Everyone's EPD (e-mails per day) is growing exponentially out of hand. Some people are now receiving in excess of 200 EPD. That's message overload.

Microsoft found that the average Outlook e-mail software user had accumulated 1,900 messages in the Inbox and Outbox folders that hadn't been deleted. That's message overload.

E-mails convey a false sense of urgency simply due to the instantaneous nature of the medium (and also the fact that the sender often knows whether or not you've read the message).

Sometimes e-mails replace other slower communication channels. But often, e-mails add an additional layer; some people will send an e-mail, for example, and then send a voice-mail message indicating they've sent an e-mail message!

Some people have been known to abuse this communication tool by sending downright nasty messages or by clogging up mailboxes with junk e-mail.

Security and privacy, too, are issues that have to be addressed.

E-mail messages can accumulate very quickly and wind up taking up too much space on computers or backup tapes if they aren't properly cleaned out.

Finally, e-mail can be too impersonal, removing the human connection and sense of relationship so important for work teams.

E-mail Management and Organization Tips

Fortunately, there are solutions that can help.

Establish and publicize **e-mail policies** in your company or at least in your immediate workgroup. One policy should strongly advise that everyone exercise the same restraint that they would show when writing memos or letters. The policy should further remind them that anything they put in writing, even on computer, could have legal ramifications and even be used against them in a court of law. I read a newspaper story about "electronic data detectives" who now make their living searching for incriminating e-mail messages on computers and backup media.

Another policy should require **resisting the urge to copy or forward** ad nauseam. The copying craze has to stop. Decide whether recipients will really need or want the information.

Limit distribution lists. If you work for a large organization, post announcements instead in a central-access area on an intranet, for example, or create your own workgroup-specific Web site.

To save computer and storage facilities space, another policy should **limit the number of e-mail messages that can be saved** and for how long. Such a policy could well relate to your organization's overall records and document retention policies.

A third policy should warn employees to **exercise caution** before forwarding any message internally or externally, especially if it contains confidential or sensitive material.

Let's face it—e-mail is not as secure nor as private as other communication methods. Perhaps you need two addresses, one public and the other a private, more restricted address. And it's a good idea to reemphasize your e-mail policies at frequent intervals; it's very easy to fall into a false sense of privacy and end up writing "personal" notes and politically sensitive messages.

Encryption, though, may be the best solution. PGP Personal Privacy (PGP stands for "Pretty Good Privacy") is a popular and trusted software program (also available as freeware) that protects the privacy of your files and e-mail messages. Powerful encryption ensures that only your intended receiver can decipher your message. An encryption program is ideal for anyone with proprietary or sensitive data. PGP is available through Network Associates, 800/338-8754 (AZ) or **www.nai.com**. Another option is HushMail (**www.hushmail.com**), a free, Web-based encryption system that lets you encrypt messages from almost any Web-capable PC, even if it's in an Internet cafe around the world. Two other popular programs are Encryption Plus for Folders by PC Guardian (800/288-8126 or **www.pcguardian.com**) and the award-winning InvisiMail Deluxe by InvisiMail International (**www.invisimail.com**).

The **electronic** or **digital signature** is another valuable security tool. It tells the recipient who "signed" the document with certainty and guarantees that nothing was changed. The electronic signature is a typical feature of encryption programs.

Passwords limit access by others to your e-mail, computer or online service. Security experts suggest your chosen password should contain at least eight characters but not many more in order to prevent typing errors. Don't share your password with anyone and change it every two months. It should be a phrase, not a single word, and shouldn't be related to your name, birth date or anything personal.

A good password contains letters (in upper and lower case), numbers and symbols. It's recommended you use a different one for each of your activities that requires a password but I personally think that's too much of an organizational challenge. Here are some examples that were included in a *Wall Street Journal* story: 2b/orNOT2b% and Alfred!E!Newman7. Store your password(s) in a secret hiding place in your house or office—just make sure the hiding place isn't so secretive that you forget where it is! A simple "low-tech" solution is on a card in your rotary card file (obviously one not called "Passwords")! For a high-tech solution consider a freeware utility called PassKeeper (**www.passkeeper.com**) or an Internet security suite as discussed in Chapter 13.

If you receive an onslaught of messages (you think you have it bad—people in public office can get tens of thousands a week!), you will probably want to install special **e-mail software** to help you manage them. A good program will have a **text editor** that works much like your word processor. Most importantly, the program should be **rules-based**. A **rules** feature lets you set up all kinds of operational parameters that can be real timesavers. It can guide you in setting up **filters** to accept or block messages from certain people or on certain topics. Filters are crucial for preventing information overload. They can alert you to e-mails marked "urgent" as well as those from key individuals, such as your boss, and can literally sound an alarm. Filters can highlight mail you want to read by sending them to a special high-priority folder. You can also use filters to scan for spam (junk e-mail), which your program will then delete.

A rules-based program can also help you with electronic filing. Your system could automatically archive messages that are older than a certain designated date or file different types of messages into separate folders. A rules-based program can help you better prioritize your messages and deal with the most important ones in a timely manner.

More E-mail Organizing Tips

In many ways, organizing your e-mail is much like organizing your paperwork.

Just like in the paper world, it's a good idea to **empty your e-mail in-box**. Easier said than done, of course! Begin by **scanning subject lines, message headers and sender names** (or set up a filter to do this). Then **prioritize** and respond to your most important and urgent messages.

Then go to those important but not urgent messages. See how many you can reply to or delegate quickly and if possible, delete them.

Take time every day to delete as many messages as possible or to file them in an appropriate folder. **Create an "E-mail Message Management System"** with electronic folders for storing and organizing messages (just as you created a "Daily Paperwork System" with paper folders for your everyday mail and paperwork described in Chapter 4). Your e-mail program may come with several generic folders and also let you create your own. (If you have no folders, then cut and paste your messages into word processing files.) Remember to work the system at least once a day and be sure to regularly clean out old messages.

Check your e-mail at set times during the day, not constantly. It's better to use set blocks of time or appointments with yourself, if possible, throughout the day. You will be more in charge of your day and control interruptions better. You will also be training coworkers and other recipients not to expect an immediate response. If you respond immediately to every e-mail, you'll find your e-mail load will increase even more.

Set up a clearly-defined message priority system with coworkers. When you use priority terms on your messages, such as "Urgent," "Regular" or "Special Attention," make sure you and your e-mail correspondents have determined in advance what these terms mean. Another option is to include a deadline date or response needed date. (See the "Response Needed" priority system described later in the "Max Your Fax" section or the work priority system described in Chapter 10.)

Postpone opening messages with attachments, unless they're from a key person. They can really eat up your time and you may also want to download them separately. Always scan them for viruses.

Use color coding for e-mail messages, if possible, particularly if you're lucky enough to have someone else screen your e-mail. One company uses "red" for urgent, "yellow" for moderate urgency and "green" for information only. By the way, 3M now has a software program called Post-it Software Notes that allows you to send colored electronic sticky notes (3M Corp., 800/328-6276 [MN] or **www.3M.com/psnotes**).

Know when to use it over another communication method. The phone may be faster, but that's assuming the person on the other end is there or regularly picks up their messages.

If possible, send e-mail messages to those who prefer this method and if you have time to wait for delivery of your message and a response.

Research also indicates that e-mail is particularly well suited for long-term projects that don't need to be rushed. Studies indicate although e-mail can be less personal and more task-oriented, it forces a better use of language and often clearer communication. Writing anything (including e-mail messages) tends to require more thoughtful reflection than say, a phone conversation.

Beware, however, of using it inappropriately as a way to avoid face-to-face dealings with workers. Don't, for example, send performance reviews and other sensitive documents by e-mail as some managers have done.

Use it to streamline your telephone messaging system. One attorney replaced telephone message slips with e-mail telephone messages in his law firm to transcribe live and voice mail messages onto an e-mail template that resembles a "While You Were Out" slip. (Many e-mail packages have such a template built in.) The big advantage is that such a system lets you sort and search messages in a variety of ways. And of course with integrated messaging/wireless communications we're seeing how voice-mail messages are sent as text e-mail messages.

Study your e-mail software. Discover the shortcuts that are built in and design ways to customize the software for you and/or your workgroup(s).

Don't give out your e-mail address to everyone. I know of a city mayor who refused to give out her address to anyone. Some experts recommend not to put it on your business card but instead to give it out selectively. In view of today's e-mail overload, that may be a good idea in theory but I don't think most people can or should do follow that approach.

Limit the number of mailboxes. If possible use just one or two. Some people have one for work and another for personal or you could have a public one for posting to newsgroups, for example, and then another one for private e-mail.

E-mail Writing Tips

You'll notice that many of the following tips also apply to business writing in general. E-mail is doing much, in fact, to revive the art of writing as well as develop clearer thinking and decision-making—all important professional and personal skills.

1. **Determine the recipient(s) of your message in advance.** Decide who really needs the message. Knowing your audience will help you better frame the message.

2. **Be very careful what you write**—Any number of others could see it, without your even knowing it. See if your e-mail program has an "Unsend" feature, too.

3. **Write a subject line that gets noticed**. It's useful to build in some kind of action and/or deadline that's required. For regular correspondents, consider also using all capitalized code words, acronyms or other abbreviations followed by a colon in subject lines that reference a project, client or subject immediately.

4. **Include the most important information right up front.**

5. **Use subheads, numbers and bullets** to break up long messages and to guide your reader through your message.

6. **Be careful about conveying negative information through e-mail**.

7. **Limit the use of capital letters**. Besides being difficult to read, overuse of caps is the equivalent of screaming at someone. Don't scream online.

8. **Check the tone and emotional content** of your messages. Avoid jokes and sarcasm unless you've clearly indicated you're joking. It may be fine to use **"emoticons,"** the use of standard keyboard symbols as graphics to indicate emotion, but I'm not sure how universal they are and whether they will be understood. (Here are two common emoticons: :) stands for a happy face and <g> signifies a grin.) If you include emoticons, do so only in more personal and informal messages.

9. **Avoid sending long messages** unless you've cleared it in advance with the recipient(s). Remote users will be particularly appreciative.

10. **Read carefully**. This goes for rereading a message you're about to send as well as reading messages you've received in their entirety.

11. **When responding to a message, clearly refer to the original message you received**, if it's not included in the reply. If it is included, be sure to use one or more greater than signs, >, before copy that the correspondent sent to you, which means "this is what you wrote." (This may be done automatically for you

when you highlight text and press "Reply.") Include only those parts to which you are responding. Less than signs before text mean "I write."

12. **Use automatic responses** if you're going to be out of town and not checking your e-mail. Electronic versions of the form letter, "autoreply" or "autoresponse" mechanisms are also good for replying automatically to common or repetitive types of messages, questions or subjects.

13. **Use a signature file** (or "sig") at the end of your message that includes your name, title, phone number and possibly your address. Limit it to no more than four or five lines. To make mine friendlier, I generally sign my messages with my first name, which I underline with the equal sign, and then I insert my sig. Omit the sig for very informal messages or for people you know well.

14. **Delete extraneous information such as cluster addresses (distribution lists)** whenever possible when you send either an original message or you forward one. Not only will it protect the privacy of those other recipients, it may prevent spammers from harvesting those addresses from your post. It also removes the need to scroll past them all to get to the message. And it's more professional as well as personal; no one likes to be on everyone's list. On the other hand, you may have certain "group lists" where you want everyone to know that they were each informed of an event, an announcement, etc.

15. **Be brief**. Learn to write brief, concise messages in short paragraphs (with no more than three sentences) that put your main points right up front so that they show up on the screen before scrolling. You may find your correspondents will copy your style. Write short paragraphs in block style that are separated with an extra blank line.

• Use bullets to list key ideas without long, wordy sentences.
• Use white space.
• Use boldface and color sparingly for highlighting key points.
• Otherwise avoid graphics, which may take too long to load.

16. **Request any action** (or indicate FYI for nonaction) that you need from the recipient. If the action item is important, try to include it up front in the subject line.

17. **Warm up e-mail by using the recipient's name** at least once. E-mail can be too cold, impersonal and autocratic otherwise.

18. **Know when to use "reply" versus "reply to all"**. You don't want to accidentally broadcast a reply that was meant for only one recipient.

19. **Avoid sending large files** that are part of the e-mail message; if you must do so, send it as an attachment.

20. **Use the appropriate tone and style for the appropriate audience.**

21. **Indicate if a message should be restricted**. Since it's all too easy these days to copy and forward messages, be sure to indicate any restrictions, confidentiality or limited access.

22. **Follow the style guide** of your organization if one exists.

23. If you need a **confirmation of receipt**, try adding the following in all caps: *** PLEASE REPLY TO THIS E-MAIL TO CONFIRM RECEIPT ***.

Instant Messaging

A more immediate, spontaneous, personal extension of e-mail, instant messaging (IM) helps to reach out and connect people. Computer columnist Lawrence Magid wrote that IM is to e-mail what e-mail is to formal letter writing.

Instant messaging lets you set up a special "buddy" or contact list that can give you and them immediate access to one another. The software indicates whether a contact is online and if so, you can then send the contact a message, which pops up on their screen in a little box right in the middle of whatever they're doing.

IM is "interrupt driven" and is analogous to someone knowing that you're at home and barging in unannounced saying "I'm here," regardless of what you're doing at the moment, asking for some of your time. It's a virtual barging into your office or cubicle.

With more and more computers connected to the Internet all the time via cable modem or DSL, IM can make you all too available.

As with all other time management interruptions (see Chapter 3), you need to have some ready responses to take control of IM as well as practice some considerate "netiquette" of your own.

Start by asking (as you should do on a phone call) whether the person is available. You could start your message by asking "Busy?" or "Got a minute?" If your buddy doesn't have time to chat, it easily lets them off the hook. And if you don't have time to chat, let your buddy know that as well. Have short reasons ready: "Sorry, on the phone" or "On a big deadline...later." When you're ready to sign off, a simple "Bye" or "Gotta go" can do the trick.

Remember that anything you write, as with all e-mail, can be saved and/or printed and leaves a cyber paper trail, so exercise caution, good judgment and restraint.

Some IM programs also have blocking features to prevent selected (or all) individuals from knowing you're online or sending you messages. You just may want to use this feature more often than not.

Just because you *can* use IM, doesn't mean you *should*. I recommend restrictive use of this channel of communication for individuals.

There's also some security concern should you be using a public IM system. An internal system could be more secure.

It's also possible to have private group IM chats. Ding from Antiverse is one such program that provides this option (**www.antiverse.com**). Ding also supports individual IM and ties into your screen saver so if there's been no activity, it will show a message that you aren't available. PowWow is an award-winning IM program that also supports collaborative, real time communication. It's available from Tribal Voice, 877/476-9969 or **www.tribal.com**.

For collaborative work or for customer support (which has its own category of real-time software) IM can be a great channel of communication.

Value Voice Mail and Telephone Time

Telecommunications are important to the bottom line. Poor telephone contact, live or voice mail, can affect customer retention. A Rockefeller Institute study found that of the eight to 15 percent of a company's annual client loss, 68 percent was due to poor telephone treatment.

Be sure your company, organization or workgroup has written telecommunications policies with regard to how calls are picked up (when and by whom/ what) as well as when they are returned. Periodically evaluate your entire phone system—the tools, the technology and the personal telephone habits you're using.

Voice mail has become a valuable, timesaving telecommunications tool. Its many advantages include: reducing telephone tag (but don't fall into "voice mail tag"!); screening calls during critical work projects; not having to return a call if a caller's message is complete enough and/or requires no response; receiving private, usually more accurate messages; and accessing messages at your convenience.

Yet, if you value voice mail itself over the needs of your customers, you can quickly lose the advantages this automated system has to offer. (For the purposes of this section, the term "voice mail" includes multi-user, computer-driven, menu answering systems—called "interactive voice response" or IVR—and also the automated answering systems found in stand-alone answering machines.)

The trick is learning how to make it serve your external as well as your internal customers. I encourage you to evaluate your system and follow the following guidelines:

1. Focus first on serving your external customer. Determine if all the options and directions of your voice mail maze encourage or discourage contact. Regularly check out the system yourself (or better yet, ask a friend who hasn't used your

system) for any bugs and survey your customers' reactions.

2. Always give your caller the option to speak to a real live person. (But make sure that the referral's voice mail isn't on, though!) Not having this live person option is sometimes called "voice mail jail." (How many times have you been transferred to someone who supposedly can solve your problem but you're connected to their voice mail and you have no idea what that person does and whether you'll ever get a return call?)

3. Limit, if possible, the number of options to no more than three. Too many choices can be confusing and impersonal. Design your "automated attendant" or "electronic menuing" feature to keep the menu simple and avoid layers of menus and choices.

4. Ideally, have a well-trained receptionist handle your company's main phone number. So few companies do anymore that you'll really stand out. (I almost always tell such receptionists how nice it is to speak with a real person and I'm often told they've heard that from other people as well.)

5. Your outgoing message should be short and inviting. Avoid generic, nonspecific messages, if possible, and give the caller specific information about your availability and other options for more immediate assistance. Give your name, job title, department, division or any pertinent information. You may also want to provide your e-mail address.

6. Be sure to tell the caller how long they have to speak. If you get many voice mails a day, **give callers a short time limit on messages they leave**. Let them know what the time limit is—for example, 30 or 60 seconds.

7. On your outgoing message always ask callers to leave the best time(s) to call them back (and to indicate their time zone) to prevent telephone tag. Assure callers that their call is important and will be handled in a timely fashion.

8. Make sure your system has an electronic telephone directory so that callers can easily get a person's extension number, even after business hours.

9. Since your system should let callers speed up or bypass an outgoing message, provide the extension number or correct code to move quickly through the system. It's great, too, if you include the option of dialing "O" for a real-life operator—or at least provide some other option of speaking with a person. I like systems that, after a few minutes, will give the caller an option of remaining on hold or leaving a message.

10. Keep your outgoing message current. It doesn't look professional to have an out-of-date message indicating for example, the dates you'll be out of town and you've been back for a week already. You may want to make a reminder in your

planner, PDA or other time management tool to change it.

11. If your system asks for information from a caller, such as an ID number, and then transfers the caller to an agent, make sure the agent doesn't ask for the same information again. Avoid such time-wasting aggravation by using "computer telephony integration" technology.

12. Periodically offer short training sessions on your telephone/voice mail system. Rarely does anyone ever read the manual and people generally need more than an initial orientation. It's time well spent to continue learning about some of the timesaving features your system just may have. Since you may have some turnover, there will probably be some new people who are depending most likely on other employees who received a brief introduction and never read the manual!

More Timesaving Voice Mail Tips

Check your voice mail at least three times a day because any less than that and you may have repeat messages from the same person either on voice mail, e-mail or another channel.

When reaching a voice mail system, try to **skip the outgoing message** by pressing either the * (star), # (pound) or 0 (operator) buttons. (Be aware, however, that some systems will disconnect you when pressing one of these buttons.)

When making a call to someone else's voice mail, **indicate how (or even if) as well as when you'd like the person to communicate back with you and the level of urgency**. Perhaps you prefer e-mail; if so, leave your e-mail address. If you're asking for a favor or you're calling someone you don't know well, **give the person a choice** of how they want to contact you. I usually leave both my phone number and e-mail address and occasionally a fax number as well.

If you don't want to reach someone in person by phone, call late at night, early in morning or at lunch time. (Make sure you're not calling a home number, though.)

When calling someone else's voice mail system, be sure to leave your name and number and a brief message that indicates the purpose of your call and any action you may need from the person you're calling and when you'll need it. You may even want to leave your phone number twice—once at the beginning and once at the end of your message. Let them know the best times to reach you. Also speak slowly and distinctly, especially when giving your name and number. Be complete and concise, yet friendly, with good, appreciative etiquette, and somehow convey what's in it for them to return your call (recognize that only one in four calls are indeed returned). Always write down an individual's extension or direct dial number for future reference so you can bypass the company-wide system.

Six Annoying Telecommunications Problems and What to Do About Them

Here are six challenging problems, along with some solutions:

1. Being put on hold for too long. **Solutions:** Get a telephone headset or use your speaker phone and do what my husband does—accumulate things to do when you're left on hold; but be sure they're quiet things if you use a speaker phone. If you've been on hold for at least 10 minutes, fax or write a note on your letterhead to the head of the organization and write simply, "I've been on hold for 10 minutes today and thought you'd like to know. I'm a current, prospective, former, customer of yours." (Use the appropriate words.)

2. I'd like a dime every time someone has a dialed a fax number instead of a phone number off of a business card or a piece of letterhead. **Solution:** Put your phone number in boldface type. (For someone else's card or letterhead, use a highlighter pen to make the phone number stand out).

3. With increasing telecommunications come new phone numbers and proliferating area codes. Major cities now often have several area codes and if you don't know a city well, it may be hard to get a correct phone number. **Solutions:** Ask your information operator to "go full book." Here's a habit to cultivate for frequent nationwide calling: give your city or state when you leave a message, and when you receive a message, jot that person's information down next to the phone number so you can return a call appropriately for a given time zone.

4. Someone's automatic fax machine keeps calling your phone line. **Solution:** When the fax call beeps on the line, dial any seven-digit number once or twice and hopefully the tones generated will signal the fax that it has reached a wrong number and cancel the redial function.

5. If you switch long distance telephone carriers, your current plan will not be automatically cancelled. **Solution:** Find out what you have to do to cancel an existing program.

6. You have call waiting but you want to temporarily disable it because you're about to make an important call or you're making a call with your modem (call waiting's beep can disrupt a modem transmission). **Solution**: Call your local phone company to see if they offer a call waiting disabling service, for which you will probably have to pay extra. You then enter a code, such as *71 or *70 to disable call waiting prior to a call. It's possible to add the code to your modem setup screen. Call waiting is reactivated when the call is complete.

How to Max Your Fax

It's amazing how in a very short period of time the facsimile (fax) machine has become almost as indispensable as the copy machine. In some offices, however, the fax machine (like the copy machine) is used too much; we don't just max the fax, we overtax it.

We have more than 25 million fax machines. And we've come a long way from the fax machines back in 1960, which weighed in at 60 pounds and transmitted only 10 pages per hour and you needed one machine to send transmissions and another one to receive them.

By the way, when you're shopping for fax machines and comparing speeds between them, you'll want to ask about and compare the "transmission" time.

But today, we're seeing other ways to send and receive faxes besides using the fax machine.

Many of us rely not only on fax machines but also on personal computers, **fax software** and **fax modems** (also called "fax boards" if they're internal modems) in order to fax electronic documents from one computer to another (or to a fax machine). This is a more efficient way to go if you primarily fax documents created on computer or receive electronic documents. It also saves paper and lets the receiving party use the information more readily (since it can be saved as a file on disk and used without rekeying in the information). Software and a modem may also cost less than a stand-alone fax machine. (Most modems sold today have built-in fax capabilities; even a nonfax modem, called a data modem, could let you send a fax using an Internet fax service or one of the commercial online services.)

Computer-based fax software helps you store, organize, retrieve, archive, recycle and keyword-search your faxes, as well as design custom cover pages. There are two types: 1) **desktop** stand-alone software for faxing from your computer and 2) **network**, which functions as a **fax server** that allows other computers called **clients** to share its resources such as fax boards and phone lines. The king of fax software is WinFax PRO by Symantec (800/441-7234 or **www.symantec.com**), which now lets you send faxes as e-mail attachments (for both editable text and electronically generated or scanned images).

Be on the lookout, too, for the HP Digital Sender, which is a fax machine for sending hard copy as e-mail attachments. By scanning pages and converting them into PDF or TIFF files, it converts a stack of paper into e-mails. (Contact Hewlett-Packard Co., 877/373-6337 or **www.digitalsender.hp.com**.)

You can also receive faxes as e-mail through a free, **Internet fax service**, which sends them directly to your e-mail account (where you can later move them to a folder). An Internet fax service is great for picking up faxes on the road. Two Internet services to check out are: EFax.com (**www.efax.com**) and CallWave (**www.callwave.com**). At the time of this writing, you can't send a fax using these two services; you'll need to use a fax machine or fax software. Also beware of the download time and space needed to receive long faxes.

If you get a lot of faxes, a fee-based service such as JFax (**www.jfax.com**) may be the way to go. JFax lets you send faxes, too. (See also what JFax can do in terms of Unified Messaging, discussed in the next section.)

If your main emphasis is on sending (rather than receiving) faxes over the Internet consider solutions from these three companies: 1) CyNet (800/964-2963, **www.cynet-fax.com**), 2) Intergram International (800/595-8977, **www.intergram.com**) and 3) ProtoNet (800/551-0636 or **www.protonet.com**).

Another option is using your PDA to both send and receive faxes. Check out Mobile WinFax from Symantec (800/441-7234 or **www.mobilewinfax.com**).

There are several advantages to using these electronic fax options. They are private and travel-friendly. They also may eliminate the need for a fax machine and a dedicated fax line. They provide better quality. They're paperless and allow for easy storage and manipulation of the data. They save time because you don't have to monitor a fax machine with its delays and jams.

Every office needs to develop suggested guidelines or a policy regarding fax use. Here are several recommended for fax machines and computer-based faxing that may apply to your office:

1. As a general rule, I advise not having your fax machine number printed on your business card or in a phone directory or newspaper unless the fax is specifically designated for a purpose, such as taking orders, or unless you prefer receiving faxes to another mode of communication such as phone calls. Putting a fax number on a card makes it too easy for others to send you unsolicited, unwanted faxes. Also it may encourage others to overtax your fax. If you do need to include your fax number on your business card or letterhead, make the phone number larger or in bold face to differentiate it from your fax number (unless you do prefer to emphasize the fax number).

2. To fax or not to fax—make fax decisions based on urgency, length of the document and the preference of the receiver, not simply because it's easier and more convenient for you to fax than mail. Faxes don't get attention; they often just get lost.

3. Machine faxing may seem very convenient but consider these downsides: a) if a fax machine is being overused, it could take many attempts and some monitoring time to get your fax through and b) if you've ever experienced difficulty with

your "automatic" document feeder in which papers don't feed correctly, it can be very labor intensive to have to feed a long document one page at a time.

4. Limit the number of pages to be faxed—before they're faxed to you. Find out how many pages will be coming. You may decide on another method. As a courtesy to someone you fax, let them know how many pages you'll be faxing and see if that is acceptable.

5. Number pages to be faxed and have the cover sheet indicate the total number of pages being faxed.

6. Don't send unsolicited faxes. I broke my own rule when contacting the manufacturers for the last edition of this book and let me tell you, it doesn't work! Call and get permission first. It will confirm that the recipient is indeed the right person and alert them in advance.

7. Make sure your fax machine has enough memory to store faxes in case your machine runs out of paper, and check the paper supply often, especially if you receive many incoming faxes. In fact, make sure your fax is automatic enough for your business—besides memory, it should have such features as an automatic document feeder, an automatic document cutter, delayed transmission (to take advantage of lower phone rates), on-hook dialing, automatic dialing and activity report (a printout of the date, time and phone number of each fax that's sent and received). This reporting feature may also be useful if you only receive part of a fax and want the fax number of the sender to let them know you only received a partial fax.

Here's one caveat about using the delayed transmission feature: try to avoid unattended faxes because if you fax a phone number by mistake and it reaches a telephone answering machine, it could rack up a hefty phone bill by redialing over and over again the phone (not the fax) number.

8. Get a fax modem for your personal computer if you: receive and send mostly electronic computer documents, prefer getting confidential fax messages, want the option to print them out and want to automate the process of sending multiple faxes.

9. When designing your own fax transmission forms, include a section called "Method/Urgency of Delivery," that has four boxes: one for "Urgent...Notify Recipient as Soon as Possible"; one for "Confidential"; one for "Regular Mail Delivery"; and another marked "Other" (Specify). You may also want to include a section called "Response Needed" with these four options: 1) Urgently, by the close of business day, 2) Tomorrow will be OK, 3) Please respond within 3 days and 4) Prefer response on or by [this date]. Also include: the sender's name and telephone and fax numbers; the company name and address; date and time sent;

recipient's name, company and fax number; number of pages, including the cover sheet; subject or "RE:" section; a "Special Instructions" section that lists options to check, e.g., "Please reply," "For Your Information" and "As You Requested"; and space for a "Message" section for a handwritten or typed message.

10. To save time and money, use Post-it Fax Notes, which measure 1½ by 4 inches and attach to a corner of the original document to be transmitted. Eliminating a separate transmittal cover sheet saves paper costs as well as telephone transmission charges and saves time preparing a cover sheet.

11. Here's another simple solution to use when a document doesn't need a cover sheet: type or print "Sent via fax" on the document along with the page number on each page, e.g., Page 1 of 2 and Page 2 of 2. Make sure your phone and fax numbers on your letterhead will fax legibly; better yet, be sure to include them clearly on the first page.

12. For plain paper fax machines, put light yellow paper in the receiving tray of your fax to alert recipients to faxes that have come in and use it for incoming faxes only. This is a good way to separate faxes, which may be more urgent, from other papers. Avoid other colors, especially pink or darker shades that aren't good if you'll need to photocopy any faxes; these colors will produce a muddied, gray shadow on copies. A light blue or green could also work; test it out on your photocopier first.

13. If a fax is confidential and you need to send it via a fax machine, call right before faxing so the recipient can pick it up right away.

14. Double check any fax number you key into a fax machine or your computer; if you make an error, it's unlikely the incorrect recipient will bother to call you.

15. If you delegate your faxing, use a fax request slip that says, "Please send this fax within the next _ hour(s) or the next __ minutes." It's easy to write in the correct number.

Unified Messaging

Despite (or maybe because of) the complexity of today's communications, the trend is to simplify and consolidate whenever possible. We're seeing more and more of this in what is called **unified messaging**, a solution in the form of a service that consolidates your voice mail, e-mail and faxes in one mailbox, which functions as one **universal in-box**.

For $10 to $20 per month, a unified messaging service gives you one phone number to call to retrieve voice, fax and e-mail messages using voice recognition technology and also gives you your own home page to actually look at e-mails and faxes and perform other communication functions. The real plus is being able to retrieve messages. You can listen to voice mail, e-mail and faxes from any phone and reply to them. If you have a PC with Internet access, you can read e-mail and faxes and listen to voice mail—all located on one Web page.

JFax.com Unified Messaging is a veteran in this new field (888/438-5329 [CA] or **www.jfax.com**). Consider also Webley from Webley Systems Inc. (888/444-6400 [IL] or **www.webley.com**) and Portico from General Magic (800/767-8426 [CA] or **www.generalmagic.com**). All of these services charge; there are free services but they aren't quite up to speed yet, as of this writing.

Collaborative Computing

One of the hottest trends today is the push to use computer technology, especially the Internet, to improve how people work together, communicate, share information and build teamwork in some new and exciting ways. Products and services are changing the amount as well as the flow of information. With information no longer in the hands of a few individuals and with the trend toward nonhierarchical, cross-functional teams, which break down barriers between departments, companies and organizations, we're seeing new teamwork possibilities where people can come together online to solve problems and create new business opportunities. Options abound for working collaboratively.

Many smaller organizations (as well as large) are opting for the collaborative features of **Web-based teamware services**, which include three core functions: 1) simple project management through shared calendars, schedules and task tracking; 2) idea management through threaded discussion groups/forums and real-time communications; and 3) document sharing, storage and management that includes routing and "versioning."

Web-based teamware is especially good for project or work teams that are scattered in different locations. Teamware helps people communicate, collaborate and save time and money, too. You can outsource teamware services through an **application service provider**, for less than $20 per user, per month. HotOffice Technologies has received notable acclaim (888/446-8633 [FL] or **www.hotoffice.com**). Other services to consider are eRoom Technology's eRoom (617/497-6300 [MA] or **www.instinctive.com**) and Lotus's QuickPlace (800/343-5414 [MA] or **www.lotus.com**).

Web-based teamware won't give you all the power and functionality of **groupware** packages. Online collaborative efforts have traditionally been facilitated with groupware applications over a network, such as Lotus Notes, Novell GroupWise, or Microsoft Exchange, which offer full-featured project and team management. Groupware is costly and usually requires extensive installation and maintenance support that includes data backup, staff and end-user training.

Whenever you mention "groupware," Lotus Notes (**800/343-5414** [MA] or **www.lotus.com**) immediately comes to mind because Notes pioneered this category. Notes is not an application but rather the leading groupware application **platform** used for building and delivering a wide range of applications. Programmers and other highly technical people can use Lotus Notes directly to build custom, corporate or groupware applications. Notes helps keep critical information (in a variety of different formats) moving to everyone in an organization who needs it, when they need it.

Web-based presentation services let you make real-time presentations and collaborate across the Web via text-based chat or companion telephone conference calls. (As of this writing, intranet and Internet bandwidths don't adequately handle streaming video or videoconferencing.) These services let you bring a PowerPoint presentation in a Web-compatible format and include chat windows, annotation tools, ad hoc audience polling and whiteboard markup (a whiteboard lets multiple users collaborate on a document or image with participants' comments clearly identified). These services use the standard HTTP protocol behind network firewalls.

Check out the following services, which have received some acclaim: WebEx.com/WebEx Meeting Center by WebEx Inc. (877/503-3239 [CA] or **www.webex.com**); Astound Conference Center by Astound Inc. (877/278-6863 [CA] or **www.astound.com**); and PlaceWare's MyPlaceWare/PlaceWare Conference Center (PlaceWare Inc., 888/526-6170 [CA] or **www.placeware.com**).

Suites combine several different software programs, such as word processing, spreadsheet, presentation graphics, e-mail, scheduling and database and are becoming increasingly more collaborative and Web-based.

An **intranet** is an internal, corporate computer network that uses Internet features such as e-mail, Web pages and browsers to build a private communications and data resource center for a specific company or organization. Built within its own secure firewall, an intranet is only accessible to the employees of that organization. Good intranets include specialized sites for different types of workers; for example, marketing and sales people would have some of their own sites, administrative people could have their own, etc. An effective, user-friendly intranet will also have simple keyword search functions. It should facilitate information sharing but not add to information overload.

An **extranet** is an intranet that's connected directly to a company's top customers and suppliers. Because it allows information to flow more freely between companies, efficiency and communication are improved.

Web-based teamware collaboration services are great for sharing information through intranets, extranets and the Internet.

All these collaborative computing options help work groups do one or more of the following: a) communicate with each other, b) share information and c) improve work process(es) for better quality products or services that satisfy customers—both external and internal.

Resource Guide

Note: Always check with vendors for the latest version of software products and the compatibility with your existing hardware and software. **See also the earlier portions of Chapter 11 and the index for other products and services.**

E-Mail, Fax and Telephone

AutoSpell is an e-mail spell checker. CompuBridge, **www.spellchecker.com**.

Coalition Against Unsolicited Commercial E-Mail (CAUCE) fights spam (junk e-mail). Visit CAUCE at **www.cauce.org**.

eGroups.com (formerly ONElist) is a free Web-based service I've used that lets you stay in touch with 12 to 1000 people. The service keeps an address file, lets you share files with everyone on your list and provides daily or digest-style e-mails. Or you can opt to visit their Web site for a weekly digest. You can use it professionally to communicate with your customers or use it personally just to stay in touch with family or friends. **www.onelist.com**

E-ttachment Opener is a viewer than decodes almost any type of e-mail attachment, letting you view and print the contents. DataViz, 800/733-0030 or **www.dataviz.com**.

Eudora is a top, award-winning program that allows users to send, receive, sort and manage e-mail and it has great filtering features to help manage and centralize several different e-mail accounts. 800/2-Eudora (CA) or **www.eudora.com**.

Interguru has a low-cost shareware service that converts your e-mail program's address book so you can use it in a new e-mail program. **www.interguru.com/mailconv.htm**

MailSpy is a free utility that checks your in-box for important e-mail messages in the background while you continue working. SaberQuest, 801/235-1738 or **www.saberquest.com**.

Whew stores all of your saved e-mail messages in one file and indexes them for easy searching, which is especially useful if you frequently need to retrieve important pieces of information, such as phone numbers. WordCruncher Publishing Technologies, 801/756-8833 or **www.wordcruncher.com**

12

THE TRAVELING OFFICE: HOW TO GET THINGS DONE ON THE ROAD OR AT HOME AND TRAVEL SMARTER

Quick Scan: If you travel a good portion of the time, you're a telecommuter with a home office, you have multiple, mobile offices or you have far-flung team members, you need special time management techniques and work tools to manage your priorities and responsibilities. Discover how to master paperwork and communications from afar. Discover high-tech telecommunications options that are now available. Read about specific tips and tricks that other professionals use when they're in the air, on the road or just on the go. Special travel tips and a resource guide round out this chapter.

More people today have the challenge of a "traveling office," of working in at least one nontraditional office—be it a car, a corner at home, a hotel room or the cramped quarters of an airplane seat. It's estimated that over 30 million people now work outside the office on a regular basis and that figure is climbing. We're seeing even more "telecommuting" (that term, by the way was coined by futurist Jack Nilles in 1973 when he was a professor at USC). More and more people are setting up home offices; more than 50 percent of adults work out of their homes at least part of the time). And business trips are on the rise. According to a recent Gallup/Air Transportation Assn. poll, 49 percent of air travel is for business reasons and 37 percent of those passengers said their business travel increased last year.

We're also seeing the mobile **virtual office**, which "nomad" workers can locate almost anywhere—their home, a hotel, their car or their customer's place of business. A virtual office is typically equipped with a laptop computer, cell phone, pager and other mobile telecommunication tools and is easy to relocate whenever the need arises. Just as Chapter 10 talked about how the term "job" is changing and is being replaced by the notion of "work," so, too, the traditional office where we used to do much of our work is changing.

Whether you "travel" 8 or 80 percent of the time for business, keeping up with all your responsibilities in multiple, mobile offices can be quite a challenge. As one executive admitted, keeping up is difficult even when you're not traveling. The tools, tips and techniques in this chapter could make the difference for you between exhaustion and exhilaration.

For some business people, traveling, particularly by plane, represents the opportunity to finally get some real work done without all the constant interruptions. Airplane travel time can be a precious respite from the more demanding everyday routine. One association executive told me a number of years ago, "The airplane is the best place to read, think and write because you're away from the telephone." That may not be as true today, what with phones on most planes and other telecommunications tools available; but some people choose not to use these tools during actual travel time.

Working on the Road

Today, because of computers and technology, and especially the Internet, you have more options than ever before in terms of the amount and kinds of work you can do.

Your first step is deciding what you need and want to do. Remember when you travel or work in other locations, there can be extra strain and pressure anyway; don't overburden yourself if at all possible. Also see what percentage of time you're going to need a "traveling office." If it's for a good chunk of your work time, then it makes sense to outfit yourself accordingly; don't use an occasional business trip, however, as a reason for getting the latest electronic gizmo or service. Make sure you really need those business tools in the first place.

Set Up a Portable Office System

You'll need to plan a system to organize your work, communications and papers. As with everything else, there's no one right way to organize this system. But having a regular system in place, with the right tools, equipment and supplies as well as the right routines, can help you be more productive and stay in touch.

Traveling Technology

Today's high-tech telecommunications make traveling or working in multiple locations and staying in touch easier than ever.

Rule Number One is how much and even whether you need to communicate at all in every given instance. Just because you *can* do it (and in exciting high-tech ways) doesn't mean you *should* do it. Many people become too busy doing things they shouldn't be doing in the first place. Many are also making too many routine things urgent—not a very effective use of time. Too many people are communicating so much of the time that they have no down time, no private time—they're always working. Multitasking has become a lifestyle, not just part of a computer operating system. Many people have even become "virtual parents" (a term coined by management consultant Gil Gordon) as real face-to-face interactions are replaced with paging, cell phone and e-mail moments.

Prioritizing is more important than ever before. Good organizational skills let you first see the big picture—your goals and values—and then design your system—the right habits and tools.

Another big problem is trying to decide which tools (or toys) to use. I did some seminar work for one Fortune 500 firm that had a problem with too many telecommunications options. Many employees had to check five or six systems several times a day just to make sure they received all their messages. Pity those employees who were less than positively organized and forgot to check every one of them! The more tools and systems you have, the more likely it is that something will slip through the cracks.

In addition, the company, through its strong emphasis on individualism, encouraged people to use communication channels that best fit them. This is a nice idea in theory, but when you have to remember how all of your colleagues like best to communicate and those colleagues are scattered across the country, your communications difficulties can easily multiply.

Unified messaging, as discussed in Chapter 11, may soon help alleviate this problem. But it won't eliminate the increasing sheer volume of messages that people are receiving each day. (So instead of all those messages in different places, they'll all be lumped together in one electronic in-box.)

Rule Number Two is use the right telecommunications tools for you and the least possible number of tools—keeping them simple but effective for your applications. Cost of the tools you select is a consideration, but be sure you measure cost in terms of time and energy savings as well as actual dollars. Use technology where it really counts.

Wireless Connections

With wireless technology, staying connected keeps getting easier and easier through **PDAs** (personal digital assistants), **Pocket PCs**, **laptop (notebook) PCs**, **cell phones**, **pagers** and ever evolving handheld wireless devices and PCDs (personal communication devices) that offer a combination of these tools.

As of this writing, **PDAs** and **Pocket PCs** (see Chapter 2) are taking center stage, especially for mobile professionals. Besides providing the standard time and personal information management features, they: a) connect you to the Internet or specially reformatted Web pages called "Web clippings," b) send and receive e-mail, c) send and receive faxes, d) do two-way paging, e) can access GPS (the Global Positioning System that pinpoints your geographical location) as well as all kinds of travel information, f) have removable plug-in software modules and g) synchronize your data with your main computer quickly and easily.

Wireless is evolving, even as I write (and you read). One device will let drivers plug their Palm PDAs into their cars and operate them by voice while driving.

Safety concerns, however, spring to my mind about the use of any communication tool while driving, even if they are hands free and voice operated. Yes, it's better than having one hand on the wheel and the other holding a PDA or cell phone. But my feeling is that all such devices are too distracting.

Let's talk for a minute about the ubiquitous use of **cell phones** in cars. A *Los Angeles Times* front page story reported that driving while using a cell phone carries about the same risk as driving while drunk. Take your pick—either driving drunk or talking on a cell phone while driving—both quadruple the risk of having an accident. Several studies back up this finding. In addition, one large study also found that hands-free phones are no safer than conventional hand-held phones when people are driving.

With over 35 million cell phones in the U.S., plus millions of PDAs and pagers, this is something to think about seriously. Some cities, in fact, are trying to ban cell phone use by drivers in a moving vehicle. If you must use a cell phone while driving, **use a headset** (Plantronics, as discussed in Chapter 6, makes all kinds of headsets). Cellular stores sell hands-free kits, some with voice activation. End of lecture.

Let's talk **pagers**, which are still a useful wireless device and have over 60 million users today. What's nice about pagers, too, besides their small, lightweight size, is you can leave them on. Compared to cell phones (the pager's major competitor), pagers tend to cost less per month and receive signals better in buildings. Pagers have broader coverage and paging services can store messages that can't be delivered. They're smaller and lighter to carry, much less expensive (typically $8 to $10 per month for basic service), are fast (most messages are received within 10 seconds of being sent) and have great battery life.

Types include the simple, easy-to-use numeric pager (which provides only a digital readout of the phone number of the person calling you), the alphanumeric pager (which provides both numeric and text messages and can also receive e-mail) and the two-way pager, which has advanced paging capability. The two-way pager has mini-keyboards that let you communicate with another pager as well as a telephone, e-mail address or fax machine; Internet news and information services are becoming an option as well. Sometimes you can get voice-mail messages on these pagers, too. Two-way pagers are a great adjunct to your existing e-mail system if senders keep their messages short.

Check to see how many messages/numbers your pager will hold. One other word of caution: pagers can drop characters when they're used in airplanes, tunnels, trains and buildings with a lot of steel.

Here's a tip: don't tell everyone you carry a pager. Some people will abuse your time and expect you to call back right away, perhaps even at night or during weekends, which may be too invasive, depending, of course, upon your work and/or lifestyle.

While many people have both a pager and cell phone, when given a choice, many more choose the **cell phone**. There are 86 million cell phone users in the U.S. and by 2007, wireless-phone use is expected to jump to over 50% of the population. Be on the lookout for smarter **Web phones** (sometimes called "smart phones") that will continue the push for greater convergence of technology. If you want to access some basic text Internet information on your standard digital cell phone for free, get Xypoint's WebWirelessNow service (**www.xypoint.com**).

Cell phones let you stay in touch with colleagues and customers and prevent voice mail backlog. Cell phones also give you the option of having voice mail when you don't want to receive calls. By the way, remember to turn your phone off during meetings or seminars; getting a vibrating page is inconspicuous but taking a call can be rude.

Here are some useful digital cell phone features to look for: easy-to-read display; recalling last numbers dialed; phone number storage (capacity can be 1,000 plus); voice mail alert; caller ID; call forwarding; call waiting; built-in date, clock and alarm; vibrating alert; scrolling keys; conference calling; programmable call timer; calendar notes; Internet access; e-mail; e-mail forwarding to a fax machine; and a service that assigns two different numbers to the same phone. If you travel abroad to different continents, look for a phone that incorporates the GSM (global system for mobile communications) digital technology that's used overseas, especially in Europe.

The Nextel Direct Connect phone includes a special pushbutton that works like a two-way radio, connecting you instantly to someone else (such as a spouse) who has the same type of phone and it works coast to coast.

As for carriers, choose one that most closely matches the areas you travel. When you travel outside your carrier's territory, you may have to pay special charges for long-distance or "roaming." If you use an outside area frequently, expand your area coverage with a different program and/or a different carrier. If you travel extensively look for fixed-rate cell-phone plans; AT&T has a national plan called Digital One.

Ask a carrier about any other special "custom calling" services that are offered, such as call waiting, call forwarding, no-answer transfer, conferencing and voice mail.

A **notebook** or **laptop PC** is central to most people's portable office system if you have some serious writing, correspondence, project, presentation, spreadsheet or Internet work to do while on the road.

Make sure you have a laptop that's suitable for travel. There are basically two different weight/size configurations for mobile users: 1) the lightweight, three-to-four-pound models, which lack internal disk drives (and often standard ports) and 2) the more equipped six-to-seven-pound models that may come with a hard disk, a CD-ROM and a floppy drive. (There are also heavy-duty, fully-equipped notebook PCs not designed for travel that weigh seven pounds or more; these models are designed as desktop-replacement PCs that should only be moved rarely.)

Other features to look for in a laptop as of this writing are: a) a 12-inch screen with a resolution of at least 800 by 600 (also called "SVGA"); b) three-hours-plus battery life (ideally at least six hours long, the time of roughly one transcontinental flight); c) at least 64 megabytes of RAM; and d) a keyboard and pointing device that feel good to you.

As for a floppy disk drive, some computer experts recommend substituting a Compact Flash (CF) memory card mounted in a PC Card holder, a PC Card hard disk, a CD-RW drive or an Iomega Zip drive.

It's generally a good idea to buy any user-replaceable accessories such as batteries close to the time you purchase a new laptop just in case they aren't available later. But if you haven't done so, try iGo Mobile Technology Outfitter, a leading provider of hard-to-find, model-specific accessories and services for mobile electronic devices (888/205-0064 [24-hour ordering and support] or **www.igo.com**).

As for using your laptop on long flights, consider either bringing along an extra battery or booking a flight on American Airlines, which offers 12-volt "power ports" on certain flights. Other airlines may also provide this option.

To discourage others from peeking over your shoulder while working on sensitive or proprietary material, use smaller fonts, a lower brightness setting on your PC and if necessary, a privacy filter on your laptop's screen.

A laptop computer can be an invaluable tool if you're in outside sales, giving you a real customer service edge. That's the case for salespeople who work for one food distributor. Armed with laptops and order-taking software, the 35 sales reps call on restaurants, hospitals and other institutions. Sales reps save customers time and money by providing on-site analyses and up-to-the-minute dollar and supply figures, transmitting and verifying orders on the spot and printing out the final order for the customer (sales reps also carry portable printers). Using technology in this way can transform your relationship with customers; you become more like partners in business.

Take care of your laptop on the road. Avoid temperature extremes and fluctuations in temperature. For example, don't leave your laptop in a hot trunk, which can cook components and screens. An icy cold environment could crack a screen. Use antiviral software to protect against viruses.

Make sure your lap top's travel case has plenty of padding, to protect your computer if it's accidentally dropped. Here are four excellent sources of well-padded cases: Brenthaven (**http://brenthaven**); Codi AirPro (**http://codi-inc.com**); Kensington (800/535-4242 or **www.kensington.com**); and Targus (877/482-7487 or **www.targus.com**).

To deter laptop theft when you're out in public, try using an inexpensive backpack bookbag to look more inconspicuous. That's what one project manager does. She securely packs the computer in the bag, surrounding it with manuals (you could use towels), puts peripherals into drawstring "stuff sacks" from a camping store and puts diskettes in a wallet with a Velcro closure (Allsop's Softpack Transportable is a great wallet that holds up to 16 3½-inch disks). Before you pack your laptop, pull the battery out a quarter of an inch because a bump during travel could accidentally turn on your computer and wear down your battery. (You should also bring an extra battery that's fully charged, as well as a recharging adapter.)

Computer columnist Walter Mossberg never uses a laptop carrying case, which advertises the fact he has a computer. Instead he uses a briefcase or small carry-on bag along with papers and magazines for padding. He puts accessories in a less-accessible bag.

The key is making your laptop inconspicuous. If possible, avoid using it in public places such as an airport or on the plane. Be sure to take it with you when you use the restroom.

You might try using security cables in your hotel room or the Kensington Lock (**www.kensington.com**). Better yet, use a safe in your room, if available, or just keep it out of sight.

Certainly affix a label with pertinent contact information (maybe include the offer of a reward for returning your computer). Put labels on peripherals, if possible, as well. Also use your laptop's password protection feature, which blocks others from even booting up your laptop but may show pertinent contact/reward information on your screen. (IBM's ThinkPads have this feature.)

A number of products and accessories will help to make your laptop more productive. Look for a mini surge protector—Curtis makes one (800/955-5544 [NJ] or **www.curtis.com**). Fellowes makes a handy clip called the Laptop Copy-Grip for holding a few sheets of paper (800/945-4545 or **www.fellowes.com**). The ASF Notebook Computer Light provides a little extra task lighting when you need it without disturbing others (ASF Lightware Solutions, 800/771-3600 or **www.readinglight.com**).

It's convenient to use **PC Cards**, which are credit-card-sized cards for "plug and play" operations that expand the capability of your laptop. You can get different cards for such things as paging, to use as modems, to provide "flash memory," to use for sound and to use for additional portable hard disk storage.

Here's another very important tip to follow when using a PC Card modem: **don't plug into a digital or PBX phone jack** (usually located in the wall), because the high current can destroy your modem. If you don't know whether a line is analog or digital, you'll want to use a digital-phone-line tester to make sure the line is safe for the modem. (If the hotel phone has a modem jack on the side, you could probably safely use that.) If the wall jack turns out to be digital, you can use the various Konexx Konnector models by Konexx Unlimited Systems Corp. (800/275-6354 [CA] or **www.konexx.com**) to connect your modem and communicate over the digital or PBX phone or to connect an analog connection to digital.

A **connector** is especially handy in a hotel room when you want to connect your modem-equipped laptop computer (or compact fax machine) into the hotel room's telephone system. Three good brands for connectors are Konexx Unlimited Systems Corp. (just mentioned), Road Warrior International (800/274-4277 or **www.warrior.com**) or TeleAdapt, which provides 24-hour international customer service, (**877/TELEADAPT** or **www.teleadapt.com**).

Here are three more tips for traveling laptops. First, make sure your laptop is covered by your insurance, no matter where your laptop happens to be (think up all the various scenarios you can). Second, if possible get 24-hour on-site service and/or replacement for your laptop. Third, take your overnight delivery service number with you (and any of their forms) in case you need to ship it back for repairs or an exchange.

Internet Options

Whether or not you take your laptop along, consider these Internet options to stay connected.

A **remote access program** lets you connect your laptop easily to an office PC over the Internet. If you're on the road with your laptop and you want to use files and applications that are on your desktop computer, this is a way to do it. LapLink provides remote control and also lets you do file transfers that easily and quickly copy files from one machine to another, also called "downloading" or "uploading" files. You could use LapLink to back up your notebook computer every day to a special directory on your desktop computer called "notebook." LapLink is a highly-rated remote access program (800/343-8080 [CA] or **www.LapLink.com**). Take a look also at CoSession, another notable program (Artisoft Inc, 520/670-7100 [AZ] or **www.cosession.com**).

Virtual desktop services provide you a Web site with common PIM applications (e-mail, calendar, to-do list and address book) along with 5 MB to 20 MB (at the time of this writing) of disk storage for files, which is great for accessing files when you're traveling. You'll find information-sharing capabilities such as sharing your appointment calendar, sending files to coworkers, having a discussion board plus other features, such as file synchronization. Two programs have received notable attention and each offer some free services: Zkey.com (213/408-4200 [CA] or **www.Zkey.com**) and Visto (650/930-5000 [CA] or **www.visto.com**).

If you're just looking for free Web storage space consider FreeDiskSpace (**www.FreeDiskSpace**) and @Backup (**www.@backup.com**).

Free **Web-based e-mail** that sends and receives e-mail from any computer with an Internet connection (at cyber cafes, airline clubs and business centers) is another way to avoid hauling around your laptop. Here are two well-known sources: Hotmail (**www.hotmail.com**) and Yahoo! Mail (**www.mail.yahoo.com**).

If you're an AOL subscriber you can access your e-mail (and send e-mail) via the Web from any computer with a Web browser by either going to **www.aolmail.aol.com** or **www.aol.com** and clicking on AOL Mail on the Web. Whether you're at work, on the road or away from your computer you can read and send e-mail. You can also see your old and sent mail. Always determine, before you travel, the least expensive way to access your e-mail.

Hand-held wireless e-mail devices (which are two-way pagers) may be the way to go if most of your communication is by e-mail and you don't want to lug your laptop. The best-known devices are the Motorola PageWriter, which has a good keyboard, and the BlackBerry by Research in Motion (RIM), which is very compact.

Jfax, which was mentioned in Chapter 11 in the discussion of unified messaging, lets you send and receive faxes and deliver voice messages via e-mail (888/438-5329 [CA] or **www.jfax.com**).

Finally look for **instant messaging**, the technology of real-time private messages that are faster than e-mail, to be incorporated in Internet-enabled devices including some cell phones and two-way pagers. Instant messages are for quick, concise messages. (For more information, see Chapter 11.)

A Word on Voice Mail

Voice mail systems or **telephone answering machines** can work great when you're out of your office. (Why is it you always seem to get even more calls when you're away?) Of course if you have a machine, you'll have one with remote access where you dial a code to retrieve messages. If you have a voice mail system or service, find out if you can arrange to have it beep you via a pager. (And of course, a voice mail or "voice messaging" system is far preferable to an answering machine because it lets several callers leave messages at the same time, especially important if you receive many calls and don't want to risk the chance of losing a call whenever your answering machine is handling another call simultaneously.)

Here's a timesaving voice mail tip if you're traveling and are fortunate enough to have an assistant. Have your assistant listen to and transcribe your voice mail and then summarize important messages for you by leaving one message on your voice mail (or e-mail).

Many hotels now have their own voice messaging systems for guests but be careful when using them because they don't offer as much privacy as other tools. It's best not to discuss any sensitive, confidential or personal matters on hotel voice mail (or on an incoming hotel telephone line for that matter). Call back on an outgoing line to discuss such matters; you'll hear a beeping sound if a third party is on an outgoing line. It's possible for a hotel employee or anyone familiar with a given hotel's system to be able to listen to messages of any guest. If the hotel voice mail system uses a code (such as your room number and the first four letters of your last name), ask if you can change the code. You could opt not to use the system at all and revert back to written telephone messages; that will discourage callers from leaving private messages.

More on Faxing

If you plan to send or receive many faxes, you have several options. Using your laptop, you could send and receive faxes via your computer. You'll need some software to help you, of course, such as WinFAX Pro by Symantec (800/441-7234 or **www.symantec.com**). It's probably more convenient to put the software on your desktop computer and then dial in for your faxes from your laptop.

If you need a hard copy fax when you're on the go, you can print out any fax stored in your modem-equipped laptop via a hotel fax machine or at a public fax station located at a quick printer or commercial mail station. Look in the Yellow Pages for "Fax Transmission Service."

Look at more options. If you're staying in a hotel, look for one that caters to business travelers with either special business floors or special equipment in the rooms. (Start with Marriott and Hyatt, which are business friendly.) By the way, if you're planning to do extensive work from your hotel room, check the status of their telephone system and rooms before you get there. Find out if there's a business center on site, available equipment, hours of operation and fees; if there's no business center, find out what the hotel charges for printing, copying and faxing as well as any special services. Some hotels have faxes sent to an electronic fax mailbox, which guests can retrieve at the nearest fax machine. Some hotels may offer a service that delivers faxes via guest-room TV sets; using a remote control, a guest can either order the fax they see or have it deleted. Some airlines now have phones with fax capabilities.

Traveling Time Management

Just as important as choosing your tech tools and services is making special use of your travel time.

While on a plane, take advantage of "creative thinking time." One consultant takes a sheet of paper and jots down ideas in the form of mind maps (visual idea outlines) and decision trees (pros and cons) for two or three of his current projects.

One association executive with an administrative assistant brings along a portable Dictaphone recorder (the size of a pager) and some pre-stamped "Jiffy" envelopes when he travels. He mails back the tapes in the padded envelopes. (If you're better at writing than dictating, you could e-mail your assistant.) For urgent dictation, he dials into his desk dictation machine, which is on 24 hours a day.

If you use dictation, then you may want to use a **digital dictation** machine, which records the voice electronically to a computer hard drive or other mass storage medium. The big advantage to digitized technology is you can use it over phone lines and dictate from any type of phone from any location. You can key in simple codes to label your dictation and indicate its priority; high priority dictation gets transcribed first. You can dictate at any speed and transcribers can set the playback to match their typing speed without distorting the tone of the voice. Perhaps the biggest advantage is the ability to edit—to insert new material at any point. Another big plus is the ability to search quickly via random access rather than having to search laboriously through a tape.

For digital dictation systems contact the following companies: Dictaphone Straight Talk at 800/447-7749 (FL) or **www.dictaphone.com** or Lanier Information Systems at 800/708-7088 or **www.lanier.com**.

Consider also DragonNaturallySpeakingMobile (800/825-5897 [MA] or **www.dragonsys.com**) which provides a hand-held recorder, a voice file transfer program and the company's award-winning speech recognition software.

You can make good use of your commuting time by dictating, making calls on your cell phone or listening to tapes. The Crucible Group (800/334-5771 [NJ] or **www.news-track.com**) publishes "Newstrack Executive Tape Service," a twice-a-month tape cassette series that summarizes newspapers and magazine articles. (Try listening to tapes such as Newstrack on a plane, too.)

Accomplish as much as you can in the allotted time by **consolidating activities** when you travel. Plan ahead all the meetings you want to have and the people you want to see in a particular location.

Consolidate similar activities while working on a plane, too. For example, group together all your writing work. Because space is at a premium, you're almost forced to work in this linear way. It's harder to jump from one thing to another when you can't spread out all your "stuff." (And if you're one of those people who accomplishes more when you travel, perhaps you should incorporate this one-thing-at-a-time work style into your back-at-the-ranch office, too.)

Keeping Up with Calls While Away

"I stay flexible about which telephone I use—I don't have to be in a hotel room. I use pay phones when I can to keep the cost down but it's nice to use a cell phone occasionally for convenience," says one director of a public health agency.

By the way, check with your hotel to see if you can access your own carrier rather than having the hotel operator route your call through a high-priced carrier. It's especially important when traveling abroad to get local access numbers in foreign cities from your long-distance carrier. Also determine before you leave whether a local access number or an 800 number will be more economical for you to use on the road in connecting with your online service .

On a more philosophical note, the public health director says that the telephone helps her "maintain the rhythm of life," no matter where she is. Besides telephoning for business, she will place "stay-in-touch" phone calls. "The telephone works from out of town. The other person doesn't really care where you are when you're calling to wish a happy birthday." She adds that personal telephoning also helps make travel less jolting.

Most business travelers will call in for messages (or retrieve them via the Internet) at least once a day and try to return calls or respond to messages the same day. If you feel a need to stay in touch with your work group, you may check two or three times a day.

Other business travelers rely more heavily on their staff or may use other communication channels, such as e-mail or faxing.

If you're **a manager in charge of a far-flung** team, you have special needs to keep up not only with phone calls but communications. "Virtual managers" who manage "virtual teams" need to make special efforts to stay in touch. Because phone calls are more personal, they offer an excellent channel of team-building communication. As *Wall Street Journal* columnist Carol Hymowitz explains it, "Voice time replaces face time as the dominant form of communication."

So you need to be especially organized when you communicate by phone with virtual team members. That means avoiding telephone tag by scheduling regular telephone appointments. That means returning calls promptly—no more than half a day later. That means planning to spend a little extra time on the phone to develop a more personal relationship and to listen carefully and empathetically.

Handling Paperwork on the Road

Planning is the secret to handling paperwork when you travel. When you book your hotel reservation, for example, make sure the room has the basic paperwork necessities: a flat writing surface (or desk) with a light, a telephone and close access to phone and electrical/modem outlets. (Isn't it inconvenient when the telephone is on the night table when you have a lot of phoning to do?) See if any in-room PCs, printers or fax machines are available. Here are some other ways to plan ahead for paperwork.

Select practical accessories to hold and transport paperwork and supplies. Try an expandable, document case that contains different colored folders. Take along a lightweight tote bag filled with reading material; when empty, the bag can be folded inside the document case or could be used for transporting other items. A large, transparent, plastic folder could hold thank you notes, sympathy cards, get well cards, stamps, number 10 envelopes and letterhead. A few Express, Priority Mail or FedEx envelopes may be useful to have on hand if you're going to be gone for a week or more and anticipate processing some paperwork on the trip and you want to mail some of it back, maybe along with dictation tapes.

Categorize different types of paper. Even your reading material for a trip can be organized into categories. One category could be "Business Reading," such as reports, industry newsletters and selected articles. Others could be specific, project related categories. Try to include a "Fun Stuff" category such as the daily paper, *USA Today* and *The Wall Street Journal*, which keep you current and are good sources of conversation starters.

If possible avoid traveling with a very heavy briefcase. Paper weighs a lot and can cause great strain. You may want to ship some papers you accumulate from a trip back to your office, after first sorting and eliminating papers.

Take pertinent resource material with you in a concise, easy-to-carry format. One regional sales manager created an alphabetical notebook system that he takes with him when he travels out in the field. He says, "I'm not at my desk that often so I can't carry the whole file cabinet with me." So instead he carries a three-ring notebook with alphabetical tabs and reinforced paper sheets that contain summaries of clients and prospects, the latest meetings, the types of programs his company is offering and sales materials.

He uses single word phrases, "buzz words" he calls them, so he can see information at a glance. Typical information includes people profile facts such as key contacts and their family members and special interests plus buzz word summaries of problems and solutions that instantly remind him of next actions to be taken. If a client calls when he is on the road, he is prepared to talk intelligently, armed with up-to-date information. When he's in the office, he uses the book there, too. You may prefer to keep such information on your PDA or laptop; but if you're very visual or kinesthetic, you, too, may prefer the "low-tech," hands-on approach. Whatever works for you is what I always say.

A **loose-leaf personal notebook organizer** can be an invaluable tool for carrying information you collect on a particular trip. Many organizers come with special expense envelopes that are great for keeping all your records and receipts together in one place. These envelopes make it easy to compile expense reports, which you should ideally do on the road.

Speaking of dreaded expense reports, here are some options for doing them on the road. You can use your PDA. If you have your laptop, use Excel or the Web site TimeBills.com.

Portable file boxes may work for you if your office is in your car trunk or you have many files to take with you on a business trip. File boxes come in all shapes and sizes and can accommodate legal and letter files and hanging file folders. Check your office supply catalog under "file boxes" or "storage files." (See also "Portable Office Products" in the chapter resource guide.)

One executive has mail and important reading material sent to him via Federal Express when on an extended trip. He says, "Nothing is more depressing than returning from a trip to a stack of papers. When I come back, rarely do I have anything on my desk."

File your paperwork as you go into active project folders or at the very least, into two colored folders, say, red for "urgent" and blue for "not urgent." If you have papers for an assistant, have a separate folder. Either jot down, note in your PDA or dictate instructions for each paper as you read it. This will save you time when you return from your trips. If you're uncomfortable with dictating machines, you could use Post-it Notes. Use different colored Post-it Notes to distinguish paperwork with different priorities or to categorize different types of work.

As for all those business cards you collect, here are some tips to try, which are especially useful at trade shows and conferences. I jot down either an "A," "B" or "C" at the top to indicate the importance of this contact. If a card doesn't rate one of these letters, it gets tossed as soon as possible. I also write the date and event or place where we met. If I need to write more background or followup information, I'll write "over" on the front and jot notes on the back. (If you learn any personal tidbit, for example, names and ages of kids, write that down, too.) "A" cards usually are ones that will need some immediate followup and are grouped together, as are Bs and Cs. If you ever use the back of your card to write someone else's name and address (because they don't have a card) cross out the front of your card so that you don't accidentally give it to someone else.

And here's a tip if you ever plan to use the hotel fax machine: check the cost first. Hotels sometimes assess high service charges—a flat rate $25 service charge per message or per-page fees of up to $10 for the first page and $1 for each additional page. An overnight mail service could be cheaper and the hotel may even have a daily pickup and delivery by such a service, which in many cases is Federal Express. (For other options see the earlier "Traveling Technology" section in this chapter.)

Seven Travel Tips You Need to Know

Let's face it: traveling is time consuming and energy draining, particularly when you're out several days at a time, working feverishly with all of your high-tech tools and you're crossing different time zones. All the more so if you tend toward disorganization. So part of maintaining an effective traveling office and staying physically effective yourself is learning to handle the logistics of travel. Here are seven travel tips that will make your trips less hectic and maybe even pleasurable.

One: Take Time to Prepare

You are only as organized as you are prepared. "I pack my suitcase, my briefcase and my mind for each trip," says publisher Mike Welch. "I really think it through. Like great athletes who picture themselves leaping over the bar, I picture myself at the business meeting." In addition to packing all the pertinent meeting materials, Welch commits to memory all the important details concerning the agenda.

Consultant Bill Butler advises, "Read any briefing papers or material pertaining to your trip before you leave. State Department research indicates information is not absorbed and retained as well when you're in a travel mode."

Take time to prepare your clients or customers when you're leaving them to go on a trip. Trish Lester, president of a business communications company, writes her clients three weeks before she leaves for an extended period of time. She encourages them to call her before she departs, but also assures them they have the option of leaving messages on her voice mail while she's away.

You can do two things to eliminate or reduce voice or e-mail messages while you're away: 1) Activate your e-mail's autoresponse feature (often called a "vacation response") to reply automatically to every message you receive, letting the correspondent know you're not on your regular schedule and possibly provide an alternate person as a contact, and 2) change your outgoing voice-mail message to spell out how long you'll be gone, whether you'll be checking messages (and if so, ask them to leave a short, concise message with a phone number) and whether there's an alternate way to either reach you (i.e., e-mail, pager or a cell phone) or contact someone else.

If you're planning to meet someone at an airport, hotel or restaurant, be sure you each have a backup plan. Having prearranged contacts, such as administrative assistants at each respective office, can help with any last minute change in plans.

Find out in advance about any timesaving services offered by your car rental agency and hotels, such as **counter-bypass programs**, to avoid standing in line and otherwise wasting your valuable time. Be sure to check all travel benefits, including rental car discounts, that are available to you through your company or any professional association memberships. Always ask about special deals, such as a "corporate rate," but don't assume that's the best deal. A discount through an association may be better.

As for hotel accommodations, you may not be aware just how much influence you can have in that area, too. For starters, you should **negotiate your room rate**. Did you know that many hotels have more than 30 different rates for each guest room? Ask about any specials—such as corporate, weekend or midweek rates or if there are any special ads or coupons running in the local paper. Some hotels offer their own clubs and extend special discounts to members. Never use a hotel chain's toll-free 800 number if you plan to negotiate. Call the hotel directly. And you can research and negotiate rates on the Internet, too.

Be sure to **spell out important room preferences** you may have—for example, nonsmoking, quiet and close to an elevator. If you need to do a lot of work from your room, find out what the setup is regarding work space, access to the phone and outlets, whether there is a data line in the room for a modem and any telecommunications equipment and services the hotel provides for business people. Call ahead to see if a hair dryer or other items are automatically provided so you don't have to pack them. If you're traveling in Europe, you may also want to request a room on a lower floor for safety reasons, as fire alarm systems are nonexistent in many foreign countries.

As for private working space at an airport, especially if you know you're going to have a layover, consider renting a Laptop Lane office which charges by the minute (the rate currently includes all long-distance and fax transmission rates). Dubbed "your smart office at the airport," each office features a 40-square-foot enclosed private workstation with a door, spacious work space and a swivel chair. Located at airport terminals, Laptop Lane private rooms are equipped with desktop PCs, notebook connections, laser printers, fax machines, multiline phones and Internet connections—in short, "multi-tasking heaven." For locations, contact Laptop Lane at 206/386-5800 [WA] or **www.LaptopLane.com**.

If you have a travel agent, make sure yours is organized and routinely remembers to handle all the details, such as crediting mileage to your frequent flyer club. This is one item that is typically missed. One agency uses a quality checklist that is printed on the front cover of a special jacket that holds airline tickets and itinerary. As a customer, you can see at a glance that indeed all those details have been handled.

The ideal agent will ask for and keep up-to-date travel information regarding your frequent flyer numbers, your billing procedures (perhaps you use two different credit cards, one for business and the other for personal travel, which is a good idea) and your travel preferences (such as airline seating, rental cars and hotel rooms). If you have to start from scratch for each trip, your agent just isn't organized enough.

Your agent should routinely provide you with seat assignments and boarding passes so that you don't have to wait in line at the airport.

For flight times to avoid, Bill Butler comments, "I look with a jaundiced eye at the first flight out, which is often a very popular flight for business. I will usually avoid it because it's too crowded and hectic." Also avoid, if possible, booking the last flight out, especially if you have a speaking engagement or a critical meeting. It's far better to spend extra time at your destination than arriving a day late because of a cancelled flight.

While you may not want the first flight out, do travel early in the day, if you can. You then have more options if a flight is cancelled. Avoid connecting flights but if you must schedule them, leave enough time between them—at least double what the airline tells you. If you must book a connecting flight, try to do so through a smaller, less crowded airport. Also avoid traveling during holidays.

Many business travelers prefer aisle seats because they offer a little more leg room and are less confining. But not just any aisle seat will do if you carry on luggage; if so, get a seat close to the boarding ramp.

Some people prefer the "bulkhead," which has seats with the most leg room—more leg room than aisle seats. The disadvantages are that you have no underseat storage and you'll have to move if you want to see the movie screen. I also read that there is a head injury hazard during sudden stops or turbulence because the bulkhead dividers are generally wall structures that don't give.

If you're safety conscious, you may prefer to take the advice of most air safety experts who recommend an aisle seat next to the rearmost overwing exit. On the subject of safety, also read the emergency card in the seat pocket to find out how to open the various door and window exits and to locate the four exits that are closest to your seat. Also recommended is counting the rows of seats to each exit; you might not be able to see the exit signs in an emergency but you could still feel and count the seats.

Before you leave for the airport, always call the airline to make sure your flight is on time. For return flights, it's also a good idea to call the day before to reconfirm your flight, even if you are ticketed.

Allow plenty of time to get to the airport and your gate, especially for larger airports. You should get to the gate at least 90 minutes before a domestic flight and two hours for an international one; you can lose your seat assignment if you don't. If you get there less than 30 minutes before the flight, you could lose your reservation altogether. (Check with your airline as these time guidelines are subject to change.)

As for hotels, avoid checking in with your MasterCard or Visa, which the hotel will use to pre-approve and set aside a dollar amount to cover your expected expenses. This pre-approval actually reduces your current credit limit. Instead, check in with a card without any credit limit such as an American Express card even if you later decide to pay with another card.

Two: Organize Your Travel Info

The more you travel, the more you need to stay current on travel trends, topics and your own travel information.

Butler stays current on flight information by subscribing to the pocket-size OAG Pocket Flight Guide (North American edition), which is updated monthly and available by subscription from Official Airline Guides (OAG), 800/DIAL-ORG or **www.oag.com**. Carry the "OAG" when you travel; if your flight is canceled, you could find an alternate on your own more quickly using it (however, it may cost you extra if you don't have your original airline reschedule a flight for you). And then to avoid waiting in line, go to a pay phone (or use your cell phone) and call the airline directly yourself. You may also be able to get this kind of travel information through your PDA.

If you have a personal wireless communicator, you can access OAG's FlightLine (which is part of FlightDisk), an on-line OAG; if you have your laptop with you and you have an on-line service, you could subscribe to Electronic Edition Travel Services (EETS), which provides not only flight information but the ability to book the reservations directly (EETS is available through OAG). FlightDisk provides monthly updated flight information giving you access to hundreds of thousands of flights across the country and around the world, as well as to travel information on the ground.

Butler stays current, also, by following industry reports included in *The New York Times* travel section. He has learned, for example, that Atlanta often shows extra delays because of a big problem with early morning ground fog. On the other hand, Memphis, which has Federal Express' major terminal, is considered the "all weather airport." Butler points out Chicago is noted for lots of traffic so you need to allow extra time between connecting flights. Butler used to travel 50 to 60 percent of the time; he now travels 30 to 40 percent. With such a heavy travel schedule, it makes good sense to have fingertip travel information. Butler maintains files on major cities he visits frequently.

Butler also keeps a travel notebook that is arranged by client and location. The notebook contains directions, places to stay, ground transportation, how long it takes to get to the airport at various times of day, the "leading food adventures to the locals," restaurants to avoid and hotel history, in particular his room preferences. (Nonsmokers may also want to request and note for future reference which hotel rooms and floors are smoke-free.)

Organized travelers have a trip form they carry with them that lists their itinerary, transportation, lodging, key contacts and phone numbers. They also leave at least one copy of their trip sheet with a staff member, as well as with their family. Butler has an expense report printed on the back of his form, which makes for a convenient system.

Mike Welch uses a sheet that lists such things as the airlines and types of planes he'll be flying, seat assignments, who confirmed his reservations, rental car arrangements and who will pick him up. Along with this sheet, Welch also brings photocopies of airline guide pages he may need. He carries these items in his pockets, which have been specially organized for travel so that he doesn't have to look in a million places. Having a simple and dependable system, even when it comes to organizing your pockets, can make a big difference when traveling.

Three: How to Select Travel Clothing

"Keep it simple" is the best advice when it comes to selecting clothes for a trip.

Buy clothing that doesn't wrinkle. If they are wrinkled on the rack, you know they will wrinkle on the road. (Anything with wool travels great, as well as knits and polyester blends.) Depending on the time of year, wear (never pack) one all-purpose coat appropriate for a particular trip.

Bill Butler simplifies his travel wardrobe. Butler packs black shoes and socks, makes sure shirts go with all suits and relies on neckties to provide color. One clothing designer limits his travel wardrobe to two basic "colors"—black and white.

A California image consultant suggests women stick with solid colors and separates. Use accessories such as belts, print scarves or necklaces to add variety and choose ones that bring up the bottom color from your skirt or pair of slacks. Some handy items to include are a dressy blouse and belt to go out in the evening and a tweed jacket that has many colors. Take no more than three pairs of shoes— one for walking or sports (such as tennis shoes), a pair of flats and a pair of low heels. Have at least one belt to match the main pair of shoes you'll be wearing.

Wear the right clothing when you're flying. Several layers of light-colored, well-fitting (but not tight) clothing are best. From a safety perspective, select clothes made of wool, a naturally flame retardant fabric. It's better than most materials, especially synthetics and leather, which should be avoided. (A good way to test flammability off the airplane is to snip off a small piece of fabric and set it afire. If it melts rather than chars, don't wear it.) Also avoid high-heeled shoes.

Four: How to Choose and Use Luggage on the Go

When it comes to luggage, I recommend and use a Travelpro Rollaboard, a compact suitcase with retractable handle and built-in wheels that you can roll through the terminal and right down a plane aisle. Travelpro invented "The Original Rollaboard," which is used by more than 425,000 flight crew members and is sold around the world under many well-known brand names. The Travelpro line is widely available in department stores, luggage and specialty retailers, catalogs and the Internet or you can contact Travelpro USA at 800/741-7471 or **www.travelpro.com**.

But you'll want to check with each airline you use to see what their specific guidelines are for carry-on luggage. In general, you're allowed to carry on no more than two pieces of baggage. According to the FAA (Federal Aviation Administration) Web site **(www.faa.gov)**, the maximum size bag for most airlines is 45 linear inches (the total of the height, width and depth of the bag). The FAA encourages you to "think small" and to remember that in certain situations an airline may require most or even all of your bags to be checked. There can be some variation in guidelines by different airlines, depending on factors such as aircraft size and the number of passengers on a flight.

Check also about personal items such as purses, coats, hats, umbrellas, briefcases, laptops and cameras to see whether they're counted or excluded as carry-on luggage. In terms of safety, always stow heavy items under the seat in front of you, not overhead.

I prefer taking luggage on board so as to avoid the hassles of lost, stolen or misdirected luggage. (It also saves you time avoiding the wait for luggage at baggage claim.) I never check luggage on my way to any destination if I can help it; occasionally, coming back I will, however, depending on my own energy level or if I have a particularly heavy load. Even if you check most of your luggage, be sure to pack toiletries, prescriptions, underwear, a change of clothing, important documents, valuables and any other critical items in a carry-on bag.

(By the way, if you're taking valuables such as electronic equipment, cameras and jewelry with you, check with your airline for their lost luggage compensation. You may want to obtain some additional insurance coverage, especially for international flights which tend to have much lower compensation.)

Five: Use Travel Checklists

It's always a good idea to maintain at least one travel checklist of items you always take on a trip. See Figure 12-1 for an example.

In addition, you may want to keep sample packing lists for different types of trips that you will take again. If you have a computer, keep your lists there. Whether you prepare packing lists manually or on computer, group items by category. Some useful categories are: clothing, personal care, business materials and recreation.

Figure 12-1. THE POSITIVELY ORGANIZED! TRAVELING OFFICE CHECKLIST

Here are some items to include in your traveling office. Check off the ones that you already have, circle the ones you want to get and add any others that would come in handy:

[] Briefcase
[] Attache case
[] Tote bag
[] Document case
[] Notebook
[] PDA
[] Calendar/appointment book
[] Telephone/address book
[] Paper—pads, loose sheets, personal or company stationery, business cards—any of these items or add what you'll need:

[] Writing tools—pens, pencils, markers:

[] Accessories: tape, scissors, stapler, clips, portable office kit

---

[] Equipment: pocket calculator, dictation machine, small tape player, laptop

---

[] Labeled file folders, file pockets, expansion pockets, plastic folders

---

[] Stamps, return envelopes, Jiffy envelopes, Express/Federal Express envelopes

---

[] Work: schedule, agenda, files/info related to business trip, reading material, paperwork, project work

---

[] Travel materials: itinerary, tickets, legal documents—driver's license, passport, visa, certificate of registration (from U.S. Customs for items such as cameras and watches made in a foreign country); travelers checks, cash, credit cards

---

[] Any extra conveniences you can think of: _____

You may want to develop your own special checklist of extra convenience items. For example, "Bill Butler's batch of things to carry" includes: the OAG Pocket Flight Guide, a small atlas, a name and address book, a list of restaurants in the major cities you'll be visiting, a digital alarm clock that keeps both current time and home-based time, a pocket calculator, extra shoelaces, a sewing kit and safety pins, aspirin, antacid tablets, foil-wrapped granola bars, a nasal decongestant in case you have to fly with a cold, cough drops, pleasure reading such as a John Macdonald or Agatha Christie book and gifts wrapped with yarn instead of ribbon, which tends to become mashed in a suitcase.

Writer David Shaw takes Scotch tape, packing tape, extra glasses and contact lenses, a Swiss army knife, a spot remover, a laptop computer, rope, his own gourmet food (he refuses to eat airline fare), pre-addressed post card labels and a small pocket tool kit with pliers, chisel, hole punch, file, stapler, screwdrivers, measuring tape and scissors.

I bring along lots of dollar bills for tipping and change for local phone calls. I also stash pre-moistened towelettes in my carry-on bag to freshen up. I usually take along my sleeping pillow.

Magellan's mail-order travel catalog features such handy items as nylon "hidden pocket" money pouches, inflatable neck pillows for long plane or train rides and emergency dental kits.

Have your doctor write up extra copies of prescriptions you may need while away or in case you lose any medication.

You may want to make a packing list that is divided into two parts: day and evening. Decide exactly what you're going to wear and which accessories will go with each outfit.

Six: Pack Systematically

Here's a very visual way to pack. (Since I've traveled a lot, I sometimes skip the list and go directly to this step.) Lay your accessories and clothes out on the bed before packing them. Try not to take too much (easier said than done, I admit!) When it comes to cosmetics and toiletries, pack each item after you use it the last time before the trip.

I keep many items in my suitcase all the time, in between trips. I have a cosmetic case that duplicates the cosmetics and toiletries I have at home. Packing time can be cut in half when you have an extra toiletry kit that is ready when you are. The ideal time to replenish any supplies that are low is when you unpack at the end of each trip. Dental, medical, body care and makeup supplies in travel-sized containers are convenient. For extra protection, fill containers three-quarters full and secure them in self-sealing plastic bags. I keep small, zip-lock bags in my cosmetic case for different types of toiletries.

I also keep a hair dryer and several brushes in the bag, too, as well a couple of large plastic bags and a bathing suit (I'm a native Californian).

Pack your wallet systematically, too, or should I say, unpack it. Leave behind unnecessary credit cards, papers or accessories. Make a list of the credit cards you decide to take and their numbers and keep that list separate from your cards. Include any phone numbers you may need to call if your credit cards should become lost or stolen. (By the way, you should already have a complete, up-to-date list of all your credit cards.) Don't keep all your money or traveler's checks in your wallet, or any one place for that matter; stash some of it in other places.

If you're going to travel with film, be sure to pack it separately and accessibly so that you can hand it to the security people at airport security or pack it in an lead-lined x-ray film bag. X-rays won't hurt computer disks or laptops but the magnetic security devices in walk-through scanners will.

Finally, pack as lightly as possible—it's better for your back and your body.

Seven: Take Care of Yourself When You Travel

To maintain your rhythm and your effectiveness throughout your trip, recognize that as you travel you are subjecting yourself to different demanding environments. Part of staying organized on the road is preparing in advance for the adjustments you and your body may need to make and then following through while on the trip.

Jet lag is not simply the result of being in a different time zone. It combines the stress from airplane travel coupled with a disruption in our body's circadian rhythms. Besides following the recommendations in this section of the book here are two other ones experts recommend. The most important one is get some sunlight. Some experts say it doesn't matter what time of day. Others insist that the timing is important but that it's complex to figure out. One guideline suggests that if you're flying east on an overnight flight then get some sun or artificial light in the mid to late morning at your destination. If you're flying west, wait until late afternoon or early evening.

A second suggestion is to switch to your new time zone schedule, especially for sleeping and eating times, as quickly as possible. (Avoid napping if you can and if you can't, rest for no more than 45 minutes to avoid REM sleep.)

Bill Butler says avoid unnecessary travel. "Make sure you need to make the trip in the first place, that there is no other way you can possibly accomplish your goal. See if they can come to you. Traveling is mean to your body." With all the technology we have available, there should be less need to travel.

Butler suggests you avoid overeating and overdrinking. He also suggests drinking bottled water wherever you go. "Just the different chemicals in the water can have an adverse effect."

Don't forget to exercise. Running or even jump roping is beneficial and a jump rope is an easy item to pack, too.

Take special care of your body when you fly. Most airlines are cramped and uncomfortable, but fortunately, there are steps you can take to help your body adjust. **Protect yourself against dehydration.** When you're on board a jetliner you will experience dehydration of body and skin because of the cabin's low humidity. Dehydration leads to weariness.

Be sure to drink enough liquid—one expert recommends one glass of water every hour. Apple juice, cranberry juice or fruit punch are also good. Avoid tea, coffee, alcohol and soft drinks, all of which can have a diuretic effect. Carbonated drinks also can cause stomach gas, which can expand in flight, creating discomfort. (I've read that drinking carrot juice before a flight can help offer resistance to oxygen deficiency, which can occur at 6,000 feet.)

Bring along lip balm and hand cream to combat cracked lips and dry skin, likely symptoms from exposure to cabin air. Don't forget a lubricant for your eyes, especially if you wear contact lenses.

Order your airline meals ahead of time, if possible. Most airlines allow you to order special meals such as fruit and cheese; vegetarian plates; low-salt, low-fat, low-cholesterol fare; and special selections for frequent travelers. Ask each airline what kinds of meals are available one or two days before you fly. Or better yet, place your order at the time you book your reservation. Remember to avoid high-fat, salty foods, which cause body swelling and retention of fluid. (I usually also bring along some unsalted dry roasted almonds and some fresh fruit.)

Keep your body limber and comfortable. Here are four steps:

First, wear comfortable shoes you can slip on and off. Remove them shortly after takeoff. Second, to reduce swelling in feet and ankles, elevate your feet. (Body swelling and bloating occur because of an airplane's lower barometric pressure.) Elevating your feet even a few inches really helps; I place my feet on the carry-on case I stash under the seat in front of me.

Third, take short exercise breaks. Frequency of breaks is more important than time duration. At least once every hour is a good idea. Take walks around the cabin and do simple stretches at your seat. Hold each stretch for 30 to 60 seconds. (You might want to tell your neighbors beforehand what you're doing.)

Fourth, improve your posture by placing a pillow in the small of your back. The pillow provides extra support and helps you sit up straighter. Also try adding a small pillow under your thighs. Pillows can help spread body weight around.

Beware of flying if you have a cold, sinus infection or allergies. You could experience ear pain as well as possibly bursting an ear drum. Check with your doctor, who may recommend a regimen of decongestants.

Keep in mind travel safety precautions, especially if you're a woman traveling alone. Request a hotel room that's close to an elevator, not remotely located at the end of a long hallway, for example. Always use the security bar lock. Don't put out that room service ticket, which shows your room number, the time of delivery and the fact you'll be dining alone. Wherever you are, stay aware of your surroundings and the people you encounter.

"You have to really pace yourself when you travel," says one business traveler. "If you have to wait," she advises, "find a comfortable place, know you're there for the duration and roll with it." If there's a delay at the airport, she likes to go to the airport restaurant to read, work or relax.

In fact, much of pacing yourself is just learning to relax. "Don't get too excited, don't rant and rave," says another frequent traveler. "A lot of people create a crisis to be a hero. Don't let anything get to the crisis stage. The whole secret boils down to good communication—up, down, sideways. Don't take anything for granted."

What do you do if, after all your planning, your airline cancels your flight? The best course of action, especially if you have a nonrefundable fare, is to have the airline place you on the next available flight. If you try to make a new reservation or rebook yourself, you may lose out on your low fare.

If you miss a flight, be sure to call the airline immediately so that all of your other reservations aren't wiped out as well. One final suggestion: Believe Murphy's Law next time you're on the road. Or as Butler says, "You have to anticipate that things won't be perfect, but most of the time you can organize and prepare."

Resource Guide

Note: Most of the following resources haven't been discussed in this chapter. Be sure to check the chapter itself for additional resources as well as Chapter 11.

More High-Tech Travel Tools, Accessories, Services and Web Sites

Cellmania.com lets you compare cell-phone plans from more than 40 national and regional plans along with phones and accessories. Cellmania sells cellular services and products. You can also buy pagers and two-way radios.

Hello Direct is an outstanding catalog of telephone productivity tools with great service. 800/444-3556 (CA) or **www.hellodirect.com**

HotPage lets you organize and send e-mail and alphanumeric pages from your PC to a pager. This is especially useful for those who send many pages to multiple recipients. Smith Micro Software Inc., 800/964-7674 (CA) or **www.smithmicro.com**.

iGo Mobile Technology Outfitter is a leading provider of hard-to-find, model-specific accessories and services for mobile electronic devices (888/205-0064 [24-hour ordering and support] or **www.igo.com**).

Intellisync gives you great control over synchronizing your PDA and your computer, especially if you use one of the 18 major PIMs on your computer. Puma Technology, 877/738-2621 or **www.pumatech.com**.

MailStart.Com is a free service that lets you get your e-mail on the road if you don't have your own computer with you. It's great in a pinch. MailStart, **www.mailstart.com**.

Map'n'Go is an award-winning travel planner that combines superb quality maps, unparalleled routing and an enormous database of roads, restaurants, hotels and points of interest throughout the U.S., Canada, Mexico and the Caribbean. It determines your best driving route, lets you attach your choices for lodging and eating and allows you to print out a detailed Travel Plan map with your highlighted route, mileage and driving time. It includes a full-size, 128-page road atlas to take along. DeLorme, 800/452-5931 (ME) or **www.delorme.com**.

MapsOnUs.com provides free directions and maps.

Motorola StarTAC with clipOn Organizer combines a cell phone with a clip-on, piggyback PDA/PIM device. Motorola Inc., 800/331-6456 or **www.motorola.com**.

Palm.Net is a wireless service that offers paging, e-mail and limited browsing of specially reformatted Web pages (Web clippings). You can find all kinds of Web clipping programs at **www.palm.net/apps**.

Rand McNally's TripMaker and **StreetFinder** programs are highly-rated, easy-to-use travel planning and mapping programs. Rand McNally, 800/234-0679 (IL) or **www.randmcnally.com**.

Roadnews is a Web site devoted to resources for keeping laptop computer users connected while they travel (**www.roadnews.com**).

Street Atlas USA is a comprehensive award-winning street level mapping program that offers extraordinary street and road detail as well as GPS support. You can search by place name, zip code or area code and exchange. It's easy to use. (See also DeLorme's other mapping and geographic database products.) DeLorme, 800/452-5931 (ME) or **www.delorme.com**.

Tucows Network has a Web site where you can download software, including PDA software. **www.tucows.com**

Voice Organizers are palm-size "offices on the run" that store phone numbers, appointments, reminders, memos and file folders and have optional PC links and recording space. Voice Powered Technology Intl, Inc., 800/255-2310 (CA) or **www.vpti.com**.

Portable Office Products

Company addresses and phone numbers are provided unless products are widely available through office supply dealers.

The **Eldon Mobile Manager** looks like a briefcase but acts as a portable filing cabinet. Molded-in rails accommodate hanging files and other documents. A zip-down supply pocket and two oversized pockets store supplies.

More portable office accessories, shown in Figure 12-2, let you take your office with you. If you need to write while on the road, consider the **Rogers Storage Clipboard** with a durable clip and pencil holder and a divided inside compartment that stores paper, pens and more small supplies. The **Eldon Box Office File Keeper** is a file/storage box with rails inside to accommodate hanging files and folders. A supply compartment in the lid holds pens, rubber bands, paper clips and other small office supplies.

For a larger number of hanging files, **Rogers Trunk Tote** is sturdy and lightweight, provides moisture-resistent storage and features a transparent, snap-tight lid for easier viewing of stored contents.

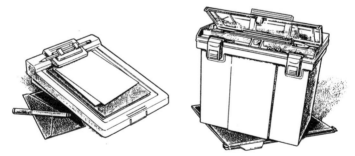

Figure 12-2. Rogers Storage Clipboard and Eldon Box Office File Keeper

Fellowes Bankers Box Hang 'n' Stor Hanging Folder Storage Box is an ideal product for storing and transporting a large number of letter-size hanging file folders. Plastic channels with a built-in track permit the files to glide smoothly. The file has a separate cover, tote handles and a large labeling area.

The **Lillian Vernon Neat Ideas for an Organized Life** catalog has some great organizers for your car—especially useful if your car is your traveling office. Be sure to check out their Web site, too. Lillian Vernon, 800/285-5555 or **www.lillianvernon.com**.

Oxford ToteFile is a compact, portable corrugated file that comes with a Pendaflex filing system—10 hanging folders in blue. The file box is white with a blue lid that matches the folder color. Also look for the **Oxford PortFile** portable file box, which comes in two sizes and includes Pendaflex hanging folders, too.

Portable Desk Accessory Kit is a zippered carry-all that packs 15 tools, including stapler, staple remover, hole punch, tape dispenser/pencil sharpener, tape, scissors, knife and notepad. Day-Timers, Inc., 800/225-5005 (PA) or **www.daytimer.com**.

Portfolio cases/notebooks are convenient tools to transport a note-taking pad and key documents. Some come equipped with a flap pocket or special pocket folders, a business card holder, a calculator and a pen/pencil strap. Look for portfolios by Hazel (**www.hazelpromo.com**). (These portfolios are not to be confused with the art portfolios discussed in Chapter 5.)

The Red Dot Portable Filing System is a versatile set of large clear files in a black case that transport project or presentation materials in a professional, organized manner. Available from Red Dot, Inc., **800/520-0010** (OR).

Rogers Auto Clipboard is a handy note pad. It attaches to a windshield or any smooth surface with a suction cup. It also features a pen on a retractable cord.

Travel Resource Information, Products and Services

Business Traveler Online (**www.biztravel.com/guide**) checks your frequent flyer balances and explores business travel trends and options.

The Center for Disease Control (the Division of Quarantine in Traveler's Health Section) can provide information on immunization or vaccinations when traveling overseas. 800/311-3435 (GA) or **www.cdc.gov**

CityNet.com is a destination search engine to nearly 5,000 places worldwide; it includes maps and links to other sites.

Encore Marketing's Short Notice Club is a "last-minute travel club" that requires a charge card number to get a booking. There is a membership fee. 800/638-8976 (MD) or **www.emitravel.com**

Arthur Frommer's Outspoken Encyclopedia of Travel is one of the best discount and budget travel sites (**www.frommers.com**).

Magellan's is my favorite travel mail-order catalog featuring hundreds of travel accessories. 800/962-4943 (CA) or **www.magellans.com**

Moment's Notice is a "short-notice" discount travel club that acts as a clearinghouse for the travel industry's unsold space. Substantial discounts apply to cruises, tours and flights. There is a membership fee. 888/241-3366 (NY) or **www.moments-notice.com**.

MSN Expedia (www.expedia.com) is a popular travel site, which also is great at comparing rental car prices.

Priceline.com lets you bid on airline tickets as well as hotel rooms to get some good deals; the downside is you don't have much advance notice and frequent flier miles aren't included.

Rand McNally Commercial Atlas and Marketing Guide features detailed and accurate maps of the 50 states, economic data, transportation and communication information, population summaries and marketing statistics. Updated annually. Rand McNally, 800/284-6565 (IL) or **www.randmcnally.com**.

Relax the Back is a great store (in 35 states and Canada) and an online catalog of products to help you sit and sleep more comfortably. I use their products at home, in my car and when I travel. **www.relaxtheback.com**.

The Road Warrior's Guide is a great pullout supplement from *PC Magazine* that they do at least once a year; also search for it online at their Web site: **www.pcmag.com**.

Smarter Living (www.smarterliving.com) gives you discounted last-minute air fares that are easily searchable.

State tourist offices for each of the 50 U.S. states are great sources of information when you're planning a trip. Many of these offices have 800 numbers. These offices are usually located in the capital city of each state and go by many a name. Key words to look for: "Department of Commerce," "Convention and Visitors Bureau" and "Office of Travel and Tourism."

Travelocity (www.travelocity.com) is a well-known online travel booking agency.

U.S. State Department (http://travel.state.gov) travel site includes foreign country entry requirements, travel warnings and consular advice.

The Weather Channel (www.weather.com) has comprehensive, up-to-date forecasts for U.S. cities and other global locations.

13

SURFING THE NET: SEARCH TIPS, TOOLS, SHORTCUTS AND SAFETY

Quick Scan: If you frequently "surf the Net" and want to learn more organized ways to tap the wealth of information on the Internet, you're on the "right page." You'll discover browsing tips, navigation shortcuts as well as some of the best Internet search tools to use—all the while protecting yourself in process.

Exploring "cyberspace," a term that novelist William Gibson coined in 1982 for the Internet, has opened up a whole new world as well as a whole new can of worms. As an organizer, a consultant and a writer, I'm both excited and concerned about the Net for myself as well as my clients.

On the plus side, you can use all this information for research, job hunting, networking to expand your business contacts (including those that are global), increasing your business, expanding customer service, collaboration, problem solving, product development, expanding your career skills and many other work-related (and personal) reasons. In researching this latest edition, I'm amazed at how quickly I can get the information I need compared to past editions. I have a vast cyberspace library at my fingertips.

On the negative side, making use of all the information you can tap can become a job in itself and can create another case of information overload. Surfing the Net can also really gobble up your time. You may find it so entertaining or compelling that you let some of your higher priority activities slip. Some people, in fact, have become addicted to the Internet according to the American Psychological Association, which said that people who spend more than 38 hours a week participating in newsgroups, chatting or sending e-mail could be at risk. Such individuals ignore their families or other personal aspects of their life and show signs of withdrawal such as anxiety or shakiness when they try to limit their Internet use. Those at risk should take "The Internet Addiction Test" by the Center for On-Line Addiction (**www.netaddiction.com**).

Besides the addiction risk, whenever you innocently use the Internet, you can open yourself to all kinds of problems—from infecting your computer system with a virus that you happen to pick up to a hacker accessing sensitive company or personal information.

Internet Safety, Privacy and Protection

From protecting company secrets and your computer system to protecting your privacy, there are some tips and tools you need to know because every time you surf commercial Web sites, those sites collect personal or demographic information. Two frightening statistics from a Federal Trade Commission study revealed that 93 percent of online businesses collect personal information and 57 percent gather demographic information from users.

Cookies Anyone?

Sometimes online sites do it with your permission (such as requesting a credit card number) but they also do it without your knowledge or permission in the form of a **cookie**, which is a block of text that is placed in a file on your hard drive by a Web site when you visit it; that cookie is then used to identify you the next time you access the site. It's a tracer on your hard drive that helps a Web site remember who you are. While cookies give you quicker access to a site without, for example, having to type in a password every time you visit, they can track all the sites you visit, giving marketers a private profile of your interests. Just as you teach your child not to accept cookies from strangers, don't let your computer automatically accept cookies from, well, strange (or even friendly) Web sites.

So how do you prevent your computer from accepting cookies? First, set your browser to warn you before letting your computer automatically accept cookies. Since most sites require that you accept cookies in order to access them, you'll probably end up accepting some or most cookies. So the next step after you've done some surfing is to delete your cookies periodically, and maybe even every day. (Cookies are stored in different locations, depending on your browser.)

While you're at it, clean out your "history" folder, which shows all the sites you've visited, and reduce the number of days that links are kept in this folder. Also clean out your "cache" folder, a temporary storage area for pages and images you've recently visited. (There is a small down side unfortunately: doing all this cleaning may slow your surfing down a bit because your browser may have to download files it would have found right away on your hard disk.)

A **cookie manager** is a program that helps you do all of these steps automatically. Cookie Pal, the award-winning program by Kookaburra Software, is a cookie manager to consider if you do a lot of surfing (**www.kburra.com**).

Finally, educate yourself on cookies by going to Cookie Central at **www.cookiecentral.com**, which tells more about how cookies work and has an excellent FAQ (frequently-asked-questions) section. (And yes, that site makes cookies, too.) But the site says that "not all cookies are bad" and that a given Web site only knows whatever information you've given it in the first place. So be careful when giving out information.

Protect Your Privacy

If you want to surf the Net anonymously, try out Anonymizer Inc.'s service at **www.anonymizer.com**, which reroutes your surfing trail through their different servers and prevents cookies. (The company's phone number is 888/746-3663.)

A software **security suite** may be the answer if you need lots of security, not only help with cookies and history files but the added protection of a **firewall** (which prevents access to your computer or your private computer network) and a **password manager** (to securely track and store all of your passwords). Some suites also speed your browsing by blocking advertisements. eSafe Protect Desktop is Aladdin Knowledge Systems's award-winning program that also provides antivirus protection (888/772-3372 [WA] or **www.esafe.com**).

Here are some other browsing tips to protect your privacy. If your ISP (Internet Service Provider) gives you several screen names, use a different screen name for browsing and/or posting to newsgroups. That way your business or personal in-box won't be flooded with spam or other mail that you don't need or want.

You may want to avoid posting to newsgroups. If you can't, then go to **www.deja.com/forms/nuke.shtml** to remove messages you posted that reside in Deja.com's archive.

To avoid getting into marketing databases, avoid having credit bureaus, motor vehicle departments and other organizations share your information with marketers. To learn what steps you can take, go to the Federal Trade Commission's Privacy site: **www.ftc.gov/privacy** .

Take advantage of automatic updates for Microsoft and Netscape security patches. Check out their respective update services: **http:// windowsupdate.microsoft.com** and **http://home.netscape.com/smartupdate**.

About two-thirds of commercial Web sites post their privacy policies. Also, look for sites that have been certified by two main watchdog groups, BBBOnline (**www.bbbonline.com**) and TRUSTe (**www.truste.org**).

Browsing/Surfing Tips

If you think that you can only open up one window at a time when you surf the Net, well, think again. Stay tuned for some simple tips for more effective browsing.

Mouse, Keyboard and Other Navigation Shortcuts

To not only save time while a site downloads, but to be able to switch between different sites or links, **open up several windows at a time**. Instead of linking to a site by clicking on the left mouse button (which removes the current site from the screen), **click on the right button**, which brings up the **"open in new window"** option. It's much easier to switch between two or more open windows than having to use the "Back" button up in far left corner. This is also a good way to download several pages simultaneously, which will save you time. Another way to open an additional window is through the "File" command up at the top.

You can **use the task bar to switch between multiple windows**, too, because each window is represented by a button on the task bar. You could also **hold down "Alt" and then "Tab" to rotate through open windows**.

To go backwards or forwards, click the **right mouse button** anywhere on an open window (except a link) and a pop-up menu lets you choose **"Back"** or **"Forward."** Or hold down the **"Alt" key and then a left or right arrow** to move backwards or forward.

If you want to see each of your open pages on the screen at one time, select "Tile" in the Window menu.

To **move quickly in a given Web site**, try these keyboard tricks: a) the **"Page Up"** and **"Page Down"** keys move you either up or down one page at a time and b) the **up and down arrow keys** move you up and down one line at a time.

To **find a word or phrase** in the text of a Web page, type **"Ctrl-F"** or click **"Find"** in the "Edit" menu.

Here's another trick to download a site faster without having to wait for all the graphics to download. **Download screens with text** by clicking your browser's Stop button or pressing "ESC" just after the page starts to appear. If you want to make this text-only loading style your default, alter your browser's options.

In fact, take a few minutes to **explore all of your browser's options and preferences**. You could save a lot of time and make your browsing more productive.

To decrease your reading time while increasing your browsing time online,

read offline as much as possible.

To prevent slowdown from "cyber traffic jams," avoid these peak times: 5 p.m. to 2 a.m. EST. (If you're on cable or DSL, you might not notice a difference.) To get the latest Internet traffic report (believe it or not!) go to **www.andovernews.com/trafficreport.html**.

To prevent the ultimate slowdown from a malfunctioning computer, always scan files (even safe-looking e-mail) for viruses before you download. (See Chapter 8 for more on antivirus software.) To be extra safe download files on a removable disk such a Zip drive or a floppy drive rather than your hard drive.

Internet Search Tools

Before we talk about search tools, let's examine the scope of what it is we're trying to search. First, the Internet is a federation of untold millions of computers in networks around the world. Unlike a network in a company that feeds into some central authority, Internet networks rely on no such authority.

The fastest-growing part of the Internet is a subsection called the **World Wide Web** or simply the **Web**, which is a vast network of documents that combine text, images, sound and video, as well as various services, including news and file transfer. (The Web was invented by Tim Berners-Lee in the mid-80s.)

As of this writing, according to one study by the NEC Research Institute in Princeton, there are over 800 million pages on the Web and of course, it just keeps growing. Most search tools are aware of no more than 16 percent of those pages and generally it's a lot less. Even if you combine all the search tools that exist, together they cover less than 50 percent of the Web. The problem lies not in having the technology to find all 800 million Web pages; rather, the problem lies in the time and money it takes to *index* all the material.

There are several different types of search tools available today: directories, search engines, metasearch engines, specialized search engines, Web databases, portals, offline search tools and Web information managers.

A **directory**, such as Yahoo!, is a hierarchical, searchable index that contains lengthy lists of categories and subcategories that are lists of Web sites. When you use a directory such as Yahoo!, you don't look for a specific word; you're looking for a **topic** or **subject**. To explore that topic, you'll "drill down" (click) your way through various categories and subcategories where you'll find lists of Web sites on different subjects related to your topic. Directories are compiled and organized by "taxonomists," people whose job it is to surf the Net and create these categories and subcategories of sites. To get to Yahoo! log on at: **www.yahoo.com**. For a Yahoo!-like business directory with a wide range of business topics, check out U.S. Business Advisor (**www.business.gov**).

Search engines use automatic software programs called "robots," "spiders" or "crawlers" that tally up which **words** appear on which sites and how many times they appear. Depending on the search engine, these robots look in different places on a given site—perhaps the title of the Web page, how many other pages link to it and/or how many times a word appears. The problem with the latter is that Web designers tend to "wallpaper" or plaster key words all over sites just so that search engines will pick up the sites. Consequently, you'll often get way too many results when you search.

A search engine is for particular words, bits of information or even specific questions, unlike a directory, which is generally better suited for subjects. Some search tools have a combination of directory and search engine features. Some popular search engines are Northern Light (**www.nlsearch.com**), HotBot (**www.hotbot.com**) and Excite (**www.excite.com**). Also take a look at Google (**www.google.com**) and Fast Search (**www.alltheweb.com**).

Metasearch engines or sites query multiple engines simultaneously. I've been using InFind for years and find it to be a handy information source (**www.infind.com**) when I want to look up specific words or names of organizations. InFind queries six different search engines and produces a one-page organized list of sites.

Specialized search engines are going to become increasingly important as the number of Web pages rapidly multiplies. Many of them have access to their own **Web databases**. Here are some good **business search engines**: Company Sleuth (**www.companysleuth.com**) provides information on companies; CorporateInformation (**www.corporateinformation.com**) gives you information on private and foreign companies from non-U.S. exchanges; Hoover's Online (**www.hoovers.com**) has good free and fee info on 14,000 companies; and for stock market info, look at TradingDay.com (**www.tradingday.com**).

For specialized news search engines there are: 1stHeadlines (**www.1stheadlines.com**), which includes business category headlines and indexes 300 newspapers and wire services; Northern Light Current News Search (**www.northernlight.com**) for free and fee archives with thousands of sources (news, books, journals and more) going back ten years; and NewsLibrary (**www.newslibrary.com**) which searches 65 U.S. and Canada newspaper archives and charges per article. (Both Northern Light and NewsLibrary let you see article abstracts before you pay.)

Web portals provide integrated tools and search services. Along with searching the Web, they also provide messaging (e-mail, chat, instant and sometimes even voice) and calendaring. Some call portals the next generation of online services. AOL is considered a Web portal as is Yahoo!, which continues to receive rave reviews not only as a directory but also as a portal.

Offline search tools are utility programs that help you manage and organize links as well as set up recurring searches. Like metasearch engines they query multiple search engines but they also help you manage the results. You'll want to take a look at the award-winning Copernic (**www.copernic.com**).

Web information managers are software programs that help you: a) capture information from the Web in a variety of different ways (for example, full page with or without graphics, highlighted sections and partial sites); b) organize it into meaningful categories usually using a hierarchical folder system; and c) easily retrieve and share data. Top programs in this young category include: iHarvest One (**www.iharvest.com**); SurfSaver (**www.surfsaver.com**) by askSam Systems; and Webforia Organizer & Reporter (**www.webforia.com**).

Resource Guide

Note: See this chapter for other tools or services not listed here.

Alexa helps you surf the Net more effectively (**www.alexa.com**).

AnyWho is a handy database of telephone information and a searchable, nationwide AT&T telephone book for individuals and businesses (**www.anywho.com**).

AskMe.com lets you ask questions of experts on virtually any topic.

Babylon.com is a free, single-click translator that turns Web English into nine other languages. (Considering 70 percent of all PC users are non-English-speaking but 80 percent of Web content is in English, this free, instant-translation software could really help a lot of people.)

Backflip provides a site to download all the Web pages you've saved as bookmarks or "favorites," letting you organize and search hundreds or thousands of them. It creates your own personal, Yahoo!-like directory (**www.backflip.com**).

Bigbook lists over 16 million U.S. businesses, letting you find services anywhere in the country (**www.bigbook.com**).

Deja News helps you locate information in Usenet communities (**www.dejanews.com**).

www.safekids.com/encyclopedias.htm provides a listing of free online reference sources.

Switchboard.com gives phone numbers and e-mail addresses for individuals.

TotalNews has newspaper and TV news sites (**www.totalnews.com**).

WorldPages has U.S. and Canadian white- and yellow-page listings, e-mail addresses, URLs and links to 200 directories.

Yahoo! People (formerly Four11) is best for searching e-mail addresses.

14

POSITIVELY ORGANIZED! IN ACTION

---

*Quick Scan: This is the companion chapter to any other chapters you've read. It is the most important chapter because this is where you commit to action. Discover how to dramatically increase your own level of organization easily and quickly. Learn how to focus on your key areas and goals for improvement to increase performance and achievement and become the **best** you can be.*

I f you want to be your best, it helps to be Positively Organized! But remember that's *Positively* Organized, not perfectly or compulsively organized.

I tell my clients, "**Be only as organized as you need to be.**" Don't become compulsive or guilty about organization. This is a tool to help you *prevent* stress, not add to it. Organization is not another thing to feel guilty about.

An Action Orientation

Now's the time to act. While organization is a process that evolves over time, you can facilitate this process by taking action and using this book as a springboard for action.

Design Evolving Organization Systems That Work for You

As you organize, focus on this phrase: "evolving organization systems."

Just as you're working in a time of change, so, too, must your organization systems evolve and change. Be sure to involve anyone who will be affected by a new organization system. If you don't, you will probably encounter great resistance. As support operations manager Stan Morel once said, "People don't like change unless they had something to do with it."

Every organization system you and/or coworkers develop should be a flexible set of tools and work habits for managing one to three of the following resources:

1. Time—planning, scheduling, recording, completing and tracking current and future meetings, appointments, commitments, activities, projects and goals

2. Information—developing productive paperwork and work flow procedures; keeping manual and computerized information accessible and up to date

3. Space—creating a functional and pleasing physical working environment both in the office and on the road.

For many, organizational systems have evolved quite by chance over the years. Your own style and degree of organization will depend on a number of factors—your level of activity, whether you have any support staff, if you deal face to face with the public, how you like to work and the "corporate culture" where you work. It's up to you just how much and what kind of organization you need.

Where to Begin

Start small but think big. If you've read more than one chapter, go back to the table of contents and look at the titles of chapters that you've read. Which chapter will make the biggest difference to you and/or others in your career or life?

Now go back to that chapter and skim the headings and subheads as well as any underlines or notes you made. What jumps out? Find a small change you can make that will make a big difference. It might be changing a work habit or using a new system. Many clients find, for example, that setting aside five minutes a day to plan the next day is helpful. Some clients decide to set up and use a daily paperwork system. Others work together jointly to create or streamline an office system or procedure.

Your Plan of Action

Dare to put your intentions in writing. When you write something down, you're giving a message to your subconscious. Besides reinforcing your subconscious, writing also helps you clarify your thinking so that you're better prepared to take action. Many, if not most people, though, are afraid that if they write something down, they'll forget about it. These people need to combine the act of writing with *reading* and *doing* what has been written. If you make a daily to-do list, for example, *read* it over several times during the day and *do* the listed activities.

Don't be afraid of change. Tropophobia, the fear of change, is the biggest stumbling block to action for most people. Once you accept and *initiate* change in your life, you'll have more control over it.

I have my clients write a **plan of action** at the conclusion of a seminar or consultation. The plan can take a number of different formats—it can be a simple letter to yourself or a prepared form such as the one on the next page.

Commit to yourself, commit to a deadline. The plan of action is basically a *written commitment to yourself.* Ideally, your first plan should focus on an organizational habit, tool, project or system that can be put into action in a *one- to four-week maximum block of time.* Create an experience of success. Don't overwhelm yourself with a six-month project where you may become discouraged or disinterested.

Be specific. Instead of the general "improving my time management skills," for your project, select something more specific, such as "I will take five minutes to plan and write tomorrow's to-do list at the end of each day." Instead of cleaning out all your file cabinets from the last 12 years, complete one file drawer in one week.

What's in it for you? Besides some hard work, you better be able to rattle off a whole list of benefits or results you hope to gain. Better yet, pick the *most important benefit.* Underline and star that benefit.

Plan step by step. If your project has more than two or three steps try "Mind Mapping" your steps before you put them in linear order. Mind Mapping is a way to pour out your thoughts and ideas in a visual, picture outline. Once you can "see" your ideas, then you can determine their sequential relationship to one another. (See Chapter 9 for a discussion of Mind Mapping and other idea organization tools.)

Make appointments with yourself. Once you've charted out your steps, schedule blocks of time to complete these steps. Schedule appointments with yourself and don't break them! Have calls screened (or let your voice mail take them), go off by yourself where no one can find you or pick a time when you won't be disturbed. Your plan of action should indicate how long steps will take—total time or time per day/week. Then write appointments in your calendar or planner based upon your plan of action projections.

Reward yourself! Make your plan of action more enjoyable by providing any or all of the three main types of rewards—tangible, psychological and experiential. Tangible rewards include physical things you give yourself—new clothes, a deluxe appointment book, or a PDA for example. Psychological rewards are positive messages you tell yourself—stating positive affirmations

Your Positively Organized!® Plan of Action

Today's Date: _____

Organization Project or Activity:

_____

Benefits or Results:

_____

Ideas/Sketch/Brainstorm:

<u>Action Steps</u>   <u>How long/often?</u>   <u>Calendared?</u>
_____
_____
_____
_____
_____
_____
_____

Reward yourself with:

_____
_____

Completion Date _____

and giving yourself little "pats on the back." Experiential rewards are a cross between tangible and psychological—getting a massage, taking a trip, dining out in a special restaurant are examples.

Getting others involved in your organization project can be a rewarding process in and of itself. Whether you engage a "buddy" who will offer positive reinforcement or you actually share the work with another, you will more likely increase your accountability and success rate as well as lighten your load. Encourage others to support you in your goals and do the same for them.

How to Change Habits

Getting more organized almost always involves habit-changing behavior. But don't worry, it doesn't take a lifetime to change a habit. Actually it takes 21 to 30 days, provided you do the following:

1. Decide what new habit or behavior you intend to practice.
2. Write it down on paper. List *how*, *when* and *why* you're going to do it.
3. Share your new habit with someone else.
4. Reward yourself. Psychological affirmations before, during and after you practice a behavior can be particularly helpful.
5. Practice, practice, practice. You need to repeat the behavior, preferably every day, to create the habit.

Commitment to Be Your Best

You will succeed with your plan of action and habit changes only if you are truly committed to being your best.

But what does being your best mean? For some, it's beating out the competition. For others, it's "doing your best"—being in competition with yourself. It's fine tuning what you're already good at. Award-winning athletes, such as world champion whitewater canoeist Jon Lugbill, are always fine tuning, looking for a better way. See if you can relate Lugbill's whitewater canoeing description to your work or life:

> I love the sport and I love being good at it. The challenge is that you constantly have to search out all the little advantages: techniques in the boat, types of boats, what you eat, how much sleep you get, everything down the line—you've got to learn to get the most out of everything you can. The combination of physical and mental goals, that's what's exciting about the sport for me.

Define it for yourself. After all, the way you live your life makes a statement about you. Why not make the best statement?

According to author David Viscott, we each have at least one special gift to give the world. I believe that those gifts should extend beyond yourself in some way to make a better world. What are your gifts and how are you making the *best* use of them?

Being Positively Organized! will help you *use* those gifts so you can indeed be your best.

A UTHOR BIO

Susan Silver is the recognized organizing expert and bestselling author of the award-winning bible of organization, *Organized to Be Your Best!* Susan is a knowledgeable, entertaining and hands-on training, coaching and speaking professional who heads the consulting firm Positively Organized! Susan's **Positively Organized!® Programs** inspire audiences to be their best by showing them essential organization skills and systems to control today's information and communications overload, accomplish more high-value work, build teamwork and reduce stress.

A Personal Note from the Author

I want to hear from you. Please e-mail me via the Adams-Hall Publishing Web site (**www.adams-hall.com**) with your results from this book as well as any comments or suggestions for future editions. You, too, could be in print!

Upcoming editions of *Organized to Be Your Best!* could feature your contributions and will keep you up to date on the latest organizational tools and techniques. You'll see how others are dealing with the challenges we all face. What's more, you'll be part of an ongoing process that's on the cutting edge of quality, innovation, performance and achievement.

You can also be part of that process even more directly. Work with my company, Positively Organized!, through a consultation or a customized training program designed to produce positive results for you or your organization in a variety of skill areas. You can find out more about Positively Organized! Programs and Services by clicking on "Susan Silver" on the Adams-Hall home page.

INDEX

A

@Backup, 149
Abbot Office Systems, 65, 114
Abledata, 201
Abodia Slide Storage Cabinets, 76
Acco (See Wilson Jones)
Accordion file, 24
Acroprint Time Recorder Co., 172
ACT!, 36, 164, 171
Action Technologies
  ActionWorks eBRM2000,
  Metro and Process Builder, 169
ADA products, 201
Adaptec, 147
AEC Management Systems
  Details, 170
  FastTrack Schedule, 168
Alexa, 258
Allsop Inc., 103, 140
All-state International
  CaseGuard, 121
  Expense Record, 167
  Tickler Record System, 24
  Time Record, 167
Alphabetic Filing Rules, 119
American Coaching Network, 6
American Productivity & Quality Assn., 200
America Online (see AOL)
anonymizer.com, 254
Answering machines (See Voice mail)
AnyTime Deluxe, 36
AnyWho, 258
AOL, 33, 230, 257

APC PowerManager, 97
APW Wright Line, 125
ARCserveit, 147
ARMA, 119
Artist & document storage, 74-77
ASF Notebook Computer Light, 229
AskMe.com, 258
askSam (askSam Sys.), 171
Association for Personal Computer User Groups, 73, 150
Astound Conference Center, 220
Atrieva Service, 149
Attention Deficit Disorder, 5
AutoSpell, 221
Avery,
  Extra Wide Index dividers, 62
  IndexMaker, 63
  LabelPro, 114
  Ready Index, 62
  See-Through Color Dots, 64
  SwifTabs, 64
  WorkSaver Inserts, 124

B

Babylon.com, 258
Backflip, 258
Backup, 142-50. (See also Computer file organization and maintenance)
Balance, 1-2, 6-7, 45-46
Bankers Boxes, 70, 109
Baumgarten's, 78
Beyond Words, 189
Bigbook, 258
Binders, 61-63 (See also Notebooks)

Bindertek Law files, 63
BlackBerry, 231
BlackIce Defender, 150
Boards, control, 159
Brenthaven, 228
Business cards, 63
Business Insight (Bus. Res. Soft.), 169
Business Traveler Online, 250
Butler, Wilford (Bill), 56, 73, 237, 238,
   240, 243, 246
Buzan, Tony, 160-61

C

Caere Corp.
   OmniPage Pro, 58
   PageKeeper, 126, 166
Calendars, 17, 18-19, 34-35
CallWave, 216
Canon, 59, 98
CaseLogic, 140
Casio, 123
CD-R, 147-48
CD-RW, 147-48, 227
CD-ROMs, 96, 126, 139-140, 147, 165
Cellmania.com, 247
Cell phones, 225-27
Center for Disease Control, 250
Center for On-line Addiction, 253
Centis, 62
Century Photo Products, 76
Charities, donations for, 73-74
Charts, 21, 154, 156-160. (See also
   Project management, Work Manage-
   ment)
Cheaney, Lee, 186
Checklists, 154-156
CityNet.com, 250
CleanSweep, 136, 141
C-LINE, 62
Clips, 63-64
Clower, Beverly, 113
Clusters, hard disk, 135
Cluster idea maps, 161
CMS Automatic Backup System, 147

Coalition Against Unsolicited
   Commercial E-mail, 221
Coastal Training Technology, 188
Codi Air Pro, 228
Collaborative computing, 219-21
Collator (Evans Coll.), 66-67, 93
Collectors, 68-78
Color Coding, 64-65, 112, 124-125, 207
Communication, 180-84. (See also
   Telephone and Traveling)
Company Sleuth, 256
Compressing data, 136
Computer accessories, 96-98
Computer Associates
   ARCserveit, 148
   Cheyenne Software, 148
Computer file organization and
      maintenance,
   backup, 127, 142-150
   CD-R, 147-48
   CD-ROM, 96, 126, 139-140, 165
   CD-RW, 147-48
   compression, 136
   data access/recovery, 166
   defragmenting, 135-136, 152
   desktop organization, 132
   directories and folders, 129-130
   disaster prevention, 141-142
   DVD, 96, 139-140
   DVD-RAM, 147
   e-mail (See E-mail)
   floppy organization, 138-139
   hard disk and, 133-135
   hierarchy, 129-130
   housekeeping, 133-141
   names, 130-13
   optimize, 135-36
   partitioning, 128-129
   path names, 131-132
   scanning, 136, 152
   shortcuts, 133
   viruses and, 137
Computers
   recycling, 73-74
Computers for Schools, 73

Connected Online Backup, 149
Connectors, 229
Conquering Chaos at Work, 201
Contact managers, 31, 164
Continuous improvement, 177
Cookie Pal, 254
Copernic, 258
Copyholders, 94
Corex CardScan, 59
CoSession, 230
Cox, Danny, 157-58
CPM chart, 157
Creative Memories, 76
Cumulative Trauma Disorders, 104
Curtis (Rolodex), 103, 229
    Curtis Clip, 94
Customer focus, 175-76
Customer service, 175
CyNet, 216

D

Daily paperwork system, 50-56
Daisy Wheel Ribbon Co., 103
    FIFO, 54
    Fox Bay Carpal Rest Wrist Support, 97
    Wrist rest, 90
DATA (TreeAge), 169-170
Data access, 166
Databases/programs, 163-65
Day Runner, 21, 29, 34
Day-Timer Organizer software, 36
Day-Timers, Inc.,
    accessories, other, 29
    calendar/master list, 20,
    charts and forms, 168
    organizers/planner, 34
    Portable Desk Accessory Kit, 250
    project lists, 21
    ruler/calculator, 28
    software, 36
    To-do list, 20
    Two-Page-Per-Week forms, 20
DaZZle Plus, 170
Defragmenting, 135-136, 152
Deja News, 258

Delegation, 40-42
DeLorme
    Map'n'Go, 248
    Street Atlas USA, 248
Desk (See also Paper/paperwork),
    accessibility, 50-51, 65-66
    accessories, 65-67, 92-94
    myth of messy desk, 47-48
    organization, 47-51
    productivity and, 47-48
    work space/surface, 49-51, 55
Desk files or sorters, 24, 54
Details, 170
Diagramming software, 160
Dictaphone, 232, 233
Dictaphone Straight Talk, 233
Dictation, 232-33
Ding (Antiverse), 211
Disk Jockey, 150
Document Control Systems, 126
Document management, 125-126
Drag and File (Canyon), 150
DragonNaturallySpeakingMobile, 233
DragStrip, 150
DSL, 210
DVD, 96, 139-140
DVD-RAM, 147

E

East-West Education Development
Foundation, 74
EFax.com, 216
eGroups.com, 221
Eldon
    Add-A-File Filing Vanes, 66
    Box Office File Keeper, 249
    The Folder File Holder, 66
    The Hanging File Holder, 66
    Mobile Manager, 249
    Mouse Tray, 97
    MouseDeck, 97
    Underdesk Keyboard and Mouse
Superstation, 97
    Underdesk Mouse Tray, 97
Electric hole punchers, 94

Electronic organizers, 32-33, 35-36, 225.

E-mail
  Attachments and, 206-07
  Color coding, 207
  Controlling, 203-211
  Encryption and, 204-05
  Filters and, 205-06
  Instant messaging and, 210
  Mailbox limits and, 207-08
  Organizing tips and, 204, 206-07
  Passwords, 205
  Phones and, 226
  Phone messages and, 207
  Privacy and, 207
  Rules-based, 205-06
  Saving, 204
  Signatures, electronic/digital, 205
  Writing tips and, 208-10

Employee involvement, 184-85, 190-193

Encore Marketing's Short Notice Club,
  250

Encryption, 204-05

Encryption Plus (PC Guardian), 205

Enfish Tracker, 150

Environment, office, 99-103

Ergonomics, 86-92, 97
  Software, 88
  Web sites, 87

eRoom, 219

eSafe Protect Desktop, 254

Esselte Pendaflex
  EarthWise, 118, 120, 121
  How to File, 119
  Oxford copyholders, 94
  Oxford DecoFile, 93
  Oxford DecoFlex, 53
  Oxford DecoRack, 67
  Oxford Manila File Jackets, 122
  Oxford Plus line, 123
  Oxford ToteFile, 250
  Pendaflex box bottom folders, 120
  Pendaflex Hanging Box File, 120
  Pend. Hang. Expandable File, 54
  Pend. Hanging File Jacket, 120
  Pendaflex hanging folder, 120

Pend. Hang. Partition Folders, 121
Pendaflex Interior Folders, 120
Pend. Links, 123
Pendaflex Printed Label Inserts, 124
Pendaflex SpeedFrame, 123
Pendaflex Sort-Pal, 54
Printed Label Inserts, 124

E-ttachment Opener, 221

Eudora (Qualcomm), 221

Excite, 33

Excite.com, 257

ExerciseBreak (Hopkins), 88

Experience in Software
  Project Kickstart, 170

Extranet, 220

Eyes, 89-90

F

FastTrack Schedule, 168

Fax, 215-18, 231, 232

Fellowes
  Bankers Boxes, 70, 109
  Bankers Box Hang 'n' Stor Hanging
Folder Storage Box, 249
  Laptop Copygrip, 229
  Literature Sorter, 78
  Magazine File, 52, 78
  Portable File & Drawer File, 77
  Roll/Stor Stands, 75
  Strictly Business Visible Folder File,
    66
  Strictly Business Mail/Literature
    Center, 78

50 Simple Things Your Business Can Do
  to Save the Earth, 201

File cabinets, 112

File Ferret 32, 150

Files 105-126. (See also Computer file
    organization. & maintenance)
  accordion, 122
  active and inactive, 108-109
  cabinets, 112
  desk, 24, 54
  expanding, 122
  frames for hanging, 123

magazine, 93
names for, 109-111
phobias and, 105-106
pockets, 67
quiz, 106
step, 56
system for, 107-119
wall mount, 67
File transfer/synchronization, 33, 225, 230, 248
Filing, 105-126
automated, 125-26
color coding, 112, 124-25
labeling, 123
maintenance, 116-117
managers and, 117-119
phobias, 105-06
supplies, 77-78, 98, 119-124
systems, special, 125-26
Filofax, 34
Finance Business Forms catalog, 124
Firewall, 220
Fix-It Utilities (Ontrack), 136
Folders, file, 112-113
Follow-up (See Tickler systems, Work/Project management)
Forms, 154-156
Franklin Covey
organizers/planner, 34
Free Disk Space, 230
Arthur Frommer's Outspoken Encyclopedia of Travel, 250
Furniture and equipment, 86-92
ergonomics, 87-92
modular furniture, 86-87

G
Gambrell, Don, 182
Gantt chart, 157, 159, 162
Geodex Systems, 34
Getting Things Done, 14
Gifts in Kind Intl., 74
Goals, 8-12
GoBack, 150

GoldMine (Goldmine Soft.), 36, 164, 172
Goodwill, 201
Google, 257
Green Disk, 74, 141
Groupware. (See Workgroup computing.)
Guard Dog, 150
Guide to Record Retention Rqmts., 119

H
Habits, 4, 5, 55
Handspring. See Visor
Hazel, 250
HelloDirect, 95, 104, 247
Hewlett Packard, 215
Hold Everything, 66
Home office, 85, 222
Hotbot.com, 256
Hotels, 237-38
Hotmail, 230
HotOffice Technologies, 219
HotPage, 247
How to File Guide, 119
How to Survive Your Computer Work Station, 104
HP (See Hewlett Packard)
HUMOResources, 201

I
IBM ThinkPad, 229
Idea tools, 160-62
iGo Mobile Technology Outfitter, 227, 247
Individual Software
AnyTime Deluxe, 36
Infind.com, 256
Information management (See Databases, Document Management, Paper/Paperwork, Personal Information Managers, Record keeping systems),
INFO SELECT, (Micro Logic), 172
Inmac, 104
In/out system, 54

Inspiration Software, 161-62
Instant messaging, 210
Intellisync, 248
Intergram Intl, 216
Interguru, 221
Internet
  addicted to, 252-53
  browsing tips, 255-56
  cache, 253
  collaborative computing, 219-221
  cookies, 253-54
  e-mail and, 204-09, 230-31
  extranets and, 220
  faxes and, 215-16, 231
  firewalls and, 220
  handheld wireless devices and, 230-31
  instant messaging and, 210
  intranets, 220
  mouse and, 255
  options, 230-31
  privacy, 253-55
  remote access programs and, 230
  searching, 256-58
  storage space on, 230
  surfing tips, 255-56
  unified messaging and, 218-19
  virtual desktop services and, 230
  voice mail and, 231
Interruptions, 37-39
Intranet, 220
InvisiMail Deluxe (InvisiMail Intl.), 205

J

Jasc Media Center, 150
JEFFCO, 121
Jet lag, 245-46
Jeter Systems, 125
JFax, 216
JFax.com Unified Messaging, 219
Job Accommodation Network, 201
Junk mail,
  Direct Marketing Assn., 58
  Privacy Rights Clearinghouse, 58
  Stop Junk Mail Assn., 58
  "Stop Junk Mail Forever," 58

K

Kardex, 125
Kensington, 140, 228, 229
Keyboards, 96-97
KidDesk (Edmark), 142
Konexx Konnector, 229
Kroy, 113

L

Labeling, 123
Label protectors, 124
Labels, folder.(See Filing supplies)
Lanier Information Systems, 233
LapLink, 230
Laptop computers, 31-32, 227-30
LaptopLane, 238
Larry's World, 152
Legal Tabs Co., 63
Letter trays, 67
Light Impressions, 76-77
  Nega*Guard System, 76
  PrintFile, 76-77
Lillian Vernon Neat Ideas for an
  Organized Life, 104, 249
Lists
  daily to-do, 19-20
  master, 17, 20-21
Literature organizers/sorters, 67, 78
Lotus Development Corp.
  Lotus Notes, 219, 220
  Lotus Organizer, 36
  Lotus Quickplace, 219

M

Magazine storage, 93
Magellan's, 250
Magid, Lawrence, 152
Magna Chart/Magna Visual, 160, 168
Magnetic Concepts, 168
Magnetic wall charts, 159
Mail, 55. (See also E-mail)
MailSpy, 221
MailStart.com, 248
Managers, 186-87

Map'n'Go, 248
MapsOnUs.com, 248
Master list, 20-21
MBA-ware, 163
McAfee VirusScan, 136
Meetings, team, 187-90
Memindex, 168
Memogenda (Norwood), 21
Memorex, 140
MemTurbo, 136
Micrografx
  iGraphics, 168
Microsoft Corp.
  Microsoft Access, 172
  Microsoft Exchange, 219
  Microsoft Office, 130
  Microsoft Project, 170
  Microsoft Visio, 83, 169
MicroTouch Systems, Inc., 190
Miller Multiplex Display Fixture Co.
  (System 4000), 77
MindManager, 161
Mind Map, 160-61, 189
Mission, company, 185-86
Mobile telecommunications, 224-32,
  233-34, 247-49
Mobile WinFax, 216
Modems, 229
Moment's Notice, 250
Monitors, 96
Mossberg, Walter S., 152, 228
Motorola StarTAC, 248
Mouse, 97, 140-141, 255
MSN Expedia, 251
MyPlaceWare/Place Ware Conference
  Center, 220

N

National Association for the Exchange
  of Industrial Resources, 74
National Business Furniture, 103
National Cristina Foundation, 74
Newell Office Products (See Eldon and
  Rogers)
  Mouse Perch, 97

Newstrack Executive Tape Service, 46,
  233
Nightingale-Conant, 46
9 to 5 Fact Sheets (National Assn. of
  Working Women), 104
Northern Light, 256
Norton software (See Symantec)
Notebooks 31-32, 227-230 (See also
  Laptop computers),
Notes (Lotus), 219, 220
Novell
  GroupWise, 219

O

Obsessive Compulsive Disorder (OCD),
  6
OC Foundation, 6
OCR, 58, 126
Office Depot, 169
Office for the Visually or Physically
  Impaired, 201
Office Hours for Windows, 180
Official Airline Guides
  EETS, 240
  FlightDisk, 240
  OAG FlightLine, 240
  OAG Pocket Flight Guide, 240, 243
OmniPage Pro, 58
On-line services, 33, 137, 149-50, 166
Ontrack Data Recovery Inc., 150
Organizers, 27-30, 34-35
  desktop file, 24, 54, 65-67, 92-94
  electronic, 17, 32-33, 35-36, 225
  literature, 78
  paper-based, 27-30
  personal, 17, 34-35
Organizing others, 195-99
Out of the Crisis, 201
Oxford (See Esselte Pendaflex)

P

PageKeeper, 126, 166
Pagers, 225-26
Palm.Net, 248
Palm PDAs, 32

PaperDirect catalog, 190
Paper/paperwork (See also Files, Desk),
  accessories, 92-94
  daily paperwork system, 51-54
  decisions, 55-56, 69-70, 105-06
  explosion, 49
  long-term, 57-58, 73
  recycle, reduce, reuse, 59-60
  scanners and, 58-59
  sorting, 70-72
  storing, 72
  tax, 60-61, 69
  tossing, 69-70
  traveling and, 234-36, 249-50
PaperPort scanner (Visioneer), 59
Partitioning computer, 128
PartitionMagic, 128, 150
PassKeeper, 205
Passwords, 205
PC Cards, 229
PC Magazine, 59, 150
PC WORLD, 59, 150
PDAs, 17, 18, 20, 21, 27, 30-31, 32-33, 35-36, 225
Pendaflex. (See Esselte Pendaflex)
Performance management, 191-92
Personal digital assistants (See PDAs)
Personal information managers (See PIMs)
Personal Technology Web site, 152
Personal Vault, 150
PERT chart, 157, 162
PGP (See ViaCrypt), 205
PhoneDisc (InfoUSA), 165
Phones (See Telephones)
Photographic storage, 75-76
PIMs (See Personal information managers), 17, 20, 30-32, 36, 164
Pioneer New Media, 139
Plan Hold, 75
PLANIT Board Systems Inc., 169
Planner Pad, 35
Planners (See Organizers)
Planning and prioritizing, 7-8, 14-17,

42, 196-97
Plantronics, 225
Pocket PCs, 17, 32, 35, 36, 225
Pocket-it Organizers, 35
Portico (General Magic), 219
Positively Organized, 3, 5, 25, 259-63
Post-it (See 3M)
Power Desk Utilities, 150
PowWow (Tribal Voice), 211
Priceline.com, 251
Priorities, 14-17, 42-43, 196-97
Process Version, 170
Project Kickstart, 170
Project management, 153-172
Project Scheduler, 170
Protonet, 216
Proxemics, 84-85

Q
Quality, 174-75, 179-194
Quality is Free, 201
Quality Press, 201
Quickplace (Lotus), 219
Quickview Plus, 150
Quill Corporation, 118
QUO VADIS planners, 35

R
Rand McNally
  Rand McNally Commercial Atlas and Marketing Guide, 251
  Rand McNally's StreetFinder, 248
  Rand McNally's TripMaker, 248
Record keeping systems, 167, 172
Records retention, 119
Records storage, 77-78
Recycling, 59-60, 73-74, 199-200
Red Dot Portable Filing System, 250
Redi-Tags (BTE Enter.), 64
Relax the Back, 251
Reliable Home Office catalog, 66, 104
Remote access programs, 230
Roadnews, 248
Rogers (See Newell Office Products)
  Rogers Auto Clipboard, 250

Rogers (continued)
  Rogers Storage Clipboard, 249
  Rogers Trunk Tote, 249
  Rogers Wire Step Sort-a-File, 66
Rolodex Corp.,
  card file and accessories, 63
Rushing, 43-44

S

Safco
  Art Rack, 75
  Corrugated Fiberboard Roll Files, 76
  5- and 10-Drawer Steel Flat Files, 75
  Giant Stack Trays, 75
  Mobile Roll Files, 76
  Portable Art and Drawing Portfolio, 75
  Tube-Stor KD Roll Files, 76
  12-Drawer Budget Flat File,
  Upright Roll Files,
  Vertical Filing Systems, 75
Safeguard, 24, 167, 172
Safeguard Interactive, 150
Sales/telemarketing, 36, 164, 171, 228
Scanners, 58-59
Scanning disks, 137, 152
SCAN/PLAN, 35, 161, 171
Schechter, Harriet, 201
Schedule boards (See Charts)
ScheduleOnline.com, 33
Scitor Corp.
  Process Version, 170
  Project Scheduler, 170
Searching Internet (See Internet)
Secure-It, 104
Service, customer, 175
Share the Technology, 74
Sheet or page protectors, 62
Sidekick, 36
Sleep, 2
Smarter Living, 251
Smead,
  Artist Portfolio, 75
  Classification Folder, 121
  Desk File, 25
  Flex-I-Vision Box Bottom, 120

Seal & View Label Protectors, 124
  self-adhesive vinyl pockets, 123
Sorters,
  desk files or sorters, 24, 54
  literature organizers/sorters, 67, 78
Soundview Exec. Book Summaries, 46
Spacesaver Group, The, 125
SpinRite (Gibson), 137
Stac Replica Tape, 147
Starfish Software, 36
State Tourist Offices, 251
Stationery holders, 67, 93
StationMate Project File, 65
StatusView, 180
Stayer, Ralph, 174
StreetAtlas, 248
Stress, 1-2
Supplies, 98
SureTrak Project Manager, 170
Surge protector, 96
Switchboard.com, 166
SYCOM
  label protectors, 124
Symantec
  CleanSweep, 136, 141
  Mobile WinFax, 216
  Norton AntiVirus, 137, 152
  Norton System Works, 136, 150
  Norton Utilities, 135, 137, 150
  Norton Web Services, 150
  WinFax Pro, 215, 232
Synchronization, 33, 230

T

TABBIES (Div., Xertrex Int'l, Inc.), 65
Tab Data File, 125
TAB Products Co., 125
Targus, 228
Tax paperwork, 60-61, 69
TeamFlow (CFM), 170
Team meetings, 187-190
TeleAdapt, 229
Telecommunications, 202-21, 224-34,
247-49
Telecommuting, 45

Telephone (See also voice mail)
  accessories, 94-95
  action, 40
  answering machine, 95-96, 211-13
  area and equipment, 92
  cellular, 225-27
  features, 94-95
  headset, 95
  location in office, 90-91
  team, 40
  time, 39-40
  training, 40
  traveling, 225-27, 233-34
  voice mail system for, 95-96, 211-213
  Web, 32
Temps, working with, 197-98
TextBridge Pro, 58
3M,
  Anti-glare/Radiation Filter, 96
  dispensers/holders, 171
  drawer organizer, 67
  Laser/Copier Labels, 171
  Organization Cabinets, 65
  personal organizer accessories, 30
  Post-it Fax Notes, 218
  Post-it Flags, 30, 64
  Post-it File Folder Labels, 109
  Post-it Labeling and Cover-up Tape,
    171
  Post-it Notes, 30
  Post-it Pop Up Notes, 64
  Post-it Printed Notes, 168
  Post-it Software Notes, 166
  Removable Magic Tape, 171
  3M Mounting Squares, Mounting
    Tape, 67
  3M tape products, 30, 67
Tickler Record System, 24
Tickler systems, 17, 22-27
Time/Design Mgmt. System, 35
Time management, 13-36
  choosing best tools, 17-33, 42
  computerized programs, 36
  interruptions, 37-39
  telephone time, 39-40
  time/energy savers, 44-45

tools, 17-36
tools and habits, 4, 5
Time savers, 44-45
Timeslips (TIMESLIPS Corp.) 172
Timewise, 169
To-do list, 17, 19-20
TopDown Flowcharter (Kaetron), 169
TotalNews, 258
Total Quality Management (See Quality)
Training, 193-94, 198-99
Training Store, The, 201
Trash to Cash, 201
Traveling (See also Telephone, travel-
    ing)
  checklists, 242-44
  FAA, 242
  health and productivity, 245-46
  Internet options and, 230-32
  jet lag and, 245-46
  office, 222-36, 247-50
  packing for, 241-44
  paperwork and, 234-36
  portable office products, 249-50
  preparations, 237-44
  resource information and services,
    250-51
  technology, 224-33
  telephone calls and, 233-34
  tips, 236-47
  voice mail and, 231
  working and, 223-39
Travelocity, 251
Travelpro Rollaboard, 241-42
Tucows, 248
24x7, 2
TypeItIn, 90

U
Unified messaging, 218-19
University Products, 77
U.S. Business Advisor, 256
U.S. State Department, 251

V
Velcro, 92, 228

Veritas Backup Exec, 147
Virtual desktop services, 231
Virtual office, 223
Viruses, 137, 152
Visio (see Microsoft)
Visor PDAs, 35-36
Visual control boards, 21, 159
Visual Horizons, 77
Voice mail
  System, 95-96
  Tips on, 211-13
  Traveling and, 230
Voice Organizer, 36, 248

W

Wall charts (See Charts)
The Weather Channel, 251
Web (See also Internet), 256
  backup, 149
  phones, 32, 226
  storage space, 230
  time management and, 17, 33
WebEx.com/WebEx Meeting Center, 220
Web information managers, 258
Webley, 219
WebWirelessNow, 226
Whew, 221
Whiteboards, 190
Windows, 152
Wilson Jones (Acco)
  Color-Life Expanding File, 121
  Color-Life Expanding Wallets, 121
  ColorLife File Pockets, 121
  MultiDex, 62
WinFAX Pro, 215, 232
Winzip, 150
WipeOut, 140
Work, 178-79
Work flow (See Work process)
Workgroup computing, 219-21
Working From Home, 104
Workload, 45-46
Work management, 154-60, 162-72
Work process, 175-90
Work space, 79-104
Work style, 5-6

WorldPages, 258
World Wide Web (See Internet)
Wright Line, 125
Writing the Natural Way, 161

X

Xertrex Intl. (Tabbies), 65

Y

Yahoo
  Directory, 256
  People, 258
  Web calendar, 33

Z

Zip drive, 147
ZIP+4 Diskette Coding, 171
Zkey.com, 230